Information management in context

Edited by Matthew Hinton

Contributors

Lynda M. Applegate

David Boddy

Albert Boonstra

Dave Chaffey

Peter Checkland

David Cobham

Graham Curtis

Matthew Hinton

Sue Holwell

Graham Kennedy

F. Warren McFarlan

James L. McKenney

James O'Brien

Elizabeth Orna

Jennifer Rowley

Steve Wood

The Open University
Walton Hall,
Milton Keynes
MK7 6AA

First published 2009

Edited and designed by The Open University

Typeset in India by Alden Prepress Services, Chennai

Printed in Great Britain by Bell & Bain Ltd., Glasgow

ISBN 978-0-7492-6836-7

1.1

Contents

Introducing *Information management in context*
Matthew Hinton   5

Organization and society   9

1   Introduction to information management
    Dave Chaffey and Steve Wood   11

2   Managing information in modern organizations
    Matthew Hinton   31

3   Organizing and leading the information technology function
    *Lynda M. Applegate, F. Warren McFarlan and
    James L. McKenney*   49

Information and process   63

4   Data, capta, information and knowledge
    Peter Checkland and Sue Holwell   65

5   The process of information management
    Matthew Hinton   73

6   The processes which information systems support
    Peter Checkland and Sue Holwell   79

7   Organizations and information
    Elizabeth Orna   89

Systems and technology   99

8   Generic types of information systems
    Matthew Hinton   101

9   Business information systems
    James O'Brien   109

10 Distributed systems, EDI and the organization
    Graham Curtis and David Cobham   133

Strategy and change

147

11 Strategy and information systems
Graham Curtis and David Cobham
149

12 The search for opportunity
*Lynda M. Applegate, F. Warren McFarlan and
James L. McKenney*
171

13 Using information systems to rethink business processes
David Boddy, Albert Boonstra and Graham Kennedy
181

14 Frameworks for e-business
Jennifer Rowley
205

15 Assessing the costs and benefits of information systems
David Boddy, Albert Boonstra and Graham Kennedy
223

Acknowledgements
247

Index
249

Introducing *Information management in context*

Matthew Hinton

The word 'information' has become much used in organizational life. It often seems to be used to refer to what is processed and provided by computers and other electronic devices. While it is true that most organizations rely on information technology (IT) to support many of their information processes, there is also a large amount of information and knowledge that is not captured by or represented in these computer-based information systems. In particular, managers must make decisions and choices about future actions. Invariably, the decisions made are based on imperfect information. In such situations managers must use their accumulated knowledge and expertise to evaluate and interpret imperfect information in choosing the best course of action in the light of objectives. In most of the organizations these decisions will be supported by information of varying degrees of accuracy and usefulness gleaned (with varying degrees of difficulty) from the organization's IT systems. However, all such systems have fundamental limitations.

It is arguable, therefore, that the majority of information that managers draw upon is not embedded in computer systems – rather, it is principally in the heads of the staff. This is particularly true of high-level information; that is, knowledge *about* the information that resides within the organization. Examples of this high-level information might include knowing where to find the required internal data or where to source external information in order to prepare a report; or knowing who in the organization last tackled a similar problem to the one you are currently being asked to solve. It has long been recognized that most managers get most of their information by talking to people, either face-to-face or on the telephone. This reflects the fact that, although managers do deal with some relatively well-defined and structured issues (for example planning budgets), many of the issues that they deal with are poorly structured, messy or fuzzy problems. In other words a manager's life is mainly about shades of grey rather than black and white. Such nuances are typically lost when information is put into writing or stored in a computer. But people are highly skilled in conveying such information, not only with the words they use but also by their tone of voice, their facial expressions and even the bodily postures they adopt. Because it is difficult to express and communicate to others, and practically impossible to express in any code, tacit knowledge is difficult to represent in computer systems. Information that is not captured in computer-based information systems is especially relied upon in decision-making processes.

Consequently, information management (IM) should be seen as the conscious process by which information is gathered and used to assist in decision making at all levels of an organization. This definition contains several points of interest. First, true information management is a *conscious* process. Information management does not just happen: it has to be thought about. This implies that it has to be planned, systematic and structured.

A second point from the definition is that the purpose of information management is *to assist in decision making*. Information is not gathered for its own sake (although that sometimes seems to be the case), but is gathered to be used. Information management therefore works best when the conscious planning process starts not with information but with the decisions that have to be made. However, although information assists decision making, it should not determine totally what decisions are made: the scope for professional expertise, intuition and discretion remains.

The third point from the definition is that information management is for the benefit of *all levels of an organization*. In many organizations, information management is often perceived as being a control mechanism for the benefit of senior managers or shareholders. Information management should be as much about aiding decision making across and between all levels of the organization as it is for senior planners and decision makers.

A final point about the definition is that it makes no reference to computers or information technology. Information management is as much about paper-based systems, or even human voice-based systems, as it is about technology-based systems.

It is a popular misconception that information management is only concerned with information technology management. Over the last four decades, the rapid expansion in the use of IT has created a raft of management concerns with respect to the use of this new technology. While it is true that some of these concerns form part of the IM agenda, there is a plethora of wider issues concerned with managing broader information resources which transcend the narrow focus on simple technology management. This book provides a set of chapters which aim to bridge the gap between the hard and soft aspects of this debate.

Chapters 1 to 3, *Organization and society*, explore the diversity and changing nature of managing the information management function. This includes how the IM function has evolved, key challenges and concepts as well as the potential impact of future developments. Distinction is made between information management and managing information technology. The chapters also address the influence of organizational structure and culture on the IM function.

Chapters 4 to 7, *Information and process*, investigate the role of information as an organizational resource. It initially establishes an understanding of how information supports purposeful action within organizations, which in turn warrants careful management attention. Given this, the concept of information resources forms a vital (if somewhat obvious) cornerstone for effective information management. From this starting point, the section explains in more detail the process of information management and how information resources support people undertaking purposeful action, by attempting to reconcile personal, social and organizational perspectives.

Chapters 8 to 10, *Systems and technology*, focus on 'managing organizational data and information'. These chapters outline the main ways that organizational data are managed prior to decision-making activity. Accordingly, the provision of information systems needed to achieve this is central to information management activities. Therefore, it is important for this section of the book to cover aspects of how information management engages with the technology. Both generic types of information systems and functionally specific systems are illustrated. In addition, the role information management plays in organizational integration and providing a cross-functional bridge is described. This section brings together key components of the technology management debate with the broader information resource management debate.

Chapters 11 to 15, *Strategy and change*, examine the role that information management plays in organizational strategy and as an agent of change. These establish that the complexity of the information management challenge increases considerably when it penetrates to the heart of an organization's activity. The strategic value of information is realized when information systems assemble the information from the various business functions and make sense of this at an organizational level. For this reason, an important part of the information management challenge is involved with the strategic perspective critical to managing and planning for the information resource. The strategic use of IT also has a far-reaching influence on organizational change. Because IT can manipulate the information resources of an organization, it is often used as an enabler for both radical and incremental business process change. Facilitating such innovation is a crucial part of the information management remit, which is often coupled with the dynamics of investing in new technology. Organizations need to foster an approach to information management that encompasses the strategic perspective if lasting organizational change is to be realized.

Together these chapters present a rich picture of the scale of information management. Given that information is the lifeblood of modern organizations, it is perhaps not surprising that information management envelops issues as diverse as managing information resources through to operational technology management through to broader strategic thinking and change. Future business achievements are now inextricably linked to successful information management.

Organization and society

Chapter 1

Introduction to information management

Dave Chaffey and Steve Wood

Introduction

Information. Technology. Both resources are increasingly important as organizations seek to improve their performance. Information and technology resources coupled with human resources help deliver value to organizations in many different ways. Applying information and technology offers new ways to do business, increases the efficiency of business processes, reduces costs, and provides the performance measures used to control improvement.

What is the relative importance of these resources to organizations? When we talk about management of information technology, with the two words coupled together, it seems that often the emphasis is firmly placed on the technology. But, as Professor Thomas Davenport has noted, the managerial emphasis should be placed more on approaches to managing information rather than technology – the stress is on the 'I' rather than the 'T' in 'IT' (Davenport, 2000). Similarly, Peter Drucker stressed the importance of information to organizational competitiveness in 1993 when he wrote:

> The industries that have moved into the centre of the economy in the last forty years, have their business, the production and distribution of knowledge and information rather than the production and distribution of things.

Ultimately, value is delivered not through technology, but through applying information; by improvement flows of information which require less resources; by better-quality information and knowledge sharing which improves decision making. In the same way that energy, water and nutrients are transported between different parts of a tree in order for it to survive, information needs to be transmitted efficiently through an organization for it to thrive.

For an organization to gain value from information raises many management issues which are not limited to technology.

Information in today's world

The significance of information in the modern world can be gauged from three terms that have been coined to highlight the importance of information in the modern world: the information society, the information economy and the information age.

The information society

The importance of information in the world today has led to social commentators and governments referring to an **information society.** Martin (1995) says of information:

> Without an uninterrupted flow for this vital resource, society as we know it would quickly run into difficulties, with business and industry, education, leisure, travel and commutations, national and international affairs all vulnerable to disruption. In more advanced societies, this vulnerability is heightened by an increasing dependence on the enabling power of information and communications technologies.

This quotation stresses the importance of information and our dependence on it as a resource within organizations and society at large. Given the importance of information to society, governments launch initiatives and pass laws to ensure that businesses use information competitively, that their citizens' personal information is protected and that relevant information is accessible to all in society. For example, the European Community Information Society initiative (www.europa.eu.int/information_society/ index_en.htm) was launched in 1998 with the aims of increasing public awareness of the impact of the information society and stimulating peoples' motivation and ability to participate (reducing social exclusion), increasing socio-economic benefits and enhancing the role of Europe in influencing the global information society. The European Community initiative describes the growth of the information society as follows:

> The last few years have witnessed a transformation in the industrial landscape of the developed world. Telecommunications liberalisation, the explosive growth of the Internet and a growing tide of mergers between computer, media and telecommunications companies all point to one thing – the birth of the information society.

The information society was defined by the UK INSINC Working Party on Social Inclusion in the Information Society in 1997 as:

> A society characterised by a high level of information intensity in the everyday life of most citizens, in most organizations and workplaces; by the use of common or compatible technology for a

wide range of personal, social, educational and business activities; and by the ability to transmit and receive digital data rapidly between places irrespective of distance.

The information economy

Information economy

An economy that is highly dependent upon the collection, storage and exchange of information

The concept of the information economy also recognizes the importance of information in the modern world, but this time with an emphasis on the impact on the economy. An information economy suggests an economy that is highly dependent upon the collection, storage and exchange of information. The dependence on information is suggested by the data in Table 1.1 and also the proportion of GDP spent on information management hardware and software, which averages 5 per cent in many countries. Additionally, many business services now deal exclusively with managing and adding value to data and by selling information derived from the data. Examples include:

- *Financial Times* (business news and information at www.ft.com)
- Factiva (detailed information about business performance at www.factiva.com)
- Experian (information about customers such as credit ratings and profiling for targeted marketing communications from www.experian.com)
- Questia (online subscription-based access is provided to published books and articles for students at www.questia.com)
- ScienceDirect.com (online journal access for science and business researchers at www.sciencedirect.com).

Evans and Wurster of Harvard Business School have argued in their paper 'Strategy and the new economics of information' that there are three characteristics of information in any market that will determine its importance (Evans and Wurster, 1997). These are:

1 *Reach*. The number or rather proportion of people in a market who are exchanging information.

2 *Richness*. This is defined by the information itself. It is constrained by *band-width* (the volume of information that can be transmitted using a communication link in a given time), hence as high-speed broadband access to the Internet increases, increasingly rich information can be delivered to customers. *Richness* is also determined by the degree to which information can be customized. For example, an e-mail received by a customer offering discounts on a product is more likely to be acted on if the product is tailored to its recipient. Interactivity is

also important to richness. A dialogue is a more effective way of exchanging information. So for a customer to solve a query about their account it will often be more efficient to speak to them by phone rather than sending an e-mail since the phone is a more interactive medium.

3   *Affiliation.* This refers to links with partners. In an online context, an organization that has the most links to other organizations will be able to gain a larger reach and influence.

In markets such as air travel, where ticket sales have been transformed by the Internet, understanding how to improve reach, richness and affiliation is crucial. This is not only because a large proportion of people buy their flights online, but because they also research their route and carrier online.

The information age

The increasing importance of information through time to both society and economies has been used to suggest that we are now in the 'information age'. When did the information age begin? Decide for yourself from Table 1.1. The 'information age' takes over from the 'industrial age' which in turn follows the 'agricultural age'. In the agricultural age, the key resources were the land and the people who worked on it and defended it. When products were first produced, it was usually one person who produced the whole product. In the industrial age, mass-production of products became commonplace with different people working on different aspects of the product, supported by machinery. Capital became a key strategic resource in addition to people. In the information age, information and knowledge are critical to organizational success and information becomes a key strategic resource also. Information is used to understand the needs of markets, support the development of products and govern and control the direction of businesses. Furthermore, in the information age, individuals and organizations pay for pure information services, ranging from online newspaper subscriptions to analysts' reports and alerts about particular industries to marketing databases to promote products to potential customers.

Table 1.1   Possible starting points for the information age

Time	Event
40,000 BC	Clay tablets from ancient Mesopotamia, where Iraq now stands, have a precursor of cuneiform writing
1300 BC	Basic Chinese characters, such as that for the horse, first formed in bone
387 BC	Plato founded his academy devoted to research in philosophy and the sciences on land which had belonged to Academos
1455	The printing of the Bible with movable type by Gutenberg in Germany
1564	Graphite is discovered
1651	John Dury first describes the role of information manager (actually a librarian at the University of Oxford, usually referred to as the first modern library)
1860	First commercial typewriters use the QWERTY keyboard
1876	Alexander Graham Bell introduced the first telephone to an audience at the Centennial Exposition in Philadelphia
1901	Marconi sends a radio signal of the Morse code letter 's' across the Atlantic from Cornwall, England, to St John's, Newfoundland
1937	Atanasoff-Berry Computer (ABC), the world's first electronic digital computer built by John Vincent Atanasoff and Clifford Berry at Iowa State University
1947	First commercial computer – ENIAC (Electronic Numerical Integrator and Computer). It weighed thirty tons and used 18,000 vacuum tubes
1953	IBM produced the first computer system that was widely adopted by organizations
1969	First node on the US ARPANET, forerunner of the Internet
1971	A computer engineer named Ray Tomlinson sent the first e-mail message. He can't remember the message, but he does remember choosing the @ symbol!
1991	First website (http://info.cern.ch) published by Tim Berners-Lee

A light-hearted guide to changes in our society is available online at www.out-a-time.com or www.futurefeedforward.com/timline.php which highlights some of the technological developments in the information age and places them in the context of earlier and later ages through to 2072!

Information in today's organization

The greatest contribution that information makes to organizations is as a resource to improve the performance of organizations and the individuals that work within them. Organizational performance can be improved by utilizing information resources to help deliver better-quality products or services more profitably. Individual performance can be improved by providing employees with more relevant, timely information to support their decisions.

The importance of information to organizational performance has been recognized by the IT Governance Institute, which has developed with its member organizations COBIT, a framework intended to assist organizations in managing their information resources. COBIT stands for Control Objectives for Information and related Technology. It was first released by the Information Systems Audit and Control Foundation (ISACF) in 1996. It is not a methodology or a standard, but a practical tool drawn from other standards and methodologies. It focuses on delivering quality information and distinguishes between 'information and related information technology (IT)'. COBIT is used by organizations in Europe, Asia and the Americas. In COBIT (2000), the reasons for the importance of managing information are stated as follows:

> Critically important to the survival and success of an organisation is effective management of information and related Information Technology (IT). In this global information society – where information travels through cyberspace without the constraints of time, distance and speed – this criticality arises from the:
>
> • increasing dependence on information and the systems that deliver this information
>
> • increasing vulnerabilities and a wide spectrum of threats, such as cyber threats and information warfare
>
> • scale and cost of the current and future investments in information and information systems
>
> • potential for technologies to dramatically change organizations and business practices, create new opportunities and reduce costs.

We will now look at how information can be used to support organizational improvement through support of business process and as a means of value creation. But, first, we highlight one of the main challenges of information management today – information overload.

Information overload

The flow of information within and between organizations and their stakeholders increases relentlessly. The amount of corporate data is doubling roughly every 6 months. A SNIA (2003) survey showed that in many European companies, data storage requirements more than doubled in the previous 12 months. The Research insight 1.1 'How much information?' further highlights the scale of the problem. Within organizations, **information overload**, or if you prefer, 'drowning in data' is a common complaint of employees as they see the potential value of information, yet are frustrated in their ability to derive benefit from it due to its volume and complexity. A simple example of this problem is e-mail. A recent survey showed that the average UK office worker spends nearly an hour of the average seven-and-a-half hour day working through their e-mails (BBC, 2002). Time spent by employees searching for information is a further and perhaps more serious problem. It is estimated that US companies spend $107 billion a year paying their employees to search for external information (Outsell, 2001). Researchers interviewed over 6,000 knowledge workers in large organisations with revenues over $10 million ranging from senior mangers to more junior staff. They found that knowledge workers spend around four hours per week looking for and gathering external information and a further four hours reviewing and applying information. An average salary of $30 per hour or $240 per week was used to estimate the total of $107 billion.

In spite of information overload, information is still a vital asset of every organization. To exploit this asset effectively, organizations have to counter information overload by improving information quality. Managing information quality will ensure that information is fit for purpose, that it is *relevant* to the needs of employees, customers and suppliers. Practical, technology-enabled techniques are available to improve information quality, such as:

- *Aggregating* – the 'big picture' is presented by summing up individual data items.

- *Summarizing* – an abstract of a technical report is one form of summarizing.

- *Filtering* – less relevant information can be removed, for example only news items that contain the company's name or competitors' names are sent through to managers.

- *Alerting* – messages are displayed on-screen or sent via e-mail to alert managers to a newsworthy piece of information.

Using information to support processes

Information is vital to all organizations since all business processes that make up an organization's operations and management make extensive use of information. Organizational performance is improved by reviewing how well processes work and making adjustments to make them operate more efficiently and effectively. Davenport and Short (1990) defined a process as

> A set of logically related tasks performed to achieve a defined business outcome.

Typical business processes involve activities to deliver a service to an internal or external customer and are illustrated in Figure 1.1.

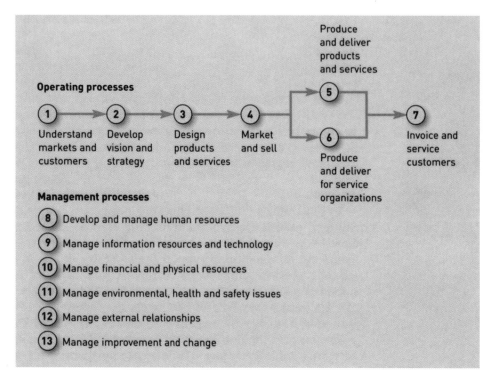

Figure 1.1　Generic organizational operating processes and management processes
Source: PricewaterhouseCoopers, 2002

There are many different types of information that support these processes. The Hawley Committee (1995), which was created to help organizations make better use of their information assets, identifies these information groupings:

- market and customer information
- product information
- specialist knowledge
- business process information
- management information and plans
- human resource information
- supplier information
- accountable information.

From these information groups it is evident that information enables organizations to:

1 *Sense* what is happening in the external environment and respond accordingly through their strategy and tactics. For example, it can monitor competitor activity such as the introduction of new products or the winning of new contracts.

2   *Research* demand for new products – customers in different markets can be surveyed for their needs for products.

3   *Monitor and control* operating processes for efficiency and improve them to save time or money.

4   *Exchange information* with partners such as suppliers as part of their operational processes.

5   *Communicate* messages about brands and products internally and externally.

We can see why Evans and Wurster (1997) wrote: '*every business is an information business ... information is the glue that holds together the structure of all businesses*'. But information is more than a glue; we will see that information management can help deliver strategic advantage to organizations through better sensing of the business environment, offering distinctive services and driving down costs. Evans and Wurster (1997) give the examples of three companies that they feel compete as much on the basis of the way they use information as through their physical products. They cite American Airlines using its control of its SABRE reservations system to achieve higher seat capacity utilization on its flights, Wal-Mart's use of electronic data interchange to increase efficiency in its supply chain, and Nike's detailed knowledge of its customer segments to produce specific products.

To illustrate the different concepts of business information management in we will use the example of a low cost airline company. Consider how this fictitious company would use information to support the processes shown in Figure 1.1. For example, the process 'understand markets and customers' requires information collected inside the company about individual customers such as where they live, the routes they fly and how much they spend with the airline. This information also needs to be aggregated (summed) so that we know the total size of a market such as the business flights market or flights originating in one country. Such internal information which helps managers review and improve the performance of an organization is known as '**business intelligence**'. The process for improving both the quality of the information and the performance of the organization is '**business performance management**'. External information is also needed to support processes. For the process 'Develop vision and strategy' it is necessary to monitor trends such as the total number of flights, market share and competitor activity, which together are known as '**market intelligence**'. The use of information and software to support business performance management is explored further in later chapters.

Using information to create value

We have seen that business information management is vital to supporting the operation of organizational processes and improving organizational performance and how organizations need to counter information overload. But, perhaps the most critical reason for the study and practice of business information management is its strategic importance to organizations. The information management capabilities of organizations impact their position in the markets in which they operate. As an example of how one company has taken information to the heart of its strategy read Mini case study 1.1 'Capital One creates value through information'.

Mini case study 1.1

Capital One creates value through information

Figure 1.2   Capital One website
Source: www.capitalone.co.uk

Capital One was established in 1995. It offers credit cards, savings, loans and insurance products in the UK, Canada and the US. It is a financially successful company achieving high returns of 20 per cent earnings per share growth and 20 per cent return on equity growth. It has been profitable in every quarter of its existence and in less than ten years it achieved net income of over $1 billion.

Capital One uses what it calls an 'Information-Based Strategy' (IBS), which brings marketing, credit, risk, operations and IT together to enable flexible decision making. It describes IBS as 'a rigorously scientific test-and-learn methodology that has enabled us to excel at product innovation, marketing and risk management – the essentials of success in consumer financial services'. For customers it is able to offer financial solutions that are tailored to individual customers' needs. It does this through mass-customization: offering different rates and fees structures to different customers depending on their risk status.

The scale of use of information is indicated by different operations in the business. In corresponding with customers, *The Banker* reported that Capital One send out one billion items of mail per year and handles 90 million inbound calls, 300 million outbound calls, 230 million Internet impressions and 40 million transactions per day. Together with its subsidiaries, the company had 45.8 million managed accounts and $60.7 billion in managed loads outstanding as of June 2003.

The IBS is managed by the Chief Information Officer, Gregor Bailar. He is in charge of operations related to computer systems, analysis of customer data, data protection, setting data standards, business continuity and information security.

According to *The Banker*, Gregor says:

CIOs today need to be technology alchemists. They need to be strong in professional technical methodologies so that their conversion is a disciplined one but, at the same time, they need to understand the business, be it banking, credit cards or loans.

Their job is not to know the future of technology, nor the latest and greatest of delivery networks, but to be focused on balancing the set of business needs, and choosing or creating the best possible solutions that can be provided from a technical perspective.

On the one hand, the CIO has to be an advocate for the business into the technology world, and on the other hand, the voice of technology in the best respect of how it can respond to the business. This is a relatively new role and the challenge is to interpret and prioritise correctly the business's needs and make the technology systems really responsive.

The CIO is expected to be involved not only in strategy development, but also in business and product innovation. Now, more than ever, CIOs are being held accountable for driving the business value, not just for keeping the lights blinking on the computers.

Source: Based on company annual reports and an article in *The Banker*, 2003

The strategic importance of business information management in an organization can be assessed using Figure 1.3. This analytic tool devised by Professor Don Marchand shows different ways in which information can create value for organizations. The main methods are:

1   *Add value.* Value is added through providing better-quality products and services to an organization's customers. Information can be used to better understand customer characteristics and needs and their level of satisfaction with services. Information is also used to sense and respond to markets. Information about trends in demands, competitor products and activities must be monitored so that organizations can develop strategies to compete in the marketplace. The *Lo-cost Airline Company* will use databases to store personal characteristics of customers and details of which routes customers have flown. Analysis of these databases can then be used to understand customer preferences and market products that better meet their needs.

2   *Reduce costs.* Cost reduction through information is achieved through making the business processes shown in Figure 1.1 more efficient. Efficiency is achieved through using information to create, market and deliver services using fewer resources than previously. Technology is applied to reduce paperwork, reduce the human resources needed to operate the processes through automation and improve internal and external communications. The *Lo-cost Airline Company* has used Internet technology so that customers serve themselves when they book tickets or make enquiries online – the concept of 'web self-service'.

3   *Manage risks.* Risk management is a well-established use of information within organizations. Marchand (2000) notes how risk management within organizations has created different functions and professions such as finance, accounting, auditing and corporate performance management. For example, the *Lo-cost Airline Company* will produce management information on the ticket sales and costs of operating the different routes which will be used by managers to assess whether their strategies are effective and revise them accordingly.

4   *Create new reality.* Marchand uses the expression 'create new reality' to refer to how information and new technologies can be used to innovate, to create new ways in which products or services can be developed. The *Lo-cost Airline Company* can also use online services to introduce new products more cost effectively, such as a holiday booking service, a car rental service or web-based services to compare the price of flights from different suppliers – all also potential value-adding activities.

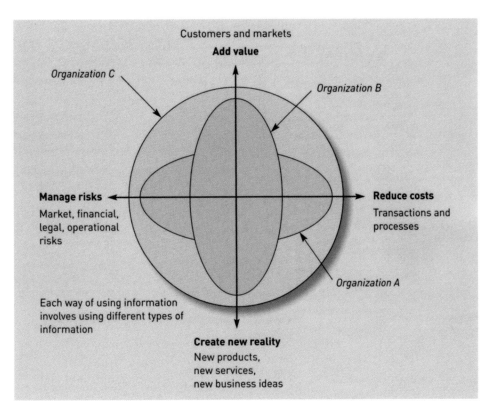

Figure 1.3   An evaluation tool relating information to business value
Source: Marchand, 2000

All organizations use a combination of these four approaches to using information. Traditionally organizations have mainly used information to reduce costs and manage risk (organization A in Figure 1.3). Risk management is essential to the operation of businesses. The availability of information technology has eased these activities. IT has also given new opportunities to create value (organization B). Organization C has a balanced approach to using information to creating business value. However, depending on an organization's characteristics, such as its size and its markets, it may not be appropriate for all companies to achieve the position occupied by organization C. Instead, Figure 1.3 can be used to assess opportunities for improved use of information.

Figure 1.4 gives insight into how business perceives the benefits of information technology. It can be seen that cost reduction is the main driver, with enhanced communication to customers, staff and suppliers also well represented. However, using the technology to gain competitive advantage is not frequently cited.

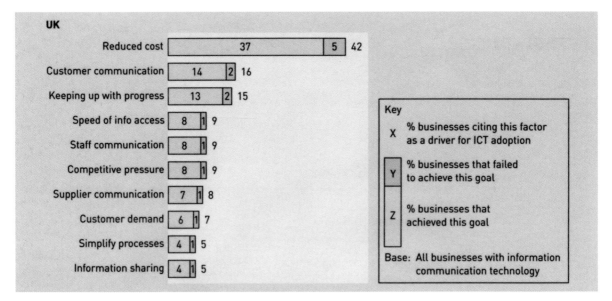

Figure 1.4   Reasons cited by businesses for adoption of information technology
Source: DT1 www.ukonlineforbusiness.gov.uk/benchmarking2003

Fundamentals of business information management

We have seen that managing information has become a significant challenge for organizations. In this section we introduce key concepts that are used as a basis for studying and improving information management. Effective BIM is dependent on effective management of different types of resources within an organization. These are information, people and technology. The elements of these three types of resources are summarized in Figure 1.5. These are portrayed as a three-legged stool, since if there are failures in the management of any one of the three of these resources, then BIM will be ineffectual. In the following sections we start by defining business information management and then explore the three different resources types and introduce some of the main issues with managing these resources.

A major challenge that every organization faces today is to develop coherent strategies that enable effective management of the different elements of the information-people-technology resources shown in Figure 1.5. The development of information management, knowledge management and information systems strategies can help harness these resources together to deliver value and support organizational processes.

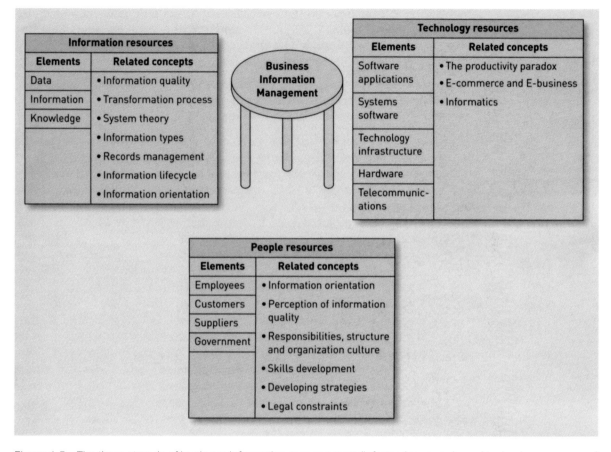

Figure 1.5   The three strands of business information management (information, people and technology resources)

What is business information management?

Business information management
The process of managing information as a strategic resource for improving organizational performance. This process involves developing strategies and introducing systems and controls to improve information quality to deliver value

'Information management' and 'business information management' are increasingly used to refer to courses and business school departments that deliver education for current and future managers. At the same time, in organizations, roles such as chief information officers (CIOs), chief knowledge officers (CKOs) and business information manager are increasing, as Carr (2003) has noted. The use of such terms is useful to suggest the need for a focus on the study and practice of managing information as a strategic resource within organizations. We define business management (BIM) as:

> The process of managing information as a strategic resource for improving organizational performance. This process involves developing strategies and introducing systems and controls to improve information quality to deliver value.

This definition emphasizes the need to treat information as a valuable resource which has an important role to play in delivering value to all types of organizations. It also suggests the need for specific responsibilities, strategies and tools to be created to manage the resource and improve its quality. Note that technology has less emphasis than in terms such as 'information technology' and information systems'. Technology is simply used as a tool to implement systems and controls which help deliver information-based value to the business.

However, the degree of adoption of this emphasis on business information management varies in different countries. In the United States, one of the leading trade publications for professionals is *CIO* (*chief information officer*) (www.cio.com) reflecting this emphasis. The role of CIO is commonplace in the US, but it has been less widely adopted in the UK. Meanwhile, in the UK, the leading trade publications read by IT professionals are *Computing* (www.computing.co.uk) and *Computer Weekly* (www.computerweekly.co.uk), reflecting a more technical emphasis. The key organizational issues related to information management, which we will cover in this book, have been usefully summarized by Elizabeth Orna (1999) of the Association for Information Management who says that information management is concerned with:

- how information is acquired, recorded and stored
- where information resources are located in the organization and who has responsibility for them
- how information flows within the organization and between the organization and the outside world
- how the organization uses it
- how people who handle it apply their skills and co-operate with one another
- how information technology supports the users of information
- what information costs and the value it contributes
- how effectively all these information-related activities contribute towards achievement of the organization's objectives.

Information resources

The discipline of business information management focuses on managing information as a resource. But what exactly is information? (We also commonly refer to 'data' and 'knowledge' in a similar context.) Distinguishing between these terms is important for understanding the nature of business information management and to enable information to be managed effectively.

How do the concepts of data, information and knowledge interrelate? Let's take the example of ticket sales for the *Lo-cost Airline Company* (see Figure 1.6).

Data
Discrete, objective facts about events. Data are transformed into information by adding value through context, categorization, calculation, corrections and condensation

Here data are recorded each time a customer buys a ticket as part of the sales process. The data will be automatically recorded in a digital form as customers or call-centre operators enter the flight booking via a Web page. Since an airline will sell millions of tickets each year, in its raw form, these data have little value to managers in the airline. The sheer volume of data means they cannot be used to access how well the processes are operating. The data needs to be transformed into information using an information system for them to be used for decision making by managers.

English (1999) defines the relationship between data and information as follows:

> Information is data in context. Information is usable data. Information is the meaning of data, so facts become understandable

Information
Organized data, meaningful and contextually relevant. Used for decision making

With this information at hand managers can use the information to ask different questions about the processes, for example:

- What is the split of revenue between sales to business and individual customers? (Operating process 1 – understand markets and customers).

- What proportion of seats do we sell on each route? (Operating process 4 – market and sell).

- What is the profitability of each route? (Operating process 5 – produce and deliver products and services).

Information systems
A computerized or manual system to capture data and transform them into information and/or knowledge

Information and communication technology (ICT or IT)
The software applications, computer hardware and networks used to create information systems

It is apparent that to answer these questions, information systems are needed to deliver relevant, timely information which is at the right level of detail to answer each question. The information from millions of ticket sales will be aggregated or summarized to produce totals and averages across the entire year for different routes. Ticket sales will also need to be compared to competitors who use these routes. Visualization using different forms such as charts and maps (see Figure 1.7) is essential to simplify the volume of data. Note that the FlightMapping service (www.flightmapping.com) is an example of an online intermediary website with a revenue model based on advertising and commission on referrals which has been created to meet online searches' need to reduce their information overload. Of course a manual or paper-based information system would be incapable of delivering these information needs, so information and communication technology (ICT or IT) is vital to modern business information management. This ICT includes software applications to capture and give access to information, computer hardware to run these applications and networks to facilitate transfer of information within the organization and beyond. Later chapters describe the different types of software or programs used to support business information management and the hardware and communications technology in more detail.

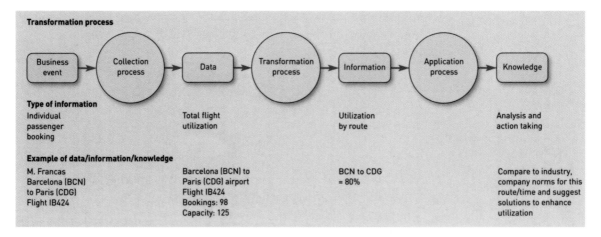

Figure 1.6   The data to information to knowledge transformation process

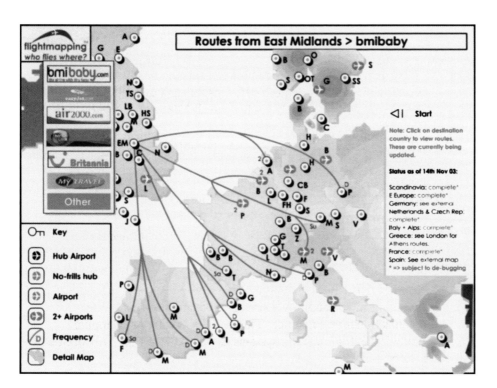

Figure 1.7   Summary information view of European flights from Birmingham International Airport
Source: www.flightmapping.com/Europe/flights.mapswf

While information from the information system will enable managers to answer the type of questions about processes given above, this, in turn, is of little value to the business if no action is taken. Managers need to apply their skills and experience to use this information to take decisions about how to change the way they use their resources to improve process performance. This application of judgement to take the best action is knowledge. For example, managers at the *Lo-cost Airline Company* will use their knowledge to act on information about unprofitable routes to attempt to improve their profitability. The concept of knowledge is less straightforward than those of data and information.

Knowledge
The combination of data and information to which is added expert opinion, skills and experience to result in a valuable asset which can be used to make decisions

English (1999) builds on his definition of information to define knowledge as follows:

> Knowledge is not just information known, it is information in context. Knowledge means understanding the significance of the information. Knowledge is the value added to information by people who have the experience and acumen to understand its real potential. Knowledge has value only to the extent that people are empowered to act based on that knowledge. In other words, knowledge has value only when acted on.

Summary

1   Information is now important to the state of every society and economy since it influences the relative prosperity and quality of living in each country.

2   Information is vital to organizations since it can deliver value, reduce costs and reduce risks.

3   Information supports business performance management where organizational processes are evaluated in order to increase their efficiency.

4   The problem of information overload, where information creation increases in organizations, needs to be carefully managed. Approaches must be found to deliver relevant, high-quality information to staff.

5   Business information management is defined as 'The process of managing information as a strategic resource for improving organizational performance. This process involves developing strategies and introducing systems and controls to improve information quality to deliver value.'

6   Business information management is supported through a range of resources including

-   information resources such as data, information and knowledge

-   people resources used to manage and use the information

-   technology resources such as the hardware and communications infrastructure and the applications resources for delivering information to users.

References

The Banker (2003) Why does the CIO have so many hats? *The Banker*, 2 December [online], http://www.thebanker.com/news/fullstory.php/aid/921/.

BBC (2002) Parenting suffers in e-mail overload, *BBC News*, 20 May [online] http://news.bbc.co.uk/1/hi/sci/tech/1998334.stm.

Carr, N. (2003) IT doesn't matter. *Harvard Business Review*, May, pp. 5–12.

COBIT (2000) Executive Summary of COBIT. Released by COBIT steering committee [online], www.isaca.org/cobit.

Davenport, T. (2000) Putting the I into IT. In Mastering Information Management, Marchand, D., Davenport, T. and Dickson, T., eds, pp. 5–9, Financial Times Prentice Hall, Harlow.

Davenport, T and Short, J (1990) The new industrial engineering: information technology and business process design, *Sloan Management Review*, 31, 4, pp. 11–27.

Drucker, P. (1993) *Post Capitalist Society*, Harper Business, New York.

English, L. (1999) *Improving Data Warehouse and Business Information Quality*, Wiley, New York.

Evans, P. and Wurster, T. (1997) Strategy and the new economics of information. *Harvard Business Review*, September–October, pp. 70–82.

Hawley Committee (1995) Information as an asset: the board agenda, KPMG IMPACT Programme, London: KPMG, 1995.

Marchand, D. (2000) Putting the I into IT. In Mastering Information Management, Marchand, D., Davenport, T. and Dickson, T., eds, pp. 295–300, Financial Times Prentice Hall, Harlow.

Martin, W. (1995) *The Global Society*, Aslib/Gower, Aldershot.

Orna, E. (1999) *Practical Information Policies*, Gower, Basingstoke.

Outsell (2001) Super information about information managers. Report on study conducted by Outsell Inc. for Factiva, Dialog and KPMG.

PricewaterhouseCoopers (2002) PricewatehouseCoopers global best practice guidelines [online], www.globalbestpractices.com/best_practices.

SNIA (2003) Storage requirements doubled in 2002. Press release – Storage Networking Industry Association Europe 4/22/03.

Source: Adapted from Chaffey, D. and Wood, S. (2004) *Business Information Management: improving performance using information systems*, Financial Times/Prentice Wall.

Chapter 2

Managing information in modern organizations

Matthew Hinton

Introduction

The last decade has seen an unparalleled increase in the use of information and communication technologies (ICT) within organizations. The expansion of computing, fuelled by ongoing technological developments in personal computing, networked communications and the explosion of the Internet, has radically altered the way organizations work. Hand in hand with the dramatic increases in the availability of the technology is the rapid diffusion of ICT to the majority of organizational members. Nearly all professional roles can no longer function without some form of interaction with ICT. The last decade has also seen a change in the application of ICT within organizations. The ability to manipulate critical management information has stimulated a progression from applying ICT to automate work, to applying it to enhance decision-making activities. This has the potential to alter the very nature of many work activities.

Few in business would dispute that ICT is essential. However, many see their use of ICT as a necessary and costly requirement for business survival, rather than a means of unleashing the untapped competitive advantage of their company. Indeed, it is argued that a gulf exists between the investment made in information and communication technology and an organization's ability to reap significant business benefit from it. Accordingly, the various changes taking place have made the management of the technology a critical concern. This concern is manifest in the inability to justify ICT expenditure, a lack of integration between the technology and business needs and a plethora of problems associated with managing the operations of the technical functions responsible for ICT. Accordingly, organizations must learn to maximize the advantages offered by ICT while avoiding the many pitfalls associated with rapid technological change.

Why is there a need for an information management function?

Modern organizations use a variety of resources in order to fulfil their objectives. Regardless of whether they are public or private, multinationals or small entities, they all share a set of common resources which they depend on to carry out their goals. These are financial resources, skilled people, physical property, time and information. Successful organizations are those that find ways to optimize the value of these resources to produce the best stakeholder value they can. So at the simplest level most managers' main task is that of asset management. While these assets are important to all organizations, their proportionate value is not necessarily the same. Nevertheless, it is a commonly held belief that information is essential to all organizations, but that skilled people are the most important asset, regardless of organizational goals or industry sector. Indeed, as we move into a more information intensive environment it is the combination of people and information resources that will deliver superior performance and competitive advantage. In fact, organizations that repeatedly deliver high performance, or are responsible for developing innovative goods or services, are likely to have motivated and empowered employees supported by well-developed information systems. As Frenzel (1999) states:

> The leverage of information and people is so powerful that managers in high-performance organizations devote considerable energy to managing information, its delivery system, the people who deliver it, and those who use it. The combination of skilled people and advanced information technology has revolutionised the concept of management.

This is an important point because the adoption of new ICT entails more than just the installation of the technology. Successful technology adoption requires organizations to assimilate the technology into their business processes and to understand how its introduction can distort the current balance of power within the organization itself. The introduction of new information systems can often redistribute knowledge among the workforce with consequences for managerial authority. Equally, employees feel a greater sense of responsibility as a result of engaging with more knowledge-based work. The growth in this type of knowledge-oriented activity means that workers and managers need to create new relationships based on participative management techniques. This should allow for a less formal management structure with greater decentralization, employee commitment and the development of self-managing teams. However, for organizations to move in such a direction they need to have strategies and plans for ICT adoption, which are developed and supported by appropriately skilled personnel. Usually expert ICT departments exist who would oversee this sort of development. Such a department would be responsible for developing the organization's strategic perspective with respect to the deployment of new technology and also for guiding its implementation and supporting and maintaining the systems once they are installed. In most organizations the ICT department is essential.

Most modern organizations have some form of ICT department. However, the growth in the use of information and communication technology has meant that there is a tendency in some quarters for people to mistake the concept of 'information management' with the practice of 'managing information technology'. While the management of the technology is no small task and one not to be underestimated, it tells only part of the story. Information management is much broader than this and should be seen as the conscious process by which information is gathered and used to assist in decision making throughout an organization. As a result, organizations have to develop an information management function which is capable of addressing this. The ICT department forms part of this response. By bringing together people with the requisite technical skills (systems analysts, programmers, Web designers etc.) an organization can support the other organizational functions with respect to their information needs. Examples of this appear in Table 2.1.

Table 2.1 Functional applications supported by the ICT department

Functions	IT applications supported
Operations	Materials logistics, factory automation, warehouse automation, shipping and receiving
Marketing	Customer relationship management systems, sales analysis systems, market research and forecasting systems
Finance and accounting	Budgetary control and planning systems, accounts payable
Human resources	Personnel records, training and development systems, compensation analysis systems

These examples are just a few of the myriad of systems that ICT departments are expected to support. Together these systems are often referred to as the *applications portfolio*, which includes the entire range of systems found within an organization. As well as the large, centralized systems (like payroll) which are the modern versions of the early computer systems, the applications portfolio also includes systems developed by functional areas for specific purposes and the communications infrastructure which binds all these systems together. An average sized organization may easily have an applications portfolio holding several thousand computer programs. The configuration of the information management function has to cater for this array of systems. Consequently, ICT departments are a mix of some centralized and some decentralized activity. Centralized functions include building new computer applications, operating and maintaining existing systems, as well as helping to develop strategic plans for the use of ICT. By contrast there may be smaller groups of ICT professionals who are responsible for supporting computer operations in other functions, say operations or marketing, or providing localized ICT training or end-user support. The structure of the information management function can vary greatly depending on an organization's culture and the characteristics of the industry sector it is in. Structures will be different depending on the variety of different organizational and department needs. Furthermore, as organizations evolve they change their business processes often through new technology adoption. The ICT departmental structures have to adapt to reflect these changes.

While a certain level of information management expertise needs to be distributed across the organization, there is a critical role for information management specialists to integrate activity throughout the organization, building and maintaining the corporate information infrastructures necessary for integrated information processes.

The history of ICT management

The history of information and communication technologies is one of phenomenal and rapid technological development. Often the potential of the technology has outstripped the ability of organizations to make use of it. The way that organizations have tried to manage this technology has gone through several distinct stages.

Computing technology has been used in organizations since the late 1950s. Initially, computers were seen as mammoth calculating machines, relevant only to scientists and code-breakers. It was not until the second or third generation of computers appeared on the market that commercial computing and data processing really emerged. The first applications of this technology were for routine business data handling and hence this phase of applications acquired the generic name of Data Processing Systems or DP for short. Early commercial computers were used mainly to automate the routine clerical work of large administrative departments. As the costs of these early computers were very high and the scope of what they could do was limited by comparison to today's standards, the business benefits were to be gained by automating large-scale administrative processing. Because of this they were used to automate existing processes, especially for tasks that were labour intensive, such as well-defined accounting operations like Payroll and general ledger systems.

By the late 1960s computers had become pervasive with large corporations having acquired big mainframe systems. Rapid advances in both the hardware (the computers themselves) and the software (the code that makes the hardware perform required tasks) meant that commercial systems became more efficient and reliable which led to further take-up of the technology. Most of these companies had large centralized computer installations which operated remotely from their users and the rest of the business. The growth in computing led organizations to question the changes that were taking place. Somogyi and Galliers (2003) state that three separate areas of concern emerged:

1   Organizations started examining the merits of introducing computerized systems. While the systems being developed were effective, given the objectives of automatic clerical labour, the financial savings were not always being realized. The reduction in the number of moderately paid clerks was more than offset by the need to employ highly paid data processing professionals, as well as the high cost of the computers themselves. In addition, the computers also required staggering maintenance costs. The remote 'ivory tower' approach of the data processing departments made it very difficult for them to develop new systems that genuinely met the needs of the users. User dissatisfaction grew with the amount of time it took for data processing departments to make system changes and their apparent inability to satisfy user needs.

2   Organizations had not anticipated that replacing manual operations with the introduction of computer systems would mean that substantial organizational and job changes would be necessary. It was becoming clear that data processing systems had the potential of changing organizational structures.

3   It was becoming clear that a lot of systems had significant limitations. This was partly due to the fact that the centralized, remote, batch processing systems did not fit many real life business situations. The output from such systems often presented historical rather than current information. This was fine for some operations but not useful for up to the minute decision-making purposes.

Consequently, organizations began to change the way they approached the management of computing technology. Software engineering emerged as a new discipline. This attempted to take a formalized and analytical approach to system development. At the same time as this, new technology was emerging, most notably the mini computer, which meant that computing power no longer had to be centralized in some remote location. This allowed organizations to place computing systems closer to the business departments they were supposed to serve. The mini computer also opened up the possibility of using computer systems in smaller companies.

As more and more routine company operations became supported by computer systems, organizations realized that there was a growing need for a more coherent and flexible approach. Holding data in different systems scattered throughout different departments meant that it was not possible to cross-reference data from various departments. This began to limit the ability of managers to make effective decisions. Two solutions to this problem arose. First, it was realized that the data needed to be separate from the systems that processed that data to create specific management information. This heralded the arrival of database technology, which is a collection of software for holding data which follows a set of basic rules about the way data should be stored. The drive for data independence brought about major advances in thinking about systems and in the practical methods of describing, analysing and storing data. The second solution centred on the development of telecommunications technology which began to allow computers at remote geographic locations to be inter-connected. During the 1980s telecommunications and networking really flourished. Coupled with the idea that data should be separate from the systems that process it, organizations were able to manage their computing resources in new ways that allowed for distributed data processing. This was dramatically enhanced by the introduction of the personal computer (PC) which put significant computing power on managers' desks. While these developments offered the potential for enormous gains from information systems, there were also a number of problems experienced as a result of the proliferation of incompatible systems and the fragmentation of data throughout the organization. It is during this period that the first information management functions begin to emerge. This function is a step beyond the traditional data processing departments and system development departments. While often including these skilled activities, the information management function was developed to manage information effectively throughout the organization. This recognized that information had become an extremely valuable resource and that a coherent approach was necessary if organizations were to achieve competitive advantage through information systems. Often the information management function was headed up by the 'chief information officer'. This was a new role that gave boardroom recognition to the importance of careful information management.

Throughout the last decade ICT have continued to advance at an overwhelming rate. Accordingly, the emphasis of what organizations seek to achieve from this new technology has changed radically since the first computers were introduced. The use of ICT is now seen from a strategic perspective as organizations rely on ICT applications to streamline structures and to link them electronically to their customers and suppliers, enabled greatly with the development of the Internet. The role of the information management function is no longer seen in isolation but is intertwined with that of the other organizational functions. Communication between the information management function and the rest of the organization is critical to reshaping business processes. Indeed, business process re-engineering has been a driving force in recent years. This uses new technology to move beyond the efficiency and effectiveness gains of earlier information systems in order to bring about radical changes in the very nature of the way organizations operate.

To summarize, the main generic benefits of ICT can be seen as:

1 *Efficiency:* a shortening of the time needed to complete a work task, i.e. doing the same job better and thus saving other resources.

2 *Effectiveness*: the ability to restructure work to allow employees to utilize their time more constructively resulting in quality, excellence and image improvements.

3 *Strategic advantage*: improving the business by exploiting the ways in which ICT can support or drive strategic business change. The application of ICT in this arena may frequently cause a restructuring or redefinition of the business, even leading an organization into new business opportunities.

These benefits can be seen as mapping onto the key stages of ICT management, described above. In the past the lack of ICT and business integration has not seemed so important or necessary. The issue has not been of overwhelming concern to either senior management or information management professionals. However, this management issue is now central due to changes in the application of ICT and changes in the competitive environment in which organizations are expected to operate. The way that information resources are managed is now inseparable from the rest of organizational activity.

Key challenges for the information management function

The historical development of information and communication technology (as described above) has meant that organizations are faced with a number of key challenges with respect to information management.

ICT resources comprise a large and often growing portion of most organizational budgets. Often the promised benefits of new information systems do not fully materialize and in numerous cases new systems are completed over time and over budget. There have even been several cases where systems have not met requirements and have had to be abandoned. Because of cost pressures and increased competition many organizations intensely scrutinize their ICT budgets. However, assessing investments in ICT generally has proved problematic as a number of intangible elements exist that cannot be measured easily if at all (Hinton and Kaye, 1996). Equally, there has been a failure to establish any relationship between ICT investments and productivity gains (Strassmann, 1999). In the past the exploitation of ICT has generally resulted in efficiency related benefits. This is appraised using well-established techniques and principles like Cost Benefit Analysis or Return on Investment (ROI). However, as the nature of ICT applications has shifted these techniques are no longer applicable. Information systems designed to support management effectiveness create problems for management as the benefits they produce tend to be qualitative in nature, for example, gains in customer service, improved management communication, or enhanced corporate image. Equally, these benefits may be cancelled out by competing organizations also investing in similar systems. Consequently, some systems become part of the operating fabric of an organization, which on the one hand do not provide any competitive benefits but, by the same token, the organization cannot do without. This is happening with much of the use of the Internet. Where once e-commerce applications would have given significant competitive benefits, they are now becoming a basic requirement for doing business in many industries.

ICT are now so widely dispersed on modern organizations that it is impossible to separate out most business processes from the technology needed to enable it. It is often the case that organizations have become so reliant on key information systems that if those systems experience any form of service disruption, for even a few seconds, it can have severe ramifications. This is particularly true as the use of new technology has facilitated global trading which has exposed modern organizations to increased competition on an unprecedented scale. Indeed, the reliance on key information systems poses another challenge. These systems clearly represent intellectual assets that are the foundation of information-based organizations, so how should these organizations value them and what measures should be put in place to protect such an asset?

A further challenge for organizations is that they now have to manage a complex network of intertwined information systems that permeate every corner of modern organizations. This brings with it a whole series of concerns. The act of developing a computer system imposes a structure on particular organizational processes which are effectively frozen in time and context. The system design is fixed at the time the design took place and within the environment which was existing then. Hence, it *concretes* in whatever is the required information systems for that time. The comparison here is that human systems have the capability to be both dynamic and diverse, while the technological rigidity of information systems tends to render them static. While the benefits of automation are initially appealing to organizations, the costs associated with the incapacity to adapt systems to a changing business environment are not considered. This *dependency* occurs when organizations fail to take into account the human elements of their business processes. A further aspect of this dependency is that organizations become reliant on the trappings needed to support their systems. For example:

1   Technology dependency: the more that the technological components of systems dominate, the greater the organizational dependency on technology. Accordingly, many organizations cannot function without access to the technology. Once organizational information is stored in a technical form it requires some sort of technical interface to access and manipulate it. System failure leads to organizational failure. This is a

hidden cost in that it requires the investment of significant organizational resources over time to ensure that technical failure is avoided.

2   Personnel dependency: technology dependency can lead to a personnel dependency. This is twofold. First, information systems require a body of technical experts (programmers, analysts and the like). These employees become critical to the functioning of the organization and some organizations feel that they have suffered a loss of control over key business systems, especially where they have outsourced their ICT operations. Secondly, the underlying skill level of the users expected to work with an information system demands a level of technical competence. An organization has little control over the level of system understanding or the diffusion of learning. Consequently, it is dependent on the users' qualities of skill acquisition as to how well their information systems will be utilized.

3   Data dependency: the issue of dependency on data, investment in them and the cost of their transfer from one system to another is a common challenge for organizations. In the majority of cases data have become a business necessity and it is seen as essential to protect them and guarantee their availability.

As organizations evolve they build up a succession of past investments in ICT. Past generations of ICT investment are known as *legacy systems*. Organizations become locked into certain technologies (both hardware and software) and ideas about design and implementation (approaches to programming, maintenance and support). Modern organizations recognize that there are key information systems which they are dependent upon. The information management challenge arises when the organization needs to change its business processes. If they were less dependent then they would simply migrate to the next technical platform with minimal effort. However, managers are constantly aware of the need for future investments to *coexist* with existing systems. New technology offers new opportunities, but organizations have to take into account the legacy of the existing structures and systems. This can only serve to restrict or, at best, channel new investment down particular technological avenues (Hinton and Kaye, 1996).

In planning for and applying ICT managers need to balance the influence and effects of the technological change on the different members of the organization. It is generally accepted that a significant source of organizational power may be derived from the control of, or access to, critical organizational information. This makes the information systems that process it critical. Indeed, determining the design, content and responsibility for such systems is frequently contentious. Furthermore, the users of an information system are critical to its success or failure. New systems can have a range of effects. For example, users may be more motivated and productive as a result of the system. On the other hand, new systems can lead to changed work roles, potentially deskilling users who may experience a degree of alienation. Despite all of this, the influence of ICT is often analysed in a fashion which depoliticizes the real processes involved. The justification for ICT can become an organizational battleground due to the political issues raised by technological change. The challenge for the information management function is to navigate a smooth path through this state of affairs.

To summarize, the challenge of managing ICT continues to be demanding. Ongoing research in this area has identified a number of key issues which continue to occupy the attention of the information management function of virtually all organizations. These are:

1   Aligning organizational goals with what the new technology can deliver.
2   Employing ICT to enhance productivity and quality.
3   Exploiting ICT to generate competitive advantage.
4   Redesigning business processes to support the organization more effectively.
5   Justifying the ICT investments needed to achieve all of this.

In addressing all of these issues modern organizations need to take into account the unique circumstances of their own organizational culture, as these provide the conditions against which new technology evolves within the organization. More often than not, these issues are managerial in nature so organizations need to find the right blend of management skills to complement an underlying technical expertise.

Key concepts in information management

As information and communication technologies become ever more diffuse within modern organizations, managers are using a variety of models to help them control and evaluate increasingly vital information assets. These models draw on a set of concepts that, at their heart, address many of the challenges presented in the last section.

Strassmann's (1995) concept of Information Management Superiority attempts to address the challenge of aligning organizational goals with appropriate ICT investments. In this framework information management superiority is maintained by five core ideas:

1   *Governance*: governance concerns power and applying an understanding of the distribution and sharing of power to the management of information and communication technologies. Information management is the process by which those who set policy guide those who follow policy and governance is central to this.

2   *Business plan alignment*: if plans for the use of ICT are to have credence then they need to be in line with organizational business plans.

3   *Process improvement*: regular analysis of all ICT activities is necessary to discover areas where improvements might be made.

4   *Resource optimization*: in seeking to maximize the benefits of information resources, managers must take into account their use of other resources (such as people, money and time). These resources may be utilized better elsewhere in the furtherance of organizational goals.

5   *Operating excellence*: operating excellence is concerned with the ongoing delivery of superior performance and quality across all business processes.

It is the constant interaction of these five core ideas that results in information management superiority. Governance is critical, however, as organizations face the challenges associated with technological change. As was previously stressed, the information management function is charged with finding a smooth path through this organizational battleground. Inevitably, there are conflicts that require resolution if organizations are to take advantage of the enormous power of new technologies. Strassmann argues that the resolution of these conflicting interests now requires the introduction of formal governance processes that will keep up with the accelerating rate of change both in technology as well as in competitive relationships. In many ways the concept of information management superiority traces the development of the information management function. Initially, organizations were generally only concerned with (4) resource optimization. As the nature of information systems development moved from automation to more strategic applications, their attention was drawn to (3) process improvement and (2) business plan alignment. The focus on business alignment and process improvement has seen organizations address (5) operating excellence as a way of refining their management of ICT. Governance encapsulates the latest phase in this development, where organizations can turn their attention to the rules governing technology dispersal and policy development. Establishing a guiding policy for ICT acquisition and deployment is now more significant than owning and operating large computer systems. Governance allows organizations to attend to policies which support the best use of their information resources without necessarily meaning they have to be responsible for the technical operations to support this. This is reflected in the significant move towards the outsourcing of these technical operations to a variety of third-party ICT service firms.

Various theories have been proposed to explain how information systems change over time. Research conducted by Nolan (1979) found that organizations tend to go through several quite distinct phases of growth. The results of their observations strongly suggest that as organizations implement new information systems and gradually assimilate this technology into their new working practices they go through six distinct and predictable stages. They showed that expenditure on new ICTs follows an S-shaped curve of increasing costs. Expenditure is gradual at first but increasing dramatically before adopting a more gradual slope again. This curve also represents a path of organizational learning about the potential use of ICT within organizations.

The characteristics of the stages can be summarized as:

1   *Initiation stage* – automation of clerical operations where some more technically minded employees use technology because they are keen, rather than use it for cost effectiveness. Usage grows slowly as people become familiar with the technologies potential.

2   *Contagion stage* – rapid growth as users become more familiar with applications and demand more and where the wider benefits of technology are perceived by more staff.

3   *Control stage* – planning and methodologies are introduced in order to assert control over developments and investment in technology is taking place in a planned manner. Controls may be introduced by setting up steering committees and project management teams. Managers become increasingly concerned about the relative costs and benefits of ICT applications.

4   *Integration stage* – the integration of the various computing functions within the organization; there is a wider user involvement in system development and a drive towards integrated systems and databases.

5   *Data administration stage* – emphasis is placed on information requirements rather than just processing requirements and there is sufficient information available to support ongoing decision-making activity. The organization is concerned with the value of its data resources and takes action to ensure the effective utilization of its databases.

6   *Maturity stage* – careful information management ensures that the application of new technology is brought into line with ongoing business planning and development. Information flows mirror the real-world requirements of the organization, which will be using a variety of applications to support its information needs. Technology and management processes are integrated into an efficiently functioning entity.

Nolan's six stage model is useful because it makes it possible to classify organizations into the stage they are presently at, thereby, being able to predict their future response to new ICT. Not all organizations within an industry sector will be at the same growth stage. Equally, within an organization different departments might also be at different stages of development. By recognizing this it is possible for an organization to understand how more advanced departments progressed and transfer that knowledge to help speed up developments in other departments still at earlier stages of development. This also means that they can produce strategic plans that are not too ambitious and anticipate possible pitfalls associated with the later stages of the model. Although this is more of a conceptual rather than a quantitative tool, the growth stage model is important for good information management because it provides critical appreciation of technology adoption processes. While the model may be criticized as not fully appreciating recent developments in ICT, the basic idea that organizations go through stages when adopting technology still applies and has been observed in a number of recent cutting edge electronic commerce applications.

Exploiting ICT to generate competitive advantage is an all consuming challenge for organizations which demands considerable management attention. Accordingly, it has been the focus for much concept development. As long ago as the 1970s Rockart (1979) developed the notion of critical success factors (CSF). Critical success factors help to focus on those few areas where things must go right. These represent the necessary conditions for organizational success. When this concept is applied to the information management function it is invaluable in detecting what information systems are vital for organizational success. Furthermore, by breaking down each factor into a set of key decision points it is possible to identify what specific actions are required to manage the use of new technologies if success is to be realized. It is true that, at a general level, critical success factors for the information management function are closely aligned with the key challenges presented earlier. However, application of this concept does allow for a very specific analysis of key challenges within a particular organizational context.

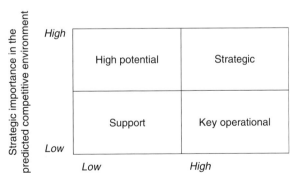

Figure 2.1   The applications portfolio grid
Source: ACCA (2001) *Business Information Management: paper 3.4 textbook*, Foulks Lynch Ltd

In trying to make sense of the strategic dimension of their information systems many organizations look at the whole portfolio of systems that they have. The applications portfolio concept looks at the strategic impact of individual applications within the organization and classifies them in terms of their current and future strategic importance.

The information management function can use the grid (see Figure 2.1) to seek out those applications that have the greatest strategic potential. The categories are:

1 *Support* – applications that improve management effectiveness but are not critical to the organization. The benefits they deliver are predominantly economic as with the cost savings realized from automation (payroll systems, accounting systems etc.).

2 *Key operational* – applications that sustain the existing business supporting core organizational activities (inventory control, order management etc.).

3 *Strategic* – applications that are critical to both current and future organizational goals.

4 *High potential* – applications that can be seen as innovative and potentially of future strategic importance, such as electronic commerce applications or expert systems.

Over time an organization can chart the evolving nature of its applications portfolio. Today's high potential e-commerce system is tomorrow's strategic necessity, which in time may become just another key operational application. A complementary approach has been suggested by Parsons (ACCA, 2001) who offers a conceptual framework that organizations can use to understand their current information systems strategy and to explore possible other strategies within their resource constraints. The framework suggests six generic strategies:

1 *Centrally planned* – information systems strategy is developed to support the greater organizational strategy and is managed at the highest level accordingly. The role for the information management function is one of service provider closely linked to the user community to deliver the business demands and combining this with significant input into the ongoing organizational planning process.

2 *Leading edge* – this strategy is implemented because the organization believes that innovative new technologies will create competitive advantage. Following this strategy can produce huge rewards but is based on a high level of risk taking for the organization. The role for the information management function with this strategy is one of experimenter and promoter, constantly pushing the technical boundaries. Likewise users are enthusiastic to utilize the new technology and incorporate it in their work practices.

3   *Free market* – ICT requirements are determined by an organization's business units (say marketing department, HR etc.) and may be supplied either internally or externally subject to best price and service. The role for the information management function is as a competitive business unit providing ICT solutions in competition with external service providers. Many organizations that employ this strategic approach outsource components of their information management structure to specialized ICT companies.

4   *Monopoly* – the organization has decided that there will be one internal source of supply for ICT. In this strategic scenario the information management function role is reactive with no requirement to direct future developments. User departments have to bid for ICT resources.

5   *Scarce resource* – there must be clearly justified returns on investment in new systems with little scope for innovation. The role for the information management function is to make the best of the limited resource, but this strategy tends to have a long-term negative effect on information exploitation.

6   *Necessary evil* – this strategy is adopted in organizations that believe that information is not important in their business. The information management function provides the minimum level of resources, just enough to meet basic needs. Users in other functions take no part in the development or management of information systems.

These days, as the importance of information is paramount, it is inconceivable that any organizations will find themselves with a 'necessary evil' strategy. When used in conjunction with some of the other concepts in this section, this framework suggests ways that organizations should structure their ICT departments and resources.

Future developments

So where next for the management of information? Modern organizations find themselves tasked with creating new business knowledge and disseminating it widely throughout the organization. Successful knowledge-creating organizations (sometimes called learning organizations) create techniques, infrastructures and systems to encourage employees to share what they know and to make better use of accumulated workplace knowledge. This simple idea is the basis for a challenging concept called *knowledge management*. A major purpose of knowledge management is to allow for knowledge sharing. Knowledge sharing is encouraged between customers, employees and business partners because it offers significant potential benefits. These come in the form of improved customer service, better supply chain management and increased collaboration both within the organization and beyond. Knowledge management systems are information systems that facilitate organizational learning and knowledge creation. Accordingly, knowledge management is fast becoming one of the major strategic uses of information systems. The new challenge of knowledge management requires that ICT departments begin providing systems that are capable of supporting knowledge management. According to Turban et al. (2001) these activities include:

- Knowledge identification – determining what knowledge is critical to decision making.

- Knowledge discovery and analysis – using tools and techniques such as databases, data mining and search engines to find appropriate knowledge and analyse it within a given organizational context.

- Establishment of organizational knowledge bases – organizational knowledge and best practice needs to be recorded, indexed and maintained in a knowledge base.

- Knowledge distribution and use – target audiences are identified and technologies adopted to facilitate knowledge delivery when needed.

The information management function has to find the right blend of new technology and creative applications to address these requirements. Many organizations are making use of a wide variety of technologies, such as data warehousing, document management, intranets and the Web (which are becoming the knowledge management infrastructure), as well as tools for data visualization and intelligent text retrieval.

The benefits to be gained from knowledge management have led many organizations to change their perspective of their information resources. The realization that there is much to be gained from sharing information across organizational boundaries has seen the development of the *virtual organization*. A virtual organization will comprise several business partners who aim to share costs and resources. Such arrangements can be temporary, as with the construction industry where partners come together for the duration of a building project, disbanding once the project is complete. The virtual organization can be viewed as a network of creative people, resources and ideas connected via online services, who group together to produce goods or services. The virtual organization combines the core competencies of the various partners as well as allowing the full utilization of resources across all partners. Frequently, this leads to the redefinition of both organizational boundaries and international business boundaries. Such close cooperation makes it difficult to see where one organization ends and another begins. The application of information systems and communications technology is vital in creating these alternative structures, but by the same token will require modern organizations radically to rethink how they go about managing information.

References

ACCA (2001) *Business Information Management: paper 3.4 textbook*, Foulks Lynch Ltd.

Frenzel, C. (1999) *Management of Information Technology*, Thomson Learning.

Hinton, M. and Kaye, R. (1996) The hidden investment in information technology: the role of organizational context and system dependency. *International Journal of Information Management*, 16, 6, 413–427.

Nolan, R. (1979) Managing the crisis in data processing. *Harvard Business Review*, March–April, p. 115.

Rockart, J. (1979) Chief executives define their own data needs. *Harvard Business Review*, March–April, p. 81.

Somogyi, E. and Galliers, R. (2003) Developments in the application of information technology in business. In *Strategic Information Management*, Galliers, R. and Leidner, D., eds, Butterworth-Heinemann.

Strassmann, P. (1995) *The Politics of Information Management*, Information Economics Press.

Strassmann, P. (1999) *Information Productivity: Assessing the Information Management Costs of US Industrial Corporations*, Information Economics Press.

Turban, E., Rainer, R. and Potter, R. (2001) *Introduction to Information Technology*, Wiley and Sons.

Chapter 3

Organizing and leading the information technology function

Lynda M. Applegate, F. Warren McFarlan and
James L. McKenney

[...] The management structures needed for guiding new technologies into
the organization are quite different from those for older, established
technologies. The corporation must encourage information technology (IT)
staff and users to innovate with the newer technologies, while focusing
on control and efficiency in the more mature technologies. In this chapter,
we will discuss two rapidly changing aspects of IT management: the range
of organizational alternatives that have emerged for effectively assigning
responsibility for IT development and the coordination and location of IT
policy formulation among users, IT and general management.

Organizing issues in IT development

Policies for guiding the deployment of IT development staff and activity in
the future must deal with two sets of tensions. The first [...] is the balance
between innovation and control. The relative emphasis a firm should place
on the aggressive innovation phase varies widely, depending on a broad
assessment of the potential strategic impact of IT on the firm, general
corporate willingness to take risk and so on. If IT is perceived to be of great
import in helping the firm reach its strategic objectives, significantly greater
investment in innovation is called for than if IT is seen to be merely helpful.
The opportunities to many firms offered by the explosion of Enterprise and
Intranet software readjusted the balance toward more innovation.

The second set of tensions is between IT department dominance and user
dominance in the retention of development skills and in the active selection of
priorities. The user tends towards short-term need fulfilment (at the expense
of long-term architectural IT structure and orderly development), while the IT
department can become preoccupied with the mastery of technology and an
orderly development plan at the risk of a slow response, or no response, to
legitimate user needs. Balancing the roles of these two groups is a complex
task that must be handled in the context of the corporate culture, IT's potential
strategic role and the urgency of short-term problem resolution.

Table 3.1   Possible implications of excess IT and user dominance

IT dominance	User dominance
Too much emphasis on database and system maintenance	Too much emphasis on problem focus
All new systems must fit data structure of existing system	IT feels out of control
All requests for service require system study with benefit identification	Explosive growth in number of new systems and supporting staff
Standardization dominates with few exceptions	Multiple suppliers deliver services. Frequent change in supplier of specific service
IT designs/constructs everything	Lack of standardization and control over data and systems
Benefits of user control over development discussed but never implemented	Hard evidence of benefits non-existent
Study always shows construction costs less than outside purchase	Soft evidence of benefits not organized
Headcount of distributed minis and development staff growing surreptitiously	Few measurements/objectives for new system
IT specializing in technical frontiers, not user-oriented markets	Technical advice of IT not sought; if received, considered irrelevant
IT spending 80 per cent on maintenance, 20 per cent on development	User buying design, construction, maintenance and operations services from outside
IT thinks it is in control of all	User building networks to own unique needs, not to corporate need
Users express unhappiness	Some users are growing rapidly in experience and use, while others feel nothing is relevant because they do not understand
Portfolio of development opportunities firmly under IT control	No coordinated effort between users for technology transfer or learning from experience
No strong user group exists	Growth in duplication of technical staff
General management not involved but concerned	Dramatically rising communication costs because of redundancy
	Duplication of effort and input everywhere because different data, hardware and communications will not allow seamless movement

Table 3.1 reveals some consequences of excessive domination by IT and by users, clearly indicating that very different application portfolios and operating problems emerge in the two settings. Given the difficulty of anticipating the implications of introducing a new technology, this chapter will emphasize the need for experimentation, as illustrated by the following [...] cases.

Some examples

Case 1: Step-by-step innovation of a new technology

A large South African retail chain installed a system of point-of-sale terminals in all of their 50-plus stores. The retail division (with the support of the IT manager) had initially funded the installation to assist store managers in controlling inventory. The terminals were to be used exclusively within individual stores to accumulate daily sales totals of individual items and permit the stores to trigger reorders in case lots at given times. The planned inventory savings were quickly achieved.

At the initiative of corporate management, these IT systems then evolved into links to central headquarters. The links fed data from the stores to new corporate computer programs that measured product performance across the stores and provided the ability to manage warehouse stock levels chain-wide much more efficiently. Because the communication protocols in the selected terminals were incompatible with those in the computer at headquarters, implementing this unplanned linkage was expensive.

Nonetheless, the possibilities and benefits of the resulting system would have been difficult to define in advance, since this eventual use was not considered important when the initial point-of-sale terminals were being installed. Further, in management's opinion, even if the organization had considered it, the ultimate costs of the resulting system would have been deemed prohibitive in relation to the benefits (in retrospect, incorrectly prohibitive). In an uncertain world, there are limitations to planning; in this case, the success of the first system laid the baseline for the next ones. The firm is now using the network to implement company-wide a customer loyalty card to enable detailed understanding of who its key customers are and their individual buying habits better to target coupons and special discounting programmes. Again, this was not anticipated at the beginning of the process.

Case 2: User innovation as a source of productivity

A large bank introduced an electronic mail system and a word processor system to facilitate preparation of loan paperwork. The two systems soon evolved to link the bank's loan officers (initially not planned to be clients of either system) to a series of analytical programs – an evolution that developed out of conversations between a loan officer and a consultant. Bundled with the word processor loan system was a powerful analytical tool that officers could use to analyse loan performance. Because of the bank's electronic mail system, loan officers (at headquarters and in branches) could easily access the analytical tool.

Three months later, the bank faced a series of internal tensions as the costs of both systems unexpectedly rose due to this added use. In addition, there were no formal means of reviewing 'experiments' or evaluating unanticipated uses of the systems by participants not initially involved. Eventually, a senior-management review committee supported the new use of the two systems and it was permitted to continue. Substantial enhancements were added to the word processing software to make it even more useful to the loan officers.

Implications

Typical of emerging new services supporting professionals and managers in doing work, the above examples powerfully convey our conviction that it is impossible to foresee in advance the full range of consequences of introducing IT systems. Excessive control and focus on quick results in the early stages can deflect important learning that can result in even more useful applications. In addition, because neither IT professionals nor users have outstanding records in anticipating how new technologies will affect organizations, a necessary general management role is to help facilitate this assimilation.

The material that follows is divided into three sections. The first discusses the pressures on users to gain control – not only over a system's development activities but, when possible, over the resulting product so it can run on a networked basis from the department. The second section identifies the advantages of strong IT development coordination and the potential pitfalls of uncontrolled proliferation of user-developed systems. The third section identifies the core policies that must be implemented by IT management, user management and general management, respectively, in order to ensure a good result. The general manager's role is particularly critical in creating an environment that facilitates technological change and organizational adaptation.

Pressures toward user dominance

A number of intense pressures encourage users to exercise stronger control over their systems development resources and acquisition of independent IT resources. These pressures can be clustered into seven categories: pent-up user demand, the needs for staffing flexibility, staff professional growth, competitive and service growth in the IT market, users' desire to control their destiny, fit with the organization, and user learning.

Pent-up user demand

The backlog of development work facing an IT systems development department is frequently very large in relation to its staff resources. The reasons for these staffing 'crunches' are many. Existing systems, for example, require sustained maintenance to accommodate changing regulatory and other external business requirements. In addition, the number of automated systems continues to grow and the maintenance time for existing systems rises as ongoing customization increases system complexity and systems' needs to be adapted to changes in the IT architecture.

The delays caused by these factors have led to enormous user frustration and a strong desire to take matters into their own hands. It has also been a driver towards outsourcing.

Staff flexibility and growth

Because the central IT department appears to be unresponsive to users' demands, user-developed systems become attractive to users as a non-confrontational way of getting work done. Deploying either their own staff or those from outside software houses, users see that they are significantly speeding up the process of obtaining 'needed' service.

Staff professional growth

An IT staff decentralized by both physical and organizational presence in the end-user department helps educate users to IT's legitimate potential; it also reduces communications problems between IT professionals and end users. Particularly important, it makes it easier to plan employee promotions that rotate IT staff to other (non-IT) jobs within the department, thus enhancing user–IT coordination. This also facilitates moving end users to IT positions.

Competitive and service growth in the IT market

Thousands of stand-alone software packages are available for specific applications, ranging from simple accounts-payable systems to complete desktop support products. These systems appear to provide beguilingly easy solutions to short-term problems. Marketed by hardware and software vendors to end-user managers, the systems' functional features are emphasized and any technical and software problems are soft-pedalled. [...]

User control

The idea of regaining control over a part of their units' operations, particularly if IT is critical, is very important to users. In many cases, this reverses a trend that began 20 years ago in a very different technological environment. Control in this context has at least two dimensions.

Development

Users can exercise direct control over systems development priorities. By using either their own staff or self-selected software houses, which may offer highly specialized skills not present in the firm, users often hope to get a system with vastly improved support features functioning in less time than it would take to navigate the priority-setting process in the corporate IT department. A user systems staff is also seen as closer and more responsive to user needs because the local manager, rather than an outsider, sets priorities. Development mistakes made by a local group are more easily accepted than those made by a remote group and they are rarely discussed; successes, by contrast, are often topics of conversation.

Maintenance

Users gain control over systems maintenance priorities, since the work will be done either by themselves or by software houses that are dependent upon them for income. Users often overlook the importance of this point at the time of initial systems installation: their assumption is that maintenance will be no problem or that it can be performed by a clerk following a manual – a rare occurrence! Needs and desires relentlessly change and they come to appreciate the need for major maintenance and desire to control it.

Fit with the organization

As the company becomes more decentralized in structure and more geographically diverse, a distributed development function becomes a much better fit and avoids heavy internal marketing and coordination expenses. Among conglomerates, for example, only a few have tried to centralize development; most leave it with the original units. Heavily decentralized companies such as Pioneer Hi-Bred have closed down the central IT development unit and placed the IT developers in key divisions. Finally, should the corporation decide to divest a unit, the process will be easier to implement if its IT activities are not integrated with the rest of the company.

User learning

Predicting the full ramifications of introducing a new technology is very difficult. On the one hand, enthusiastic user experimentation with work under their control can stimulate creativity and produce new approaches to troublesome problems. Systems developed by a central IT unit, on the other hand, must overcome greater user resistance in adoption. This IT challenge simply reflects research in the fields of organization development and control, which has identified organization learning as a principal benefit of organizing in multiple profit centres, rather than by function. [...]

Summary

In aggregate, these seven pressures represent a powerful argument for a strong user role in systems development and suggest when that role might be the dominant one. The pressures driving users toward purchase, development, and/or use of local systems and software can be summarized as short-term user control. [...]

Pressures toward IT control

Countering the arguments of the previous section, pressures exist in many settings to consolidate a firm's IT development resource into a single unit or to at least keep it in two or more large clusters.

Staff professionalism

As noted, a large central IT development staff enhances the organization's ability to recruit and retain (attract and keep challenged) specialized technical personnel. A central unit also provides useful support for a small division or unit that does not have its own IT staff and needs occasional access to IT skills.

Additionally, it is easier to modernize a centralized unit than one in which the development staff are scattered throughout the firm. [...]

Developing and enforcing better standards of IT management practice is also easier in a large group. Documentation procedures, project management skills and disciplined maintenance approaches are examples of critical infrastructure items in IT systems development departments. [...]

Central staff expertise is particularly important for reviewing user-designed systems before they go live. Lacking practical systems design experience, the user often ignores normal data-control procedures, various corporate standards and conventional costing practices.

For example, a large financial organization discovered that all the people involved in software design and purchase for three of the departmental systems used to process data on a daily basis had left the company. Further, no formal documentation or operating instructions had been prepared and all source programs had been lost. What remained were disk files with object programs on them. The system ran, but why it ran no one knew; and even if the company's survival depended on it, changes would at best have been very difficult and time-consuming to execute. [...]

Feasibility concerns

A user-driven feasibility study may contain major technical mistakes that will result in the information system's being either inadequate to handle growing processing requirements or not easily maintainable. Because of inexperienced staff, the feasibility study may underestimate both the complexity of the software needed and the growth in the number of transactions to be handled by the system. (The risk increases if competent technical staff inputs to the feasibility study were limited and if the real business needs were not well understood.) [...]

Particular care must be taken on local systems development projects, since uncoordinated user groups tend to buy or develop systems tailored to very specific situations, creating long-term maintenance problems. In many environments characterized by such local development, there is poor technology transfer between similar users and a consequent lack of corporate leverage, an issue of low importance to the local unit but a great concern from the corporate viewpoint.

A large forest products company, organized geographically, combined a system-minded regional manager with an aggressive growth-oriented IT manager who was responsible for all administrative support in the region. Within three years, the region's IT budget was double that of a comparable region; however, although their applications were extraordinarily effective, only one was exported to another region. Subsequent review indicated that nearly half of the systems developed were focused on problems of potentially general interest and could have been exported to other parts of the company.

Corporate databases

A corporate database strategy involves both collecting a pointer file (or files) at a central location for reference by multiple users and developing client-server networks and procedures that allow users, regardless of physical location, to access these data files easily. A central development staff provides a focal point for both conceptualizing and developing the architecture of these systems to serve multiple users across the firm. The need for database sharing varies widely with the nature of the corporation's activities, of course. A conglomerate usually has much less need for data sharing across the firm than does a functionally organized, one-product company. However, electronic mail, videoconferencing, video streaming and shared financial performance information have become legitimate needs in most organizations and only a central department can cost-effectively develop and distribute such systems to users or coordinate a process whereby key parts of the system development efforts are outsourced to local development units in a way that ensures easy coordination between them. [...]

Fit with the corporate structure and strategy

Centralized IT development's role is clearest in organizations characterized by centrally managed planning and operational control. A large farm equipment manufacturer with a tradition of central functional control from corporate headquarters successfully implemented a program wherein the corporate systems group developed all software for factories and distribution units worldwide. As the company grew in size, however, its structure became more decentralized; in turn, the cost of effective central systems development was escalating. The firm had to implement a marketing function to educate users on the virtues of central services and to decentralize some development functions. It is becoming increasingly common for centralized development groups to have an explicitly defined and staffed internal marketing activity to ensure appropriate coordination with the decentralized units.

Cost analysis

Given its practical experience in other systems' efforts, a centralized IT development group can usually produce realistic software development estimates [...] that take into account the company's overall interests. Software development estimates are problematic in user feasibility studies for two key reasons. Most new systems are more software-intensive than hardware-intensive; software costs are typically 75–85 per cent of the total cost for a customized system. Few users have had experience in estimating software development costs and an order-of-magnitude mistake in a feasibility study – particularly if it is an individually developed system and not a 'turnkey' (i.e. general-purpose) package – is not unknown. [...]

Much of corporate IT is fixed costs in the short run, consequently appearing to the individual user, courtesy of the charge-out system, to be an opportunity to reduce costs. However, in reality, individual user cost reductions may be a cost increase for the company – more hardware/software acquired locally and no possible savings at the corporate IT facility. Policies for ensuring that appropriate cost analyses for decentralized activities are prepared must be established.

Summary

The pressures toward centralized IT control can be summarized by the words *long-term information architecture building*. Inexorably, over the long run, most (but not all) stand-alone units will become part of a network and need to both receive and share data with other users and systems. In many respects, these pressures are not immediately evident when the system is installed but tend to grow more obvious with the passage of time. Policies for managing the trade-offs between the obvious short-term benefits and long-term risks are delicate to administer, but necessary.

Coordination and location of IT policy

The tension between IT and users can be effectively managed by establishing clear policies that specify the user domain, the IT domain and senior management's role. Senior management must play a significant part in ensuring that these policies are developed and that they evolve appropriately over time. Both IT and users must understand the implications of their roles and possible conflicts.

IT responsibilities

The following tasks constitute the central core of IT responsibilities – the minimum for managing the long-term information hygiene needs of an organization:

1   Develop and manage the evolution of a long-term architectural plan and ensure that new projects fit into its evolution as much as possible.
2   Establish procedures to ensure that, for potential IT projects of any size, internal development versus purchase is compared. [...]
3   Maintain an inventory of installed or planned-to-be-installed information services.

4 Create and maintain a set of standards that establishes:
  (a) mandatory telecommunications standards
  (b) standard languages for classes of acquired equipment
  (c) documentation procedures for different types of systems
  (d) a corporate data dictionary with clear definitions of which elements must be included
  (e) identification of file maintenance standards and procedures
  (f) examination procedures for systems developed in local units to ensure that they do not conflict with corporate needs and that any necessary interfaces are constructed.

5 Identify and provide appropriate IT development staff career paths throughout the organization. [...]

6 Establish appropriate internal marketing efforts for IT support. These should exert catch-up pressure and coaching for units that are lagging and slow down units pushing too fast into leading-edge technologies they do not understand.

7 Prepare a detailed checklist of questions to be answered in any hardware/software acquisition to ensure that relevant technical and managerial issues are raised. [...]

8 Identify and maintain relationships with preferred systems suppliers. [...]

9 Establish education programmes for potential users that communicate both the benefits and the pitfalls of a new technology and that define users' roles in ensuring its successful introduction in their departments.

10 Set up an ongoing review of systems for determining which ones have become obsolete and should be redesigned.

These issues apply with particular force to the design of systems that become embedded in the company's daily operations. Decision support systems do not pose quite the same problems, although the need to obtain data from the rest of the organization is rapidly putting them in the same situation.

These core responsibilities, of course, can be significantly expanded to impose much tighter and more formal controls if the situation warrants.

User responsibilities

To assist in the orderly identification of opportunities and implementation of new IT services and to grow in an understanding of their use, cost and impact on the organization, the following responsibilities should be fulfilled by the user of IT service:

1 Clearly understand the scope of all IT activities supporting the user. [...]

2 To ensure satisfactory service, realistically appraise the amount of user personal investment required for each new project, both to develop and

to operate the system. These costs are often much higher than planned and are frequently ignored.

3   Ensure comprehensive user input for all IT projects that will support vital aspects of the unit's operations. [...]

4   Realistically ensure that the IT–user interface is consistent with IT's strategic relevance to the business unit. If it is very important, the interface must be very close. If it is less important, more distance between the parties and more friction can be tolerated.

5   Periodically audit the adequacy of system reliability standards, performance of communications services and adequacy of security procedures.

6   Participate in the development and maintenance of an IT plan that sets new technology priorities, schedules the transfer of IT among groups and evaluates a portfolio of projects in light of the company strategy.

These represent the very minimum policies that the users should develop and manage. Depending on the firm's geography, corporate management style, stage of IT development and mix of technology development phases, expanded levels of user involvement may be appropriate. [...]

General management support and policy overview

Distinct from the issues involved in the distribution of IT services is a cluster of broad policy and direction activities requiring senior management perspective. In the past, these activities were built into the structure of a central IT organization. Now, given the need to link IT to business, IT operations are frequently separated from IT planning. [...] For example, a major conglomerate whose development staff and hardware are distributed to key users has a three- to four-person group at headquarters level. Firms that outsource most or all of their IT operations, development and maintenance activities still need this policy group.

Key responsibilities of a corporate IT policy group should include:

1   Ensure that an appropriate balance exists between IT and user inputs across the different technologies and that one side is not dominating the other inappropriately. Initiate appropriate personnel and organizational transfers if the situation is out of balance. [...]

2   Ensure that a comprehensive corporate IT strategy is developed.

3   Manage the inventory of hardware and software resources and assure that the corporate view extends to purchasing relationships and contracts. [...]

4   Facilitate the creation and evolution of standards for development and operations activities and ensure that the standards are applied appropriately. [...] This [...] requires a technically competent and interpersonally sensitive staff.

5   Facilitate the transfer of technology from one unit to another. This occurs through recognizing the unit's common systems needs as well as stimulating joint projects. [...]

6   Actively encourage technical experimentation. [...]

7   Assume responsibility for developing an appropriate planning and control system to link IT firmly to the company's goals. [...]

As these responsibilities imply, the corporate IT policy group needs to be staffed with individuals who, in aggregate, have broad technical backgrounds and extensive practical IT administrative experience. [...]

Summary

This chapter has focused on the key issues surrounding the organization of IT development activities for the next decade. A significant revolution has occurred in what is regarded as good managerial practice in this field. Important contributors to this change have been the development of new hardware and software technologies and managerial experience with IT. These technologies not only permit quite different types of services to be delivered, but also offer the potential for quite different ways of delivering these services. Consequently, what constitutes best practice has changed considerably and the evolution seems likely to continue; many IT organization structures that were effectively put together in the 1970s were found inappropriate for the 1990s and those that fitted the early 1990s are inappropriate as we enter the world of the intranet in the early 21st century.

Determining the appropriate pattern of distribution of IT resources within the organization is a complex and multifaceted subject. The general manager should develop a programme that will encourage appropriate innovation on the one hand while maintaining overall control on the other. How these organization and planning issues are resolved is inextricably tied to non-IT-oriented aspects of the corporate environment. The leadership style of the person at the top of the organization and that person's view of the future provide one important thrust for redirection. A vision of tight central control presents a different context for these decisions than does a vision emphasizing the autonomy of operating units. Closely associated and linked to this are the corporate organizational structure and culture and the trends occurring within it. Also, the realities of geographical spread of the business units heavily affect IT organizational and planning possibilities; the corporate headquarters of a large domestic insurance company, for example, poses different constraints than do the multiple international plants and markets of an automobile manufacturer.

On a less global scale are the present realities of quality and location of existing IT resources (organizational and physical), which provide the base from which change must be made. Equally important is how responsive and competent current users perceive these resources to be. The unit that is seen (no matter how unfairly or inaccurately) as unresponsive has different organizational challenges than the well-regarded unit. [...]

In dealing with these forces, one is seeking an appropriate balance between innovation and control and between the inputs of the IT specialist and the user. Not only do appropriate answers to these questions vary among companies, but also different answers and structures are often appropriate for individual units within an organization. In short, there is a series of right questions to ask and there is an identifiable but very complex series of forces that, appropriately analysed, determine for each organizational unit the direction in which the correct answer lies – for now.

Source: Adapted from Applegate, L.M., McFarlan, F.W. and McKenney, J.L., 'Organizing and leading the information technology function' in Hinton, M. (2006) *Introducing Information Management: the business approach*, Elsevier.

Information and process

Chapter 4

Data, capta, information and knowledge

Peter Checkland and Sue Holwell

[The concept of information is a subtle one and one on which there is by no means complete agreement. However, this concept is needed if we are to understand how information supports purposeful action within organizations.]

There is at present no well-defined definition of such terms as 'data' and 'information' upon which there is general agreement. It is noteworthy that a current encyclopaedia of software engineering (Morris and Tamm, 1993) contains no entries for either 'data' or 'information'. Indeed one entry asserts that

> Computer programming is concerned with the processing of information *or* data.

If there were general agreement on the meaning of 'data' and 'information', the terms could be taken as given. Without such agreement, some analysis is necessary. [Some definitions from the literature of 'data' and 'information' are shown in Tables 4.1 and 4.2.]

Anderton (1991) gives some useful examples which illustrate that there are subtleties associated with the idea of information and its communication to others.

1   A motorist is travelling at 30 km/h. The speedometer indicates 30 km/h. Does the motorist have information about his speed? Apparently, yes. But actually the mechanism is stuck and although the indication happens to be correct, *the driver receives no information.*

2   A traveller plans to fly to another country but can do so only if she is free from smallpox. She has some medical tests in the afternoon and arranges with her doctor that if the results are positive the airport desk will be called before 5 p.m. At 5 p.m. she checks with the desk and finds that no message has been received. She thus receives the information that she is free of smallpox. Yet *no physical event has occurred*; nothing, apparently, has carried the information.

Table 4.1   Some literature definitions of 'data'

Avison and Fitzgerald (1995)	Data represent unstructured facts (p. 12)
Clare and Loucopoulos (1987)	Facts collected from observations or recordings about events, objects, or people (p. 2)
Galland (1982)	Facts, concepts or derivatives in a form that can be communicated and interpreted (p. 57)
Hicks (1993)	A representation of facts, concepts or instructions in a formalized manner suitable for communication, interpretation, or processing by humans or by automatic means (p. 668)
Knight and Silk (1990)	Numbers representing an observable object or event (fact) (p. 22)
Laudon and Laudon (1991)	Raw facts that can be shaped and formed to create information (p. 14)
Maddison (ed.) (1989)	Natural language: facts given, from which others may be deduced, inferred. Info. processing and computer science: signs or symbols, especially as for transmission in communication systems and for processing in computer systems; usually but not always representing information (sic), agreed facts or assumed knowledge; and represented using agreed characters, codes, syntax and structure (p. 168)
Martin and Powell (1992)	The raw material of organizational life; it consists of disconnected numbers, words, symbols and syllables relating to the events and processes of the business (p. 10)

3   A newspaper arrives at a football supporter's house. In it he reads the score: England 1 Italy 2. The supporter has the information that Italy has won the game. Five minutes later a friend arrives with a Xerox copy of the newspaper report. The supporter receives *no information about the game*, he knew the result already. His brother, incidentally, who has not seen the newspaper, receives the information from the Xerox that England played Italy yesterday, a fact he had not previously known (p. 57).

To these instructive cameos we may add a further real but somewhat bizarre example.

At a conference held at Edinburgh University, one of the authors of this chapter occupied a room in the Pollock Halls of Residence. From the room there was a good view of some of the rock faces known as Salisbury Crags in Holyrood Park. These have attracted rock climbers for many years and details of 20 climbs here were published as long ago as 1896. It was therefore amusing to read in the present rock climbing guide, which describes 50 climbs in detail, that

At present climbing on any cliff in the park is strictly illegal and anyone caught doing so is likely to be prosecuted. The route descriptions in this section of the guide are reproduced purely for their historical interest ...

Table 4.2 Some literature definitions of 'information' (after Aiba, 1993)

Avison and Fitzgerald (1995)	Information has a meaning ... [it] comes from selecting data, summarizing it and presenting it in such a way that it is useful to the recipient (p. 12)
Clare and Loucopoulos (1987)	A pre-requisite for a decision to be taken. Information is the product of the meaningful processing of data (p. 2)
Galland (1982)	Information is that which results when some human mental activity (observation, analysis) is successfully applied to data to reveal its meaning or significance (p. 127)
Hicks (1993)	Data that has been processed so that it is meaningful to a decision maker to use in a particular decision (p. 675)
Knight and Silk (1990)	Human significance associated with an observable object or event (p. 22)
Laudon and Laudon (1991)	Data that have been shaped or formed by humans into a meaningful and useful form (p. 14)
Maddison (ed.) (1989)	Understandable useful relevant communication at an appropriate time; any kind of knowledge about things and concepts in a universe of discourse that is exchangeable between users; it is the meaning that matters, not the representation (p. 174)
Martin and Powell (1992)	Information comes from data that has been processed to make it useful in management decision making (p. 10)

Now, to any red-blooded climber the message conveyed is perfectly clear, though it is not what the words say. To a rock climber, the guidebook is saying: here are descriptions of some good climbs, go and enjoy them, but be discreet, keep a low profile and have a good story ready! In other words the information the guidebook conveys is virtually the opposite of what the text actually says! Clearly, creating and conveying information is not a simple business.

We need to find an account of 'data', 'information' and the relation between them which will make sense of examples such as these. This will need a careful use of language beyond that in normal everyday conversation. And the exploration should not start from the words themselves, such as 'data' and 'information', asking: what do they mean? Rather, we should take Popper's advice (1972):

> One should never quarrel about words, and never get involved in questions of terminology ... What we are really interested in, our real problems, ... are problems of theories and their truth (p. 310).

Popper suggests that if you find yourself arguing about the meaning of words, always a fruitless exercise, the thing to do is to accept your opponent's definitions and get down to arguing about the real problem!

Here the problem is to develop at least a skeleton theory of *what distinctions it is useful to make* in order to understand the business of arriving at 'knowledge', the theory including an account of what the process is that leads us to make use of the words which mark the distinctions, such words as 'data', 'information' and 'knowledge'. In the words of Winograd and Flores (1986): 'As observers we generate distinctions in a consensual domain' (p. 50), that is to say, a cognitive domain in which knowledge can be shared. Let us see what distinctions it may be useful to make in order to understand IS.

From data to capta

We can start by accepting the obvious: that there are myriad facts about the world. It is fact that the authors of this chapter were born in Birmingham, England and Melbourne, Australia, and that they are both, at the time of writing, working at Lancaster University. Such facts are in principle checkable; if disputed, evidence can be produced to support or refute them. There is a plethora of such facts, some agreed by all, some disputed, some accepted as meaningful by all, some private to an individual or group who defines them as a result of particular interests. Consider an example of this latter category. There must in principle exist the following fact: the number of octogenarian widows living alone in Wigan. This is a meaningful concept, though it may be the case that no one has ever ascertained the actual number of such widows. Most people would not want to know this fact anyway; but it could be a significant fact to which attention is paid by a researcher examining the operation of geriatric support services in Wigan.

This suggests that there is a distinction to be made between the great mass of facts and the sub-set of them which we select for attention, those to which we pay heed. The obvious word for the mass of facts is 'data', from the Latin *dare*, meaning 'to give'. But there is no ready-made word for the small fraction of the available data which we know about or pay attention to, or create. We refer to such data as 'capta', from the Latin *capere*, meaning 'to take' and that is the word we shall use here.

Data are a starting point in our mental processing. Capta are the result of selecting some for attention, or creating some new category – such as 'the number of octogenarian widows living alone in Wigan' in the example above – or being so surprised by some items of data which pass across our gaze that we begin to pay them attention. In the first of the earlier examples from Anderton, (1) above, the position of the speedometer needle at 30 km/h is an item of data; it becomes part of the driver's capta when he pays attention to it – though that example also reminds us that we may need to check that the apparent facts of the situation are what they seem to be.

Turning data into capta is a very familiar mental process, so familiar in fact that it has become completely transparent to us: we do it all the time without noticing the process occurring, which is presumably why we have here found it necessary to make up the word 'capta'. Also, it is by no means the end of our mental processing.

From capta to information and knowledge

Having selected, paid attention to, or created some data, thereby turning it into capta, we enrich it. We relate it to other things, we put it in context, we see it as part of a larger whole which causes it to gain in significance (Holwell, 1989). The phrase which best captures this is probably 'meaning attribution'. The attribution of meaning in context converts capta into something different, for which another word is appropriate: the word 'information' will serve here, this definition being close to the way the word is often used in everyday language.

This process, which can be both individual and/or collective, by which data are selected and converted into meaningful information, can itself lead to larger structures of related information for which another word is needed; we may use the word 'knowledge'. Such structures of information may be expected to have greater longevity than many items of information which are only ephemerally meaningful and relevant. For example, at a particular point in time in a home furnishing company, managers might select as *capta*, from all their sales *data*, the figures concerning the sales of a new expensive kitchen chair, aggregated separately for each sales area over the last three months. In the context of introducing this new product, these capta would yield *information* concerning, for example, the readiness of people in different geographical areas, classified socioeconomically, to buy a basic but expensive product. This would itself contribute to updating the company's larger-scale slower-moving *knowledge* of the home furnishing market.

The process by which data are turned into knowledge is shown in Figure 4.1. It is suggested that in this process it is useful to mark or highlight three distinctions created by our actions of selecting data; attributing meaning to these selected data; and building larger structures of meaningful data. And it is further suggested that we use the words data, capta, information and knowledge to describe the four products defined by making these three distinctions.

The scheme of Figure 4.1 allows us to make sense of Anderton's intriguing examples quoted above. The first one (in which the speedometer is stuck) reminds us that apparent facts are not necessarily true: there is in principle a need to have available processes by means of which we can try to check the accuracy of data. In the second example, (2) above, the absence of any message conveys information to the traveller, so that nothing, apparently,

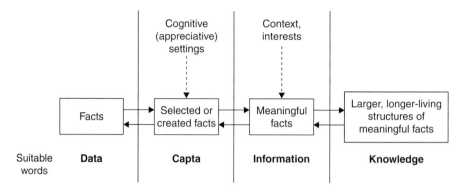

Figure 4.1   The links between data, capta, information and knowledge

has carried the information. This emphasizes the importance of context in acquiring information from data. The arrangement made by the traveller with the doctor establishes a context in which the *absence* of any message before 5 p.m. itself conveys meaningful information. In the third example the existence of the match and the final score are part of the football supporter's capta and he will no doubt convert the score into information of interest to him – such as, perhaps, England's prospects of qualifying for the World Cup. Neither the existence of the match nor the score were part of his brother's capta. The score tells the brother who won the match but also that the match itself had taken place, a new item of capta for him. Of course, if he is not interested in football he will not attribute the same meaning to it as his football-follower brother, so meaning attribution may be personal or shared.

This illustrates a very important point. The analysis has led us to use the word 'information' to describe 'capta' (itself selected 'data' which gets our attention) to which meaning has been attributed in a context which may be any or all of *cognitive*, *spatial* and *temporal*.

In the final example above, in which the anonymous writer of the rock climbing guide to Salisbury Crags manages to convey a message which is virtually the complete opposite of what the words say, we have a very subtle situation. It is another example of the important part which *context* plays in creating information. Many people glancing at the guide would of course accept at face value the statement about the illegality of climbing in Holyrood Park. But the writer, being embedded in the culture of rock climbing, knows its knowledge base, its attitudes and its values. He knows that fellow climbers will get the message; what is more, if challenged at the crag he or she will no doubt adopt an air of injured innocence! This example is the equivalent on paper of situations familiar enough in everyday life: situations in which information (in the full sense of the word) can be passed between knowing members of a particular culture by no more than a tone of voice, the gesture of a hand or a wink.

The most important feature of this analysis of data, capta, information and knowledge is that the act of creating information is a *human* act, not one which a machine can accomplish. It is the human being who can attribute meaning to the selected data which have been highlighted for attention, this being done in a context which may well be shared by many people but may also be unique to an individual. Of course the *designer* of a system which processes focused-on data (i.e. capta) into a more useful form will have the aim of making the processed capta correspond to some obvious categories of information which will be meaningful to many different people. But attributing meaning to the processed data is a human ability and a particular attribution may be unique to one individual. No designer can *guarantee* that his or her *intended* attributions of meaning will be universally accepted. In the house furnishing example discussed above, the geographically tabulated capta concerning the sales of the new chair in the three months after launch will yield different information to different people. The salesman will gain information about his bonus payments; the managing director will learn something relevant perhaps to the strategic future of the company; the production planner may take from it the need to recruit more process workers or obtain more raw materials for the furniture factory.

This emphasizes that the phrases in common usage, 'information system', or 'management information system', are ill-chosen. What such systems cannot do, in a strict sense, is provide unequivocal information; what they can do is process capta (selected data) into useful forms which can *imply* certain categories of information. They cannot, however, guarantee that the capta will be interpreted in this way by people making use of the system's outputs. In fact the phrases in common use in the early days of computers, namely 'data processing (DP) system' or 'electronic data processing (EDP) system', were more accurate than the phrases which have unfortunately replaced them both in everyday speech and in the professional field of IS. It would be a good idea to return to the earlier language, but this is unlikely to be achieved. After all, people working in IT will probably wish the word 'management', as in 'management information system', to be associated with their activity since it implies a higher-level activity and maybe better career prospects!

References

Aiba, H. (1993) The conceptualising of 'organization' and 'information' in IS work, MSc. Dissertation, Lancaster University.

Anderton, R.H. (1991) Information and systems. *Journal of Applied Systems Analysis*, 18, 57–60.

Avison, D.E. and Fitzgerald, G. (1995) *Information Systems Development: methodologies, tools*, 2nd edn, McGraw-Hill.

Clare, C. and Loucopoulos, P. (1987) *Business Information Systems*, Paradigm.

Galland, F.J. (1982) *Dictionary of Computing*, John Wiley & Sons.

Hicks, J.O. (1993) *Management Information Systems: a user perspective*, 3rd edn, West Publishing.

Holwell, S. (1989) Planning in Shell: joint learning through action research, MSc. Dissertation, Lancaster University.

Knight, A.V. and Silk, D.J. (1990) *Managing Information*, McGraw-Hill.

Laudon, K.C. and Laudon, J.P. (1991) *Business Information Systems: a problem solving approach*, Dryden Press.

Maddison, R. (ed.) (1989) *Information Systems Development for Managers*, Paradigm.

Martin, C. and Powell, P. (1992) *Information Systems: a management perspective*, McGraw-Hill.

Morris, D. and Tamm, B. (eds) (1993) *Concise Encyclopaedia of Software Engineering*, Pergamon Press.

Popper, K.R. (1972) *Objective Knowledge: an evolutionary approach,* Oxford University Press.

Winograd, T. and Flores, F. (1986) *Understanding Computers and Cognition*, Addison-Wesley.

Source: Adapted from Checkland, P. and Holwell, S., 'Data, capta, information and knowledge' in Hinton, M. (2006) *Introducing Information Management: the business approach*, Elsevier.

Chapter 5

The process of information management

Matthew Hinton

The process of information management can, at a conceptual level, be broken down into a set of key phases which cover the gathering, storing, analysing and communicating of information. These form a generic framework for information management activity.

Gathering information

This process includes all the activities you engage in to collect the information you need. In some cases these information-gathering activities may involve no more than receiving the information that other people give you or send to you, in others you may have actively to seek out the information. Information gathering may be routine (for example, staff completing and submitting weekly time-sheets or expense claims) or it may be *ad hoc* (for example, a customer calls to say they have not received their order). They can be small-scale (for example, an employee credits an expense to a budget code) or very large-scale (for example, marketing data for potential new customers in the whole of the European Union).

Information gathering is perhaps the most critical of the information management processes: if things go wrong here, all the other processes are working with information of inferior quality. Common problems are:

- that the required information is simply not gathered at all

- gathering is done poorly so that there are gaps and errors in the information

- information is gathered but nothing is then done with it

- too much information is gathered, so that what is needed is hidden by all the irrelevant information

- a lot of time is spent gathering information for the use of others, but nothing of value for you is achieved by this.

Part of the answer to these problems of information gathering – and one that is consistent with the definition of information management as 'the conscious process of gathering information' – is to plan your information gathering thoroughly. The following steps will help to achieve this:

- accountability – responsibility for who collects what should be made clear

- data definition – agreement on what items a particular type of information should include

- standardization – ensuring everyone is collecting the same information in the same way

- quality monitoring – ensuring that information of the right quality is being collected

- skills – helping staff improve their information-gathering skills.

There is also scope for imaginative thinking in information gathering. For example, supermarkets need to keep track of how many of each item have been sold. This used to be done by having staff count the numbers of each item on the shelves each day and comparing today's count with yesterday's. This was labour-intensive and prone to errors. Nowadays, most supermarkets use bar-coding to capture this information directly at the cash desk, so that the act of purchase also generates information for stock control, reorder decisions and ascertains profitability for different products. An important principle illustrated by this example is that it is more efficient to capture information at source as a by-product of some other necessary activity.

Analysing information

The purpose of analysing information is to make it more useful for decision making. This can be considered as a process of transforming 'raw data' (isolated items of information with little or no meaning in themselves) into meaningful information. Analysing information may involve a variety of manipulations of the raw data, which may take place at a number of levels, each resulting in something that is more meaningful. The manipulations can range from simple operations that can be done in a person's head to complex calculations requiring the use of sophisticated computer software. A comparison can be made here with the process of reading. Individual letters are combined into recognizable words which may convey a measure of meaning. Words can then be combined into sentences, which convey still more meaning. It is this process of transforming raw data into meaningful information that can be managed for such purposes as planning, decision making, evaluation and audit.

To provide a complete basis for decision making another necessary transformation should be mentioned. This is the transformation of *information into knowledge*: the process of integrating new information into the rich framework of knowledge already possessed by the decision maker. This last process cannot be directly managed, although it can be managed indirectly through training.

In some cases the use of computers can help to reduce the time spent in data analysis, especially where purely numerical calculations are involved. However, the process of entering data manually into the computer can be prone to errors and the use of electronic techniques can save time and increase accuracy. Where some form of statistical analysis of data has been conducted, there may be an issue about whether the right statistical technique has been chosen and whether the analysis has been correctly carried out. A more subtle issue arises where data have been analysed by computer. Can you believe the results from the computer? The trouble here is that the process of computerized analysis is largely invisible. It may be difficult to know exactly what the computer has done with the data and therefore to judge how correct the processing has been.

Communicating information

Problems with communication are probably the most frequently expressed complaint by people working in large organizations. The general nature of the communication process is shown in Figure 5.1.

Formulation involves three main steps: deciding what to say, to whom and how to say it. Deciding what to say requires a selection to be made. There are probably many things that *could* be said, but what absolutely *needs* to be said *now?* The more focused a communication is, the more likely it is to be successful. Communication needs to be correctly targeted. Whom is this communication really intended for? Does it matter if others receive it as well? How the message is expressed is also a key factor in successful communication. This entails consideration of both the message content and who its intended recipients are.

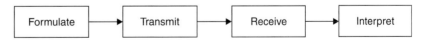

Figure 5.1   The communication process

Transmission involves the choice of means of communication (leaflet, fax, team meeting and so on) and the timing (for example send an e-mail now or make an announcement at the beginning of next week's inter-departmental meeting). These choices will be influenced by considerations from the formulation stage: whom the message is for, how it is to be expressed, how urgent it is, how confidential it is. Sometimes it is necessary to make trade-offs between these considerations. Other considerations are the reliability and 'noisiness' of each transmission option. Reliability refers to the risk that the message may get lost. 'Noise' refers to how likely a message is to disappear among all the other traffic a transmission channel may be carrying: from your perspective as the sender of the message all other messages are noise. For example, notice boards full of a great variety of notices are noisy channels: a message may get lost unless it is made so striking that it stands out from the other notices. Likewise it may be difficult to get an important message across at a meeting with many agenda items and many participants.

Successful *reception* is affected by choices about formulation and transmission. You can do your best in focusing and expressing your message and in choosing the right time, place and means of transmission, but the recipient may still not attend to your message. The more the intended recipient is overloaded with incoming information, the greater the risk. The risk is also greater the more tired or stressed the recipient is. As people become tired or stressed, their capacity to take in new information decreases, sometimes dramatically. They tend to concentrate only on the things right in front of them. Things at the periphery of their concern just do not get through. Subtle nuances are lost. In such cases you have to make extra efforts to ensure that you have the recipient's attention and to keep your message very simple.

In some cases you may have to overcome resistance to hearing messages that the intended recipient just does not want to hear. A related issue has become known as 'groupthink'. Here a group of people strive for consensus among themselves and treat this as a higher priority than considering evidence from outside the group and coming to an objective conclusion (but more on this in Part 3). These kinds of situation mean that careful presentation of your information is vital if it is to be acted upon.

Interpretation involves the issue of whether the recipient understands the message in the way you intended. In normal spoken and written communication there is always some measure of ambiguity, which offers scope for misinterpretation. Agreed definitions are critical when communication is very formalized, for example in management reporting or in the electronic exchange of data between computers. But most everyday communication cannot achieve this degree of precision. Where accuracy of interpretation is especially important, it is necessary to implement a procedure through which you can confirm that your message has been correctly interpreted.

Storing information

A lot of the information generated in an organization is ephemeral: it is gathered, used and forgotten. But there is a great deal that has to be preserved. Information needs to be stored, both for use in later activities and for submission to higher management and auditing bodies. For some types of information, there are statutory requirements determining what must be kept and for how long.

The information-gathering issues discussed earlier need a complementary plan for information storage. For each type of information you need to store, the key issues are:

- the form in which you originally obtain this information

- the volume of information

- who needs access and are they close to or remote from the site where the information is stored

- how long the information needs to be kept

- what kind of protection the information requires.

How people make sense of information

Every organization needs information in order to function and the type of information required depends on the organization's activities. As you have already seen, information management is about the gathering, analysing, communicating and storing of information to assist in decision making. Organizations need to create systems that facilitate these processes. Consequently, they devise or employ a suitable series of routine and non-routine processes collectively referred to as an Information System. An information system is a social system which *may* have embedded in it information technology; however, 'it is not possible to design a robust, effective information system incorporating significant amounts of the technology without treating it as a social system' (Land, 1985).

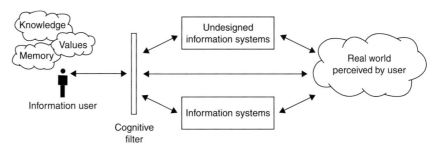

Figure 5.2   The context of the concept 'information system'
Source: Land, 1985

Several factors influence the way people interpret information. Clearly, the *nature of the problem* influences the way information is interpreted. How serious is the decision? What are the consequences of an incorrect decision and how do they compare to the benefits of a correct one? An important decision may require more care in analysing the information.

Organizational setting is critical to interpretation, as individuals become socialized by the organization. That is to say that, over time, we are influenced by our organizations in the way we approach problems. Lucas (2000) suggests that personal and situational factors also influence interpretation. Consequently, decision makers interpret a problem differently depending on their position. Studies have shown that managers are heavily influenced in problem diagnosis by their backgrounds and position, so that marketing executives see marketing problems, accountants see accounting problems and so on. In all these scenarios, the information was the same, it was just interpreted differently. The concept of *cognitive style* has also been suggested as an influence on interpretation. One of the simplest distinctions is between analytic and heuristic decision makers. Where the former concentrates on quantitative information, the latter is interested in broader concepts and is more intuitive. Research suggests that people are not analytic or heuristic in every problem but that they do have preferences and tend to approach the same type of problem with a consistent cognitive style.

Lucas (2000) suggests that these factors can be combined to represent how an individual might construct their own interpretational model. This model acts as a way of filtering data, so that to interpret information a decision maker draws on current data as well as a history of past decisions and their results.

References

Land, F. (1985) Is an information theory enough? *The Computer Journal*, 28, 3, 211–215.

Lucas, H. (2000) *Information Technology for Management*, 7th edn, McGraw-Hill, Boston.

Chapter 6

The processes which information systems support

Peter Checkland and Sue Holwell

Given [...] the idea of 'information' as selected data (or capta) to which meaning has been attributed in a particular context [and] the basic premise that information systems exist to serve and support people taking purposeful action, we can now begin to enrich the concept of what is conventionally referred to as 'an information system'. This we shall do by exploring the nature of the processes that go on within organizations and between different organizations, processes in which information will play an important role.

The intention is to build a concept which is rich enough both to make sense of, and to guide work within the IS field, irrespective of whether that work is practical or conceptual. Such a concept needs to be at the same time broad enough to encompass a range of ideas about organizations and their information support and sharp enough to provide guidelines which are usable in practice.

The personal process

Consider first ourselves as individuals in the world, having self-consciousness. We are all conscious of a world outside ourselves; we are also conscious of ourselves and others as part of that world. To be aware of that means that we have already performed the remarkable mental trick – which we do so often that we pay it no attention – of thinking about ourselves thinking about the world. The trick is 'remarkable' in that it seems to be a uniquely human skill. To explain all the observed behaviour of cats and cuckoos, barn owls and badgers, you have to assume only that they are programmed to cat-like, cuckoo-like, owl-like and badger-like behaviour, not that they are conscious of their own relation to the world, of which they are themselves a part. The fact that we *are* conscious in this way, however, means that we can think about the world in different ways, relate these concepts to our experience of the world and so form judgements which can affect our intentions and, ultimately, our actions.

This line of thought suggests a basic model for the active human agent in the world. In this model we are able to perceive parts of the world, attribute meanings to what we perceive, make judgements about our perceptions, form intentions to take particular actions and carry out those actions. These change the perceived world, however slightly, so that the process begins again, becoming a cycle.

However, this simple model requires two amplifications. First, we always *selectively* perceive parts of the world, as a result of our interests and previous history. Rock climbers visiting the island of Lundy in the Bristol Channel will tend to see it as a set of granite crags and their eyes will at once begin to scan for the climbable routes. They would probably not notice the Lundy Cabbage, an unprepossessing plant, which is in fact unique to the island and which might be the very reason for a visit by a botanist. The rock climber and the botanist each have a framework derived from their interests and experience which structures their perceptions. They create different capta and hence different information and knowledge.

Secondly, the act of attributing meaning and making judgements implies the existence of standards against which comparisons can be made, standards of good/bad, important/unimportant, etc. Finally, the source of the standards, for which there is normally no ultimate authority, can only be the previous history of the very process we are describing and the standards will themselves change over time as new experience accumulates. [...] Taking these considerations into account yields the picture in Figure 6.1, which is a process model of the active human agent in the world.

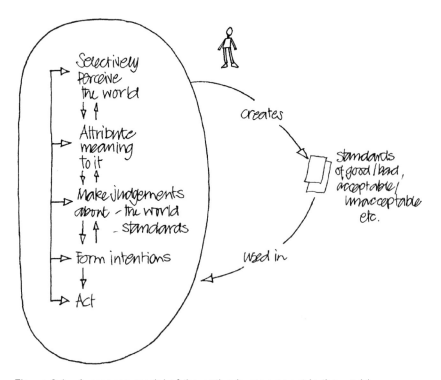

Figure 6.1   A process model of the active human agent in the world

It will be noticed that there are multiple pathways available within the process illustrated. This is because of the great flexibility of the human mind. Thus, for example, the mere fact of making the judgement 'botanically interesting' about the island of Lundy will cause subsequent perceptions and attributions of meaning to be different from those which would have been made in the absence of that judgement. Note also that the judgements made may concern either what is perceived or the standards by which what is perceived is judged: we may begin to notice as significant something we have hitherto passed by, or we may begin to judge differently something we have always paid some attention to.

The model in Figure 6.1 applies to an individual who selectively perceives his or her world, judges it and takes intentional (purposeful) action in the light of those perceptions and judgements. The model has to allow for the visions and actions which ultimately belong to an autonomous individual, for individuals do not *have* to conform to the perceptions, meaning attributions and judgements which are common, even though there may be great social and/or political pressure to do so, even though we are a social animal. (We are, ultimately, simultaneously both autonomous and gregarious, which is one reason why human affairs are so complex – and interesting.)

In general, the thinking and actions of the individual may have negligible or profound effects on others: sometimes what is initially the vision of an individual becomes that of very many people. An example of this is the reaction to the publication of Rachel Carson's famous book *Silent Spring* in 1962. Her perception, not at all common at the time, was that the excessive use of chemical pesticides was having seriously bad effects on the environment. She was noticing as significant, and attributing new meaning to, observations which were in general not much noticed at that time. And she was judging them by standards which were not at all usual at the time, 'the environment' not being perceived as 'a problem' in the early 1960s. Thirty years later we can see that Rachel Carson's act in publishing her persuasive book was one of the earliest and most significant steps in the rise of the 'environmental movement' (Hynes, 1989). This has seen the gradual establishment of an influential ecological ethic, one very different from that which previously dominated western culture, namely an ethic grounded in 'exploiting nature'.

The social process

What has just been described is an example of an individual's thinking and action having a profound effect on the mind set and actions of a very large number of people and of their governments. Nevertheless, we can be sure that, though Carson wrote the book which acted as such a powerful trigger, she would no doubt agree that she had developed her ideas in dialogue with others. Although each human being retains at least the potential selectively to perceive and interpret the world in their own unique way, running the risk of being regarded as 'weird', the norm for a social animal with sophisticated language is that our perceptions of the world, our meaning attributions and our judgements of it will all be strongly conditioned by our exchanges with others. The most obvious characteristic of group life for a social animal with highly developed language is the never-ending dialogue, discussion, debate and discourse in which we all try to affect each other's perceptions, judgements, intentions and actions. This means that we can assume that while Figure 6.1 continues to apply to the individual, the social situation will be that much of the process will be carried out inter-subjectively in discourse – which is the word we adopt here to cover all communications, verbal and written, between individuals, between individuals and institutions and between institutions, the purpose of which is to affect the thinking and actions of at least one other party. To cover this we need the modified form of Figure 6.1 shown in Figure 6.2; this is the inter-subjective, or social, version of the previous figure. In it, previously personal cognitive acts are now embedded in discourse. Thus, two strangers could enact their own versions of Figure 6.1 but, once they have met and started to communicate, they will, in general, have to construct through communication a version of Figure 6.2, with the most extreme possible version of that 'communication' being the complete domination of one by the other.

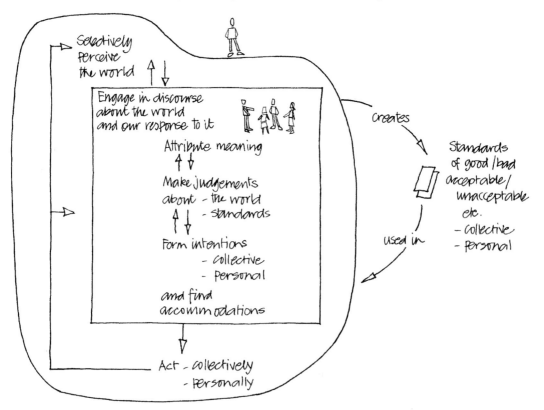

Figure 6.2   A process model of active human agents in the world

In the example just given, Rachel Carson's act in publishing *Silent Spring* became the subject of much discourse. It turned out to be very persuasive, something which could not have been precisely predicted: we now know, with hindsight, that it did in fact affect, on a grand scale, the mental states of many people who took part in the discourse or were affected by its course and products. It helped to change what Vickers calls the 'appreciative settings' which we bring to the discourse, whether as individuals or as groups. Since taking part in this process is the very essence of being human, Vickers (1972) finds it very remarkable that our language deals with it in such a poverty-stricken way. He writes:

> ... we have not even a name for this state of affairs in our heads which is the fruit of past communication and which is both the target and the interpreter of present communication. This nameless state accounts for nearly everything which we and others do – and, more important, are. Our assumptions about it are basic to nearly all our explanations of the feelings, thoughts and doings of ourselves and our fellows ... I have taken to calling it an appreciative system, because the word *appreciation*, as we use it when we speak of appreciating a situation, seems to me to carry with it those linked connotations of interest, discrimination and valuation which we bring to the exercise of judgement and which tacitly determine what we shall notice, how we shall discriminate *situations* from the general confusion of ongoing event[s], and how we shall regard them ... I call it a system because these categories and criteria are mutually related; a change in one is likely to affect others.
>
> Vickers, 1972, p. 98

Our model of the social process which leads to purposeful or intentional actions, then, is one in which appreciative settings lead to particular features of situations (as well as 'the situations' themselves) being noticed and judged in particular ways by standards built up from previous experience. As a result of the discourse which ensues, accommodations may be reached which lead to action being taken. Equally, the appreciative settings and the standards by which judgements arc made may well be changed. They will certainly change through time as our personal and social history unfolds: there is no permanent 'social reality' except at the broadest possible level, immune from the events and ideas which, in the normal social process, continually change it.

The organizational process

The idea of appreciative settings is not restricted to individuals. Our personal settings may well be unique, since we all have a unique experience of the world, but often they will overlap with those of people with whom we are closely associated or who have had similar experience. Indeed, appreciative settings may be attributed to a group of people – to members of a team, for instance, or members of a department of an organization – though we must remember that there will never be complete congruence between individual and (attributed) group settings. We can also attribute appreciative settings to that larger abstraction, the organization as a whole. Indeed, the conventional wisdom on organizations can be seen as a rather naive assumption that all members of an organization share the same settings, those which lead them unambiguously to collaborate together in decision making in pursuit of organizational (corporate) goals. The reality [...] will be more complex. Although the idea of 'the (attributed) appreciative settings of an organization as a whole' is a usable concept, the content of those settings and whatever attributions are made, will never be completely static. Changes both internal and external to the organization will change individual and group perceptions and judgements, leading to new accommodations related to evolving intentions and purposes.

Given this concept of organization and the concepts of data, capta, information and knowledge developed earlier, together with the accounts of the processes, individual and social, which work done in the IS field will support (the process shown in Figures 6.1 and 6.2), we are now in a position to give an account of the overall organizational process in which the design and implementation of so-called 'information systems' (which, more precisely, are systems which process capta) have a part to play.

The process will be one in which the data-rich world outside is perceived selectively by individuals and by groups of individuals. The selectivity will be the result of our predisposition to 'select, amplify, reject, attenuate or distort' (Land, 1985, p. 212) as a result of previous experience and individuals will interact with the world not only as individuals but also through their simultaneous membership of multiple groups, some formally organized (such as a department in an organization), some informal, such as a group of friends. Perceptions will be exchanged, shared, challenged, argued over, in a discourse which will consist of the inter-subjective creation of capta and meanings. Those meanings will create information and knowledge which will lead to accommodations being made, intentions being formed and purposeful action undertaken. Both the thinking and the action will change the perceived world and may change the appreciative settings which filter our perceptions. Thus the process will be cyclic and never ending: it is a process of continuous learning and will be richer if more people take part in it.

Adjunct to this process will be another in which the IS needed to support the action will be defined and realized using, usually, appropriate IT and telecommunications, the role of IT-based IS being to serve and support people taking purposeful action in their situations.

The whole process envisaged is shown in Figure 6.3. It is a model which relates to the *processes* in which *organizational meanings* are created: the POM model. Element 1 consists of the people as individuals and as group members, element 2 the data-rich world they perceive selectively through their various taken-as-given assumptions. In the language being used here these are 'appreciative settings'; they play the role of Land's 'cognitive filters'. The organizational discourse (element 3) is the arena in which meaning is created inter-subjectively, leading to the attributions of meaning which yield information and knowledge, element 4. This is a very complex social process in which persuasion and/or coercion is attempted, battles are fought and scores settled – the whole process embodying politics as well as, perhaps, rational instrumental decision taking! Organizations have to be able to encourage but at the same time contain such a process to survive. They have to enable assemblies of related meanings, intentions and accommodations between conflicting interests to emerge (element 5) so that purposeful action (element 6) (best thought of and expressed as a managing of relationships) can be taken. Formally organized information systems (element 7a) based on IT and telecommunications (element 7b) support organization members in conceptualizing their world, finding accommodations, forming intentions and taking action (elements 5 and 6). The technology (element 7b) will also require the availability of professional knowledge of the technology and its possibilities so that suitable configurations can be proposed. This professional know-how will also include the knowledge needed to operate, maintain and, if necessary, modify the technology. This knowledge constitutes element 7c in Figure 6.3.

Sometimes the 'support' the technology offers may include, or comprise, taking over and carrying out, by making use of technology, actions previously in the hands of people – such as doing calculations or drawing graphs. This kind of automation is an obvious radical kind of 'support'; but the more subtle aspects of support are likely to reside in the provision of processed capta which enable the users to modify the way they think about their world – that is to say, help both to sustain and to change the perceived world (element 2).

Several broad features of this model, the POM model, are worthy of comment.

1   It cannot be overemphasized that this model does not purport to be a descriptive account of *the* organizational process. What it does purport to be is a defensible device with a structure and language which can be used to *make sense of* life in real organizations and their provision of information systems (Weick, 1995). Real life itself is always richer and more complex than any of our images of it. Thus, though we could argue that Figure 6.3 broadly represents aspects we can observe and analyse, the detailed reality will always be less clear-cut than the

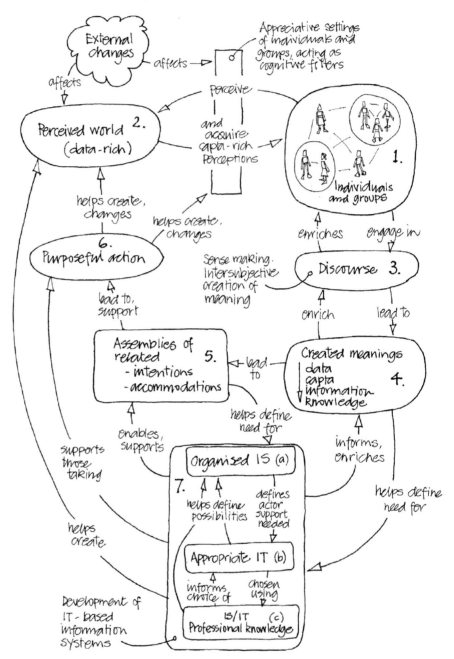

Figure 6.3   The 'organizational' form of the model of the social process in which meanings are established and lead to information support for people undertaking purposeful action: the 'processes for organization meanings' (POM) model

model; a terrain is never the same as a map which relates to it. After Checkland and Casar (1986) had represented Vickers' writings in the form of a model of what he meant by 'an appreciative system', Casar 'tested' the model in the company in which he worked in Mexico City

(Casar, 1990). This was a financial services company and Casar's professional task at that time was to set up a strategic planning function. As he did that Casar kept a detailed diary of what happened and used the 'appreciative system' model to try to make sense of his experience. He found that the model was very useful for that purpose (and hence helped him to plan and monitor what he was doing) but that the real-world happenings represented an incredibly complex flux in which many appreciative systems, both individual and group, were operating simultaneously and interactively. The complexity derived from the fact that many different appreciative systems, operating simultaneously, were doing so both over different timescales (from within an hour to over several months) and at different levels, from the tactical to the strategic. Such experience provides useful reminders to us to beware of reifying what are bound to be rather simple models when compared with complex real life!

2   In connection with the first point, it is important not to think of the model as implying a particular set of *structures*. Its elements define a set of connected *processes*. In a real situation these would have to be somehow embodied in structures, but many different structures could be chosen to encapsulate the set of fundamental processes in the model. In terms of the old question from biology: does form follow function or does function follow form? (a real chicken-and-egg question), it is clear that as far as purposeful organizations are concerned, function (i.e. process) is prime, not form (i.e. structure). (The fact that in everyday life in organizations more attention is devoted to structure than process is probably due to two things: ways of thinking about process (such as by building activity models) are unfamiliar to many managers; and in any case forming particular structures is usually a part of political power play in organizations and hence receives a disproportionate amount of attention. In everyday life, form is 'sexier' than function.)

3   It is worth noting that because the model is cyclic, with pathways which link all elements with each other, there is no clear starting point for use of the model. In a particular situation the initial focus might, for example, be on action (element 6). It might be found to be inadequately supported by the IS in element 7a, or it might be found that some boring action previously taken by people could now be automated. In another situation a new development in IT (elements 7b and 7c), such as, for example, the development of groupware (Grudin, 1991) might cause a re-think of possible knowledge (element 4), intentions (element 5) and action (element 6). In general the cycle of Figure 6.3 might be dominated, in particular circumstances, by changes in (or changed perceptions of) any of the elements in the model.

4   The process in Figure 6.3 can encompass any way of conceptualizing an organization. It is certainly not necessarily linked to the conventional wisdom. It could encompass it, however, just as it could

encompass treating the organization as a political arena, as an organism, or according to any other organizational metaphor which seems appropriate in a particular case, whether drawn from Morgan's proposed menu of such metaphors (1986) or freshly coined.

5 Finally, we may note that the model enables us to define what the phrase 'an information system' refers to (or ought to refer to) as well as implying that the process to develop information systems ought to exhibit certain features which may or may not be present in the current processes by which IS are developed.

References

Casar, A. (1990) Human action and social process: a systemic perspective, PhD Dissertation, Lancaster University.

Checkland, P. and Casar, A. (1986) Vickers' concept of an appreciative system: a systemic account. *Journal of Applied Systems Analysis*, 13, 3–17.

Grudin, J. (1991) Groupware and CSCW: why now? In *Groupware '91: the potential of team and organizational computing*, Hendriks, P., ed., Software Engineering Research Centre, Utrecht, Netherlands.

Hynes, H.P. (1989) *The Recurring Silent Spring*, Pergamon.

Land, F. (1985) Is an information theory enough? *The Computer Journal*, 28, 3, 211–255.

Morgan, G. (1986) *Images of Organization*, Sage.

Vickers, G. (1972) Communication and appreciation. In *Policymaking, Communication and Social Learning: essays of Sir Geoffrey Vickers*, Adams, G., Forester, J. and Catron, B., eds (1987), Transaction Books.

Weick, K.E. (1995) *Sensemaking in Organizations*, Sage.

Source: Adapted from Checkland, P. and Holwell, S., 'The processes which information systems support' in Hinton, M. (2006) *Introducing Information Management: a business approach*, Elsevier.

Chapter 7

Organizations and information

Elizabeth Orna

This chapter covers:

- What makes an organization?
- What do organizations need to know to survive?
- Why organizations need to define knowledge and information for themselves
- Why organizations need a policy and a strategy for information
- Whose business is information policy and strategy?

What makes an organization?

Organizations are everywhere today. Input 'organization' as a subject or title search term in any Internet search engine or large public library and you will get hundreds of hits; add 'organizational' and you will get a few hundred more, from 'organizational behaviour' to 'organizational structure' via 'organizational culture' and 'organizational learning'. But had you made the search 60 years ago, you would not have found anything like that, as Drucker (1995a, p. 76) reminds us, the word 'organization' did not come into common use in that sense until after the Second World War (though according to the *Shorter Oxford Dictionary*, it was used to mean 'an organized body, system or society' in 1873).

We all know what organizations are; we work for them, we use their services, pay our taxes to them, belong to them to pursue our hobbies or hobby-horses. And yet ... not long ago I had occasion to try to find an acceptable definition that would cover any kind of 'organization', from business to religious body, from charity to pressure group, as a preliminary to trying to define what all organizations need to know. In the end, I arrived at the 'necessary and sufficient conditions' summarized as:

- a grouping of human beings
- for explicit or implicit purposes
- creating 'offerings' of products and/or services
- interacting, internally and with its environment

- seeking sustenance to keep itself in being
- having a structure and a boundary
- embodying both social and technical systems.

This seemed to make sense when tried out on people interested in organizations and information in the light of their own experience, so I offer it here as the basis for thinking about what organizations need to know, the information they need to maintain their knowledge in good health and the reasons why each organization needs its own definition of information and its own policy/strategy for using it.

What do organizations need to know to survive?

If those are the distinguishing characteristics of organizations, then in order to keep alive and well, there are certain things that every organization needs to know [...]:

- What is happening inside its boundaries.
- What is happening in its 'outside world' of customers, members, clients, competitors, suppliers, markets, providers of grants-in-aid, supporters, donors, institutions and individuals it needs to influence.
- How to recognize, interpret and act on significant change, within and without.
- How to create appropriate 'offerings'.
- How to communicate, with itself and with its outside world. [...]

Why organizations need to define knowledge and information for themselves

For a long time, I have been trying to find an organization that has formulated its own definition of what information means for it, in the light of what it needs to know in order to succeed in its purposes, but so far I have not found one. This is odd, because if you start from the top-level definition that fits any organization, you quickly realize that the content of each clause will be different for each organization: organizations will seek people of different specialisms, skills and values according to their various purposes; their offerings will differ; so too will their internal structures and external environments and the kind of interactions appropriate to their purposes; the nature of the sustenance they need and its sources will vary; and both the internal social relationships and the technology will differ from one to the next. That being so, the *content* of the knowledge and know-how – and consequently of the information they need to maintain it in good health – will also be highly specific to how individual organizations define what they are in business for.

Arriving at an organizational definition of knowledge and information, of how the organization needs to use them and of how they need to flow inside the organization, is a complex process. Here, it is sufficient to quote two examples of very different organizations (see Table 7.1), [...] to show just how different are the kinds of information which they need to take in from their outside world to maintain their knowledge. They exemplify the points made by Drucker (1995b), that core competencies vary according to the nature of the organization, so too does the environmental information which he says is neglected in many companies, though necessary for strategy development – as exemplified by US companies which went into Europe in the 1960s without even asking about labour legislation.

Table 7.1   Information from the outside world as defined for two organizations (Credit Union Services Corporation, Australia; Surrey Police, UK)

Credit Union Services Corporation	Surrey Police
Credit Unions, in Australia and world-wide	Trends in crime – local, national, international
Developments in the economy, finance, industry, sociodemographic trends	Local population: age profile, employment
Legislation and compliance requirements	Local geography, land use, vehicle movements
Relevant IT developments, e.g. Internet banking, electronic commerce	Local industry and commerce
Customer response to products	Relevant IT developments, e.g. for tracking crime, imaging
Competitors – banks and building societies	Research in criminology
Existing and potential markets	Local organizations/institutions
Contacts and organizations it needs to communicate with/influence	Legislation Other police forces in the UK and abroad Contacts – individual, and in local and national organizations

I have come to believe that many of the conceptual difficulties which organizations, and especially their senior managers, experience in trying to come to grips with information arise from being content with a general belief that it is quantitative, about the past and present of their own organization, and lives in databases, and from being unaware of the full range that emerges once one starts 'unpacking' the meaning of mission statements or corporate objectives. As Farkas-Conn (1989) put it, 'Managers subscribing to the notion that companies must use their capabilities and their resources to the fullest are still thinking of information in a disjointed manner of collections, interactions, and a growing world of hardware and software, rather than of an interconnected dynamic whole ... we must now develop an extended view of what constitutes corporate information.'

Yet an appropriate definition of knowledge and information for *this* organization at *this* point in its development is an essential part of the foundation for any attempt to create and apply an information policy or strategy.

Why organizations need a policy and strategy for information

If the knowledge organizations need and the information resources they need to keep their knowledge in good health are so extensive in range and so specific and individual in content, the management of them must be based on a clear policy. The investment of effort in developing first a policy and then a strategy for using knowledge and information can bring both avoidance of dangers and positive benefits.

Risks/losses to avoid

It is commonplace today to speak of information as a potentially profitable resource and so it is indeed. But without a policy that compels attention to the nature and extent of the resource, how it is used and how it contributes to corporate objectives, the potential will go unrealized and loss rather than profit will be the likely outcome.

These are some of the dangers identified from actual observation of enterprises (summarized in Table 7.2):

- Uncoordinated information activities and systems, resulting from lack of policy about the use of information technology, with left hands and right hands unacquainted with one another's actions, leading to incomplete exploitation of information and to anarchic use of information.

- The control of information activities by people who have, by the nature of their professional background, a limited understanding of how organizations work and are managed and a restricted conception of what information is and how it can be used. There are, for example, a lot of people with 'information' in their job titles, who are well qualified in such fields as mathematics, computing, accountancy and engineering, but whose education and work experience has not included the theoretical basis of information, or modern methods of

Table 7.2 Risks and losses that information policy can help to avoid

Situation	Consequent risks and losses
Uncoordinated information activities and systems	Incomplete exploitation of information, anarchic use
Information activities controlled by people with restricted understanding of organizations and information	Important kinds of information overlooked entirely, or managed without professional skills to exploit them
Inappropriate information activities; inappropriate formats for information	Organization wastes time on things it no longer needs to do; people's time wasted in disentangling information they do need from inappropriate presentation
Poor communication of essential information for creating organization's offerings	Failures in attempts to innovate
Systems and IT investment without strategy related to overall business objectives	Systems and IT cannot make maximum contribution to core competencies of organization
Not possible to bring together relevant information from different sources	Bad decisions, missed opportunities for initiatives, losses
Managers do not fully understand what they need to know to foresee dangers, how to make good use of it	Inability to anticipate and respond appropriately to internal or external threat
Organization does not understand the importance of accurate and ethical use of information in dealing with its outside world	Loss of reputation, of customers, of money in compensating and rectifying

handling the textual information which is such an important part of the information resources of enterprises. (Davenport, 1993, suggests that as much as 85 per cent of the important information in organizations is too unstructured to be captured or distributed electronically – and argues from this against the common managerial assumption that information acquisition, analysis and distribution is low-level work.)

- Inappropriate information activities, unrelated to the organization's main objectives: for example, information products which once had a justification, but which no longer serve any useful purpose; or the presentation of information in formats that make it very difficult for those who need it to use for their own purposes.

- Failures of attempts to introduce innovative products or processes. Rothwell in the 1980s (1983) analysed a number of such failures in British industry and found that poor communication of information was a major cause of failure in all of them. The weaknesses included poor internal communication of technological, management and economic information; poor communication with external sources of scientific and technological information and with users about what they needed; deliberate ignoring of outside advice; and failure to provide information to the users of the product. Sillince (1994) suggests, in a study of production management systems in relation to innovation and organizational design, that to succeed in innovation, organizations need to develop an 'information model which considers the following elements: work units, information needs, goals, inputs and outputs', which needs to be continually monitored and updated. And a recent book on technology, globalization and economic performance argues that the 'short-termism' characteristic of British shareholders operates against the production and use of knowledge for innovation in UK firms (Michie, 1997).

- Systems and IT investment pursued without a strategy related to overall objectives and so unable to make its maximum contribution to the organization's 'core competencies' where it could add most value. Holohan's (1992) research on how organizations defined the performance indicators presented on their Executive Information Systems (EIS) shows the consequences: 'Unfortunately, not one organization which took part in the research modelled its EIS on its overall business strategy, thus limiting the use of their EIS to that of a glorified fire extinguisher rather than using it to help bridge the gap between formulating and implementing a business strategy.'

- Inability to bring together relevant information from a number of different sources and disciplines in a coherent form to bear on problems to which they are relevant. For example, plant investment proposals unsupported by in-depth marketing information and strategic plans which are short on information about the human resources and training requirements on which their fulfilment depends.

- Inability to anticipate and respond appropriately to threatening situations, internal and external. King's (1996) study of declining and failing medium-large firms in the USA, for instance, indicates that 'failures are often caused from within the company and by intrinsically interrelated factors that frequently are rooted in the faulty acquisition and use of information by managers'.

- Loss of reputation among customers and the community, resulting from not having a policy for ethical use of information, or from having a policy but failing to ensure that staff follow it in their dealings with customers. The insurance industry, for example, will not quickly forget the damage and loss that certain companies suffered through the dishonest and misleading use of information by pensions salesmen.

Benefits to gain

The advantages are much more than just the avoidance of the dangers of being without a policy. They can be expressed briefly as follows (see also Table 7.3 for a summary):

- It becomes possible to integrate all information activities and to mobilize all sources of information to contribute to the totality of the organization's objectives.

- The information policy provides the basis for objective decision making about resources for information activities and about the management of information, because it is integrated within the framework of corporate objectives and priorities. So any proposed development in the management of information can be considered in relation to how it will contribute to overall objectives and priorities.

- A policy for information allows for continuity in development; it reduces the danger of information initiatives being cut short and the resources invested in them wasted – a hazard to which information services are particularly susceptible in organizations in search of quick cuts in apparent expenditure. The fact that the policy embodies criteria for assessing the contribution that information makes to fulfilling the objectives of the enterprise means that it is possible to judge the real gains and losses that would follow from a proposed change in resources.

- Because an information policy is developed by bringing together distributed knowledge of all information resources and activities in the organization, it is capable of promoting cooperation and openness rather than hostility or concealment among those who are responsible for different aspects of information management. (There is a lot of uplifting managerial talk these days about information sharing and being a learning organization, but it will stay at the level of cynicism-promoting talk without an actual policy for information.) It is also an essential step on the way to combining the benefits of diffused responsibility for knowledge and information with a dynamic, unified view of the organization's total resources and with ready access to all of them.

- The free flows of information that result favour successful innovation, as suggested both by the Rothwell studies mentioned above and by more recent research such as that presented by Bowden and Ricketts (1992), which indicates that the factors associated with effective implementation of innovation are parallel to those associated with effective implementation of information policy, for example cross-functional teams and good intra- and inter-firm communications. They also support productivity and competitiveness. Koenig's (1992) studies of productivity in the pharmaceutical industry revealed differences in the information environment of more and less productive firms, with the more productive showing greater openness to outside information, less concern with protecting proprietary information, greater effort devoted to developing information systems and more uses of them by end-users. Bowonder and Miyake (1992) made similar findings, with particular emphasis on the importance of environmental scanning, about the relationship between information management and competitiveness in Japanese companies. [...]

- An information policy makes the basis for a sound strategy for investment in information systems and technology, because it allows the options to be evaluated in relation to the organization's key objectives and to its human resources. [...]

- Finally, the constant monitoring involved in applying an information policy means that the organization is capable not only of timely response to changes in the internal and external environment, but of moving ahead to *initiate* change that will allow it to take advantage of changing environments. [...]

Table 7.3 Positive benefits which information policy can help to promote

Situation	Benefits promoted by information policy
Integrated information activities	All resources of information can contribute to all organization's objectives
Information policy integrated within corporate policies and priorities	Decisions about resources for information activities can be taken in relation to how they contribute to corporate goals
Policy embodies criteria for assessing how information contributes to achieving organizational objectives	Off-the-cuff decisions to cut information resources become less likely, because likely effects can be predicted
Policy brings together distributed knowledge of all information resources and activities	Promotes cooperation, negotiation and openness among people responsible for different aspects of information management
Information flows more freely	Innovation, productivity and competitiveness are better supported
Options for investment in systems and IT can be evaluated in relation to key organizational goals and to what people need to do with information to achieve them	Basis for sound systems and IT strategy, supporting corporate goals and allowing productive use of technology
Intelligence gathering and constant monitoring of internal and external environment as part of information policy	Not only timely response to change, but chance to initiate change so as to take advantage of changing environments

Whose business is information policy and strategy?

Information policy and strategy are too important for the well-being of the organization to be left to a limited group of people, or developed without close attention from top management and/or board level. The process should involve everyone who manages resources of information which are essential to the organization in the light of its definition of what it is in business for; the senior managers to whom they are responsible; representatives of 'stakeholders' who use or contribute to the resources; and those who manage the systems and technology which support people in doing things with information. And it should be under the aegis of the top management team.

This is in line with ideas advanced by Marchand (1997) and by Japanese-American thinkers like Nonaka and Takeuchi (1995) about the value that can be created by diffusion of responsibility for knowledge and decision making throughout organizations, rather than concentrating it at the top.

References

Bowden, A. and Ricketts, M. (1992) *Stimulating Innovation in Industry: the challenge for the United Kingdom*, Kogan Page/NEDO.

Bowonder, B. and Miyake, T. (1992) Creating and sustaining competitiveness: information management strategies of Nippon Steel Corporation. *International Journal of Information Management*, 12, 39–56.

Davenport, T.H. (1993) *Process Innovation: re-engineering work through information technology*, Harvard Business School Press.

Drucker, P. (1995a) *Managing in a Time of Great Change*, Butterworth Heinemann.

Drucker, P. (1995b) The information executives truly need. *Harvard Business Review*, January–February, 54–62.

Farkas-Conn, I. (1989) Information as a corporate resource. *Information Services and Use*, 9, 205–215.

Holohan, J. (1992) Use of executive information systems in measuring business performance. *Journal of Information Technology*, 7, 177–186.

King, A.S. (1996) Organon of business failure: phase model of organizational decline. *Journal of Information Science*, 22, 4, 259–276. (Useful analysis of how lack of strategic use of information contributes to decline and fall of businesses exhibiting various syndromes.)

Koenig, M.E.D. (1992) The importance of information services for productivity 'under-recognised' and underinvested. *Special Libraries*, Fall, 199–210.

Marchand, D.A. (1997) Managing strategic intelligence. *Financial Times Mastering Management*, Financial Times/Pitman ('sharing strategic intelligence rather than processing it centrally encourages a diversity of interpretations and views about the future'; helps to cope with rapid change in the environment; strategic intelligence should not be confined to the top of the company, but should be distributed in line with more lateral approaches).

Michie, J. (1997) Innovation the key to growth for any nation (article on Archibugu, D. and Michie, J. (eds) *Technology, Globalisation, and Economic Performance*, Cambridge University Press). *The Guardian*, 21 April.

Nonaka, I. and Takeuchi, H. (1995) *The Knowledge-creating Company: how Japanese companies create the dynamics of information*, Oxford University Press.

Rothwell, R. (1983) *Information and Successful Innovation*, British Library R&D Report 5802, The British Library and the Technical Change Centre.

Sillince, J.A.A. (1994) A management strategy for innovation and organizational design: the case of MRP2/JIT production management systems. *Behaviour and Information Technology*, 13, 3, 216–227.

Systems and technology

Chapter 8

Generic types of information systems

Matthew Hinton

An information system collects, processes, stores, analyses and disseminates information for a specific purpose. At its simplest level, an information system processes a set of inputs (like data and instructions) and produces a variety of outputs (like reports and calculations) within a given environment. This chapter sets out to explore the generic types of information systems that are used for storing and processing information. To begin with, it describes the important role played by databases, as arguably the single most significant component in most information systems. This is followed by a breakdown of the generic types of information systems that can be identified in virtually all organizations. System classifications are derived from their various attributes, such as organizational purpose and value, and the nature of the business processes they support.

Databases

Databases are the most widespread form of information store and are commonly employed throughout organizations. As such, they often form the building blocks of management information systems. Essential to the idea of a management information system is the ability to retrieve data and use them for the production of targeted information for management decision making. Much data will be created and stored as a result of the ongoing processes and transactions taking place within an organization. This activity takes place regardless of the type, size or industry sector the organization finds itself in. The commercial operation of a retail store will produce data every time goods are delivered, staff employed to place stock on shelves, or groceries paid for by customers. In the same way a public service like a hospital will generate data which show its 'transactions'; how many patients on a waiting list, the allocation of key resources like an operating theatre or the stock of medical supplies. It is important that such data are seen as a central resource for the entire management information system and not solely connected to the application that produced it:

> ... Sales transaction data used to update the sales ledger will be stored after the updating process. This data should be available for other purposes. It can be used to provide reports on sales personnel performance as part of the HR management function. Alternatively, it can be fed into models that use data and information from other sources to forecast cash flows and aid cash management.
>
> Curtis and Cobham, 1998, p. 25

In order for data to be commonly available, special software, known as the database management system, is required to control access to the various data stores. Figure 8.1 shows how the ongoing organizational processes are fed into the database and the data are passed on to managers via the database management system. Managers may make direct enquiries of the database or, more commonly, some form of management information system will process data as required.

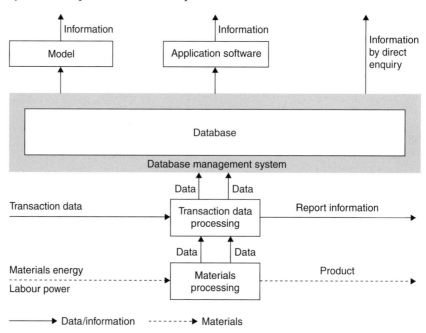

Figure 8.1   The provision of information from a database

Access to accurate and timely information needed for decision making has become increasingly important for modern organizations. Unfortunately, it has not always been easy to identify and retrieve the required information. Organizations have accumulated vast database systems containing gigantic volumes of data, so the emphasis has shifted to efficient organization and access management of this resource. The focus of technology has changed from simple data input and capture to information access and availability provided by an organization's data warehouse. A *data warehouse* is a relational or multidimensional database management system designed to support decision making (Turban et al., 2001). The data warehouse transforms data into a more useful resource by grouping them more conveniently for users, standardizing data formats to enable better data analysis and increase the availability and accessibility of data to appropriate working groups. The intelligent management of data in many different databases, using a data warehouse, has many business advantages. These include:

- removing barriers among functional areas, thus providing a look at cross-functional activities

- consolidating data about individual customers

- providing users with an integrated, customer-centric view of the organization's data, compiled from data in different systems

- providing added value to customers by allowing them to access better information when data warehousing is coupled with communications technologies such as the Internet.

Types of information systems

Business information systems are designed to produce information that is of value to the organization. So that the user organization can be persuaded to invest money in this type of undertaking they must be persuaded of the value of the information produced. The value of this information is in turn dependent on the purpose of the information. For example, the system may produce information that enables the user to keep control of the organization's payroll or enables management to make better decisions so giving the organization a competitive edge. In terms of business objectives, information systems fall into three major categories: operational, tactical and strategic (see Figure 8.1).

Operational systems

Information systems of this type concern those operations carried out by the organization in its normal trading environment. These systems perform necessary routine activities and include applications such as stock control, order processing, retailing systems, on-line booking systems and so on. Operational systems can be unexceptional but they are usually critical to the organization's endeavours (Cleary, 1998).

Tactical systems

Tactical systems are usually associated with those processes that supply information for immediate decision making. Such decisions usually refer to management activities involved with the monitoring of financial budgets, pricing levels, human resourcing, production schedules, stock level planning and so on.

Strategic systems

Strategic systems are invariably concerned with those decisions that affect the long-term policy objectives of the organization. Such decisions usually regard matters like determining the types of products/services supplied by the organization, the organization's centre of activities, investment plans in research and development and issues concerning the financing of the enterprise.

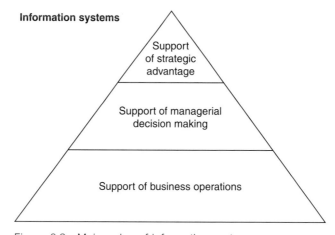

Information systems

Support of strategic advantage

Support of managerial decision making

Support of business operations

Figure 8.2   Major roles of information systems

Strategic systems frequently depend on information sources that are usually beyond the influence of the individual organization. For example, borrowing requirements and export policies could depend upon national factors such as interest rates and levels of unemployment, or international factors such as currency exchange rates or commodity prices. So useful models such as sophisticated spreadsheet scenarios incorporating data of this type have enabled users to make better decisions than might otherwise have been the case (Cleary, 1998).

So information systems perform three vital roles in any type of organization:

- support of its business processes and operations
- support of decision making by its employees and managers
- support of its strategies for competitive advantage.

The categorization of information systems is a matter of debate. Indeed some regard it as a fruitless debate since change is so rapid, but it can be helpful to sort information systems into levels according to use. With this in mind, O'Brien (2000) offers a classification of information systems that distinguishes between operational and management support systems (see Box 8.1).

Box 8.1 Classification of system roles

Operational support systems

Information systems have always been needed to process data generated by, and used in, business operations. Such operational support systems provide a variety of information products for internal and external use. However, they do not emphasize producing specific information products that can be best used by managers. Further processing by management information systems is required. The role of an organization's operational support systems is to efficiently process business transactions, control industrial process, support enterprise communications and collaboration. *Transaction processing systems* are an important example of operational support systems that record and process data resulting from business transactions. For example, point of sale systems at many retail stores use electronic cash register terminals to electronically capture and transmit sales data over telecommunication links to regional computer centres for processing. *Process control systems* monitor and control physical processes. For example, a petroleum refinery uses information systems to monitor chemical processes and make instant adjustments that control the refining process. *Enterprise collaboration systems* enhance group-working activity. For example, a project team may use electronic mail to send and receive messages and to coordinate their activities.

Management support systems

When information systems focus on providing information and support for effective decision making by managers, they are called management support systems. Conceptually, several types of information system support a variety of managerial responsibilities. *Management Information Systems* (MIS) provide information in the form of reports and displays for managers. For example, sales managers may use their personal computers to get displays about sales results of their products and to access sales reports evaluating sales made by each salesperson. *Decision Support Systems* give direct computer support to managers during the decision-making process. For example, advertising managers may use an electronic spreadsheet package to do sensitivity analysis to test the impact of alternative advertising budgets on forecasted sales. *Executive Information Systems* provide critical information in easy to use displays. For example, top executives may use touchscreen terminals to instantly view text and graphics displays that highlight key areas of organizational performance (O'Brien (2000), pp. 33–34).

As mentioned above, the term *Decision Support Systems* (DSS) covers any computerized system that supports decision-making activity. A DSS is intended to support rather than replace decision-making roles. Computerized systems can replace the human decision maker in structured decisions but are of little help in completely unstructured situations. In addition, decision makers encounter a variety of decisions which comprise a structured element, where data are transformed, and an unstructured non-rule-governed element. It is just these decisions that can be aided by DSS (Curtis and Cobham, 1998). Many decisions taken within an organization will be taken not by a single individual but as a result of group deliberations. Group decision support systems (GDSS) deliver computer-based support for group decisions. Given their purpose, decision support systems require flexible interactive access to data. In addition, DSS are designed with an understanding of the requirements of the decision makers and the decision-making process in mind. This has implications, two of the most important being:

1   *Flexible access to data*: many semi-structured decisions are only possible if the decision maker has immediate access to *ad hoc* data retrieval and report generation facilities. For internal decisions this means that access by powerful query languages of existing data held in a corporate database is required.

2   *The need for interactive support*: typically many of the semi-structured decisions for which DSS are relevant involve the decision maker in asking questions that require immediate answers. As a result of this, further interrogation is made. Examples are:

    Sensitivity analysis (sometimes called 'what if?' analysis) – as in 'what would the effect on profits be if we were to be subject to a 5 per cent material cost rise?'

    Goal seeking – as in 'what would be the required mix in the liquidation of short-term and medium-term assets to reduce a projected cash deficit to zero over the next six months?'

    Optimization – as in 'how do we ensure optimum utilization of our machines?'

The development of artificial intelligence techniques has given rise to two final categories of information system you will encounter in organizations: *Expert Systems* and *Knowledge Management Systems*. An expert system is a knowledge-based information system that uses its knowledge about a specific, complex application area to act as an expert consultant to decision makers and other system users. As O'Brien (2000) explains, 'Expert systems provide answers to questions in a very specific problem area by making human like inferences about knowledge contained in a specialized knowledge base.' They must also be able to explain their reasoning process and conclusions to a user (Egan, 1995). The major limitations of expert systems are the result of their limited focus and inability to learn. So expert systems excel only in solving specific types of problems in a limited domain of knowledge. They fail where a broad range of knowledge is needed to solve a problem and are weak when dealing with subjective managerial decision making.

References

Cleary, T. (1998) *Business Information Technology*, FT Prentice-Hall.

Curtis, G. and Cobham, D. (1998) *Business Information Systems: analysis, design and practice*, Addison Wesley Longman.

Egan, R. (1995) The expert within. *PC Today*, January.

O'Brien, J. (2000) *Introduction to Information Systems*, McGraw-Hill.

Turban, E., Rainer, R. and Potter, R. (2001) *Introduction to Information Technology*, Wiley and Sons.

Chapter 9

Business information systems

James O'Brien

IS in business

Business managers are moving from a tradition where they could avoid, delegate, or ignore decisions about IT to one where they cannot create a marketing, product, international, organizational, or financial plan that does not involve such decisions (Keen and Ballance, 1997).

There are as many ways to use information technology in business as there are business activities to be pursued. As a business end user, you should have a basic understanding and appreciation of the major ways information systems are used to support each of the functions of business. Thus, in this chapter we will discuss business information systems, that is, a variety of types of information systems (transaction processing, management information, decision support, etc.) that support the business functions of accounting, finance, marketing, operations management and human resource management.

Analysing Amazon.com

We can learn a lot about how information technology empowers the strategic moves and e-commerce success of Amazon.com (see Box 9.1).

Box 9.1 Amazon.com: success and expansion in electronic commerce

[...] Originally, it seemed as though the major Internet portals – with Yahoo! and America Online leading the way – held most of the keys to the future of retail commerce. As the biggest online magnets for potential shoppers, portals charge retailers dearly – in either long-term, multimillion-dollar sponsorship deals or shares of sales revenues – to stake out small plots of valuable portal real estate and drive more customer traffic to their sites.

Consumer-agent technology and price-comparison sites such as Junglee and CompareNet, on the other hand, have always held the promise of a direct consumer–retailer relationship – with shopbots (shopping software robot programs) available 24 hours a day to find any product at the best price. But it was not until Amazon made two major acquisitions that industry observers caught a glimpse of how the balance of retail power might shift.

Amazon's pace was blistering. In June 1998, the company added music to its offerings. In one quarter, it became the leading Internet music seller, with more than $14 million in sales, much to the chagrin of stunned competitors such as CDNow and N2K. In the fall, it launched European book sites in Germany and Britain and added videos to its 'media suite'. Then came the acquisitions.

In August 1998, Amazon gobbled up Junglee and PlanetAll (an online address book and organizer for some 1.5 million users) for $280 million in stock. By November 1998, Amazon announced it would add software to its product line and it opened a gift centre, adding such items as Barbie dolls, watches and PalmPilots to its array of offerings. Online auctions began a few months later.

In creating this potential powerhouse of shopping services and offerings, Amazon.com looks to be moulding itself into not simply a Wal-Mart of the Web but rather a next-generation, retail commerce portal.

Imagine a customized site where, through a Junglee-like shopping service, you will not only shop easily with a trusted brand for books, videos, gifts and more, but you will also research the features, price and availability of millions of products from a single storefront that has Amazon's – and your – name on it. That is the promise and the challenge of Internet retailing in the future.

That is what has got Amazon this far in its first three years of business: exhaustive focus on convenience, selection and personalization. It lived up to its billing as Earth's Biggest Bookstore by building an inventory of more than 3 million titles. It was also among the first Internet stores to facilitate credit-card purchases, greet customers by name and offer customized homepages, send purchase recommendations via e-mail and number and explain each step in the purchasing process.

But it has not been all roses in Seattle, either. Amazon has been criticized for inefficient inventory management while the company continues to post multimillion-dollar losses each quarter. According to an IceGroup study of Amazon's business model in 1998, losses were running at the equivalent of $7 per transaction. (Its gross profit margins and customer-retention rates, on the other hand, continue to improve steadily, factors that keep investors happy.) The company needs to ready logistics and backend systems to handle an expansion of product offerings. Transaction costs need to be cut to ensure the seemingly unattainable: a profitable quarter.

Amazon remains the dominant player in e-commerce, despite German media giant Bertelsmann and Amazon competitor Barnes & Noble's joint Web venture. Amazon's four-month jump to the top of the music category proved how extensible the Amazon brand is, especially as the company builds out from books, music and videos. A profitable quarter is not due till 2000, but if Amazon decides to begin selling ad space – which it hasn't done yet – that might change quickly. (Source: Adapted from Jeffrey Davis, 'Mall Rats,' *Business 2.0*, January 1999, pp. 41–50)

For three years Amazon.com concentrated on becoming the best online bookstore on the Web and one of the best websites for customer service. They invested heavily in electronic commerce software and other information technologies to offer top-rated convenience, selection and personalization to their customers. Then they leveraged this investment in IT and retail e-commerce to support a strategic expansion into music, videos, software, gift items and online auctions. In addition, they have made investments in new e-commerce technology by acquiring companies that provide shopping agent software and online organizer services.

These capabilities enabled Amazon to transform itself into a retail commerce portal for all types of products and services. Thus, now they have solved their inventory and logistics management problems, Amazon should continue to be a dominant player in electronic commerce.

Cross-functional information systems

As a business end user, it is important that you have a specific understanding of how information systems affect a particular business function – marketing, for example – or a particular industry (e.g. banking) that is directly related to your career objectives. For example, someone whose career objective is a marketing position in banking should have a basic understanding of how information systems are used in banking and how they support the marketing activities of banks and other firms.

Figure 9.1 illustrates how information systems can be grouped into business function categories. Thus, information systems in this section will be analysed according to the business function they support to give you an appreciation of the variety of business information systems that both small and large business firms may use.

However, [...] information systems in the real world typically are integrated combinations of functional information systems. Such systems support business processes, such as product development, production, distribution,

Figure 9.1   Examples of business information systems. Note how they support the major functional areas of business.

order management, customer support and so on. Many organizations are using information technology to develop cross-functional information systems that cross the boundaries of traditional business functions in order to re-engineer and improve vital business processes. These organizations view cross-functional information systems as a strategic way to use IT to share information resources and improve the efficiency and effectiveness of business processes, thus helping a business attain its strategic objectives (Figure 9.2).

For example, business firms are turning to Internet technologies to integrate the flow of information among their internal business functions and their customers and suppliers. Companies are using the World Wide Web and their intranets and extranets as the technology platform for their cross-functional and interorganizational information systems.

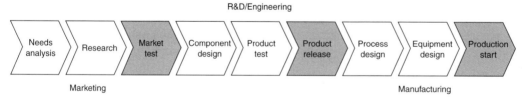

Figure 9.2   The new product development process in a manufacturing company. This business process must be supported by cross-functional information systems that cross the boundaries of several business functions. Source: Adapted from *Process Innovation: Reengineering Work Through Information Technology* by Davenport, T.H. (Boston: 1993), p. 222. The Harvard Business School Press. Copyright © 1993 by Ernst & Young.

Enterprise resource planning

In addition, many companies have moved from functional mainframe legacy systems to cross-functional client/server network applications. This typically has involved installing enterprise resource planning (ERP) or *supply chain management* (SCM) software from SAP, Baan, PeopleSoft, or Oracle Corporation. Instead of focusing on the information processing requirements of business functions, ERP software focuses on supporting the business processes involved in the operations of a business. [...]

Marketing information systems

The business function of marketing is concerned with the planning, promotion and sale of existing products in existing markets and the development of new products and new markets better to serve present and potential customers. Thus, marketing performs a vital function in the operation of a business enterprise. Business firms have increasingly turned to information technology to help them perform vital marketing functions in the face of the rapid changes of today's environment.

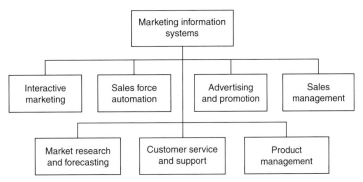

Figure 9.3   Marketing information systems provide information technologies to support major components of the marketing function.

Figure 9.3 illustrates how marketing information systems provide information technologies that support major components of the marketing function. For example, Internet/intranet websites and services make an *interactive marketing* process possible, where customers can become partners in creating, marketing, purchasing and improving products and services. *Sales force automation* systems use mobile computing and Internet technologies to automate many information-processing activities for sales support and management. Other marketing information systems assist marketing managers in product planning, pricing and other product management decisions, advertising and sales promotion strategies and market research and forecasting. Let's take a closer look at these computer-based applications.

Interactive marketing

The explosive growth of Internet technologies has had a major impact on the marketing function. The term interactive marketing has been coined to describe a type of marketing that is based on using the Internet, intranets and extranets to establish two-way interaction between a business and its customers or potential customers. The goal of interactive marketing is to enable a company profitably to use those networks to attract and keep customers who will become partners with the business in creating, purchasing and improving products and services.

Table 9.1 outlines the steps of the interactive marketing process on the Internet. Notice that the Internet has become the primary distribution channel of the new online marketing environment. Customers are not just passive participants who receive media advertising prior to purchase, but are actively engaged in a network-enabled proactive and interactive process.

Table 9.1   The interactive marketing process on the Internet

Step 1	**Segment and identify potential customers** (Initial market research done by reaching relevant groups – WWW servers, listservs, newsgroups)
Step 2	**Create promotional, advertising and educational material** (WWW page with multimedia effects – audio and video) (Product information and complementary products, order forms and questionnaires)
Step 3	**Put the material on customers' computer screens** Push-based marketing – direct marketing using Web broadcasters, newsgroups, listservs and e-mail Pull-based marketing – indirect (static) marketing – WWW pages
Step 4	**Interacting with customers** Dialogue with the customer, interactive discussion among customers about various features offering endorsements, testimonials, questions/answers
Step 5	**Learning from customers** (repeat customers are 80 per cent of the customer base) Incorporating feedback from customers in advertising, marketing strategy Identifying new markets, using experience in new product development
Step 6	**Online customer service** Fast, friendly solutions to customer problems

Source: Adapted from Kalakota, R. and Whinston, A. *Frontiers of Electronic Commerce*, Addison-Wesley, 1996, p. 499.
© 1996 Addison-Wesley Publishing Company, Inc.

Notice that interactive marketing views prospective customers as belonging to many distinct market segments that must be approached differently online through targeted marketing techniques. Interactive marketing also encourages customers to become involved in product development, delivery and service issues. This is enabled by various Internet technologies, including chat and discussion groups, Web forums and questionnaires and e-mail correspondence. Finally, the expected outcomes of interactive marketing are a rich mixture of vital marketing data, new product ideas, volume sales and strong customer relationships (Halper, 1997).

Sales force automation

Increasingly, computers and networks are providing the basis for sales force automation. In many companies, the sales force is being outfitted with notebook computers, Web browsers and sales contact management software that connect them to marketing websites on the Internet, extranets and their company intranets. This not only increases the personal productivity of salespeople, but dramatically speeds up the capture and analysis of sales data from the field to marketing managers at company headquarters. In return, it allows marketing and sales management to improve the delivery of information and the support they provide to their salespeople. Therefore, many companies are viewing sales force automation as a way to gain a strategic advantage in sales productivity and marketing responsiveness.

Table 9.2   Some of the benefits of web-based sales force automation

Shorten the sales cycle through prequalification of prospects

Increase revenue through targeted marketing

Automate the management and qualification of Web leads

Capture all customer information directly into a sales database

Enhance order management with access to data on pricing, promotions, availability, production schedules, export regulations, carriers and transportation schedules

Source: Adapted from Kalakota, R. and Whinston, A. *Electronic Commerce: a manager's guide*, Addison-Wesley, 1997, p. 325. © 1997 by Addison-Wesley Publishing Company, Inc.

For example, salespeople use their PCs to record sales data as they make their calls on customers and prospects during the day. Then each night sales reps in the field can connect their computers by modem and telephone links to the Internet and extranet, which can access intranet or other network servers at their company. Then they can upload information on sales orders, sales calls and other sales statistics, as well as send electronic mail messages and access website sales support information. In return, the network servers may download product availability data, prospect lists of information on good sales prospects and e-mail messages (Table 9.2).

Sales and product management

Sales managers must plan, monitor and support the performance of the salespeople in their organizations. So, in most firms, computer-based systems produce sales analysis reports that analyse sales by product, product line, customer, type of customer, salesperson and sales territory. Such reports help marketing managers monitor the sales performance of products and salespeople and help them develop sales support programmes to improve sales results.

Product managers need information to plan and control the performance of specific products, products lines and brands. Computer-based analysis can provide price, revenue, cost and growth information for existing products and new product development. Thus, providing information and analysis for pricing and product development decisions is a major function of a product management system.

Advertising and promotion

Marketing managers try to maximize sales at the lowest possible costs for advertising and promotion. Marketing information systems use market research information and promotion models to help (1) select media and promotional methods, (2) allocate financial resources and (3) control and evaluate results of various advertising and promotion campaigns. For example, the INFOSCAN system of Information Resources Incorporated (IRC) tracks the sales of over 800 000 products by their universal product code (UPC) to more than 70 000 US households at over 2400 retail stores. INFOSCAN measures the effect of promotional tactics such as price discounts, coupon offers and point-of-purchase (POP) promotions. Then INFOSCAN's computer-based marketing models produce sales forecasts and other analyses of marketing strategy.

Targeted marketing

Targeted marketing has become an important tool in developing advertising and promotion strategies for a company's electronic commerce websites. As illustrated in Figure 9.4, targeted marketing is an advertising and promotion management concept that includes five targeting components.

- *Community.* Companies can customize their Web advertising messages and promotion methods to appeal to people in specific communities. These can be *communities of interest*, such as *virtual communities* of online sporting enthusiasts or arts and crafts hobbyists, or geographic communities formed by the websites of a city or local newspaper.

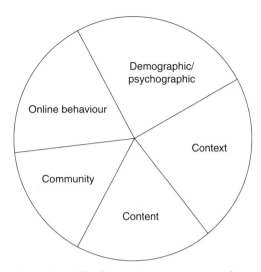

Figure 9.4   The five major components of targeted marketing for electronic commerce on the World Wide Web
(Source: Adapted from Martin, C. *The Digital Estate: strategies for competing, surviving, and thriving in an Internetworked world* (New York: McGraw-Hill, 1997), pp. 124–25, 206)

- *Content.* Advertising such as electronic billboards or banners can be placed on various website pages, in addition to a company's home page. These messages reach the targeted audience. An ad for a movie on the opening page of an Internet search engine is a typical example.

- *Context.* Advertising appears only in Web pages that are relevant to the content of a product or service. So advertising is targeted only at people who are already looking for information about a subject matter (vacation travel, for example) that is related to a company's products (car rental services, for example).

- *Demographic/psychographic.* Marketing efforts can be aimed only at specific types or classes of people: unmarried, twenty-something, middle income, male college graduates, for example.

- *Online behaviour.* Advertising and promotion efforts can be tailored to each visit to a site by an individual. This strategy is based on 'web cookie' files recorded on the visitor's disk drive from previous visits. Cookie files enable a company to track a person's online behaviour at a website so marketing efforts can be instantly developed and targeted to that individual at each visit to their website.

Market research and forecasting

Market research information systems provide marketing intelligence to help managers make better marketing forecasts and develop more effective marketing strategies. Marketing information systems help market researchers collect, analyse and maintain an enormous amount of information on a wide variety of market variables that are subject to continual change. This includes information on customers, prospects, consumers and competitors. Market, economic and demographic trends are also analysed. Data can be gathered from many sources, including a company's databases, data marts and data warehouse, World Wide Web sites and telemarketing services companies. Then, a variety of statistical software tools can help managers analyse market research data and forecast sales and other important market trends.

Manufacturing information systems

Manufacturing information systems support the production/operations function that includes all activities concerned with the planning and control of the processes producing goods or services. Thus, the production/ operations function is concerned with the management of the operational processes and systems of all business firms. Information systems used for operations management and transaction processing support all firms that must plan, monitor and control inventories, purchases and the flow of goods and services. Therefore, firms such as transportation companies, wholesalers, retailers, financial institutions and service companies must use production/operations information systems to plan and control their operations. In this section, we will concentrate on computer-based manufacturing applications to illustrate information systems that support the production/operations function.

Computer-integrated manufacturing

A variety of manufacturing information systems is used to support computer-integrated manufacturing (CIM) (Figure 9.5). CIM is an overall concept that stresses that the objectives of computer-based systems in manufacturing must be to:

- *Simplify* (re-engineer) production processes, product designs and factory organization as a vital foundation to automation and integration.
- *Automate* production processes and the business functions that support them with computers, machines and robots.
- *Integrate* all production and support processes using computers, telecommunications networks, and other information technologies.

The overall goal of CIM and such manufacturing information systems is to create flexible, agile, manufacturing processes that efficiently produce products of the highest quality. Thus, CIM supports the concepts of *flexible manufacturing systems*, *agile manufacturing* and *total quality management*. Implementing such manufacturing concepts enables a company to respond quickly to and fulfil customer requirements with high-quality products and services.

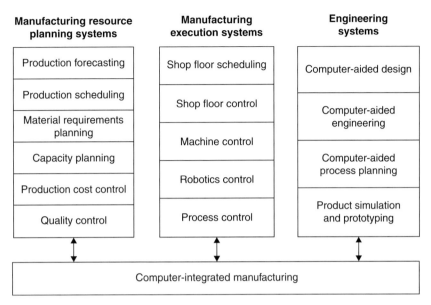

Figure 9.5   Manufacturing information systems support computer-integrated manufacturing.

Manufacturing information systems help companies simplify, automate and integrate many of the activities needed to produce products of all kinds. For example, computers are used to help engineers design better products using both computer-aided engineering and computer-aided design and better production processes with computer-aided process planning. They are also used to help plan the types of material needed in the production process, which is called *material requirements planning* (MRP), and to integrate MRP with production scheduling and shop floor operations, which is known as *manufacturing resource planning*.

Computer-aided manufacturing (CAM) systems are those that automate the production process. For example, this could be accomplished by monitoring and controlling the production process in a factory through *manufacturing execution systems*, or by directly controlling a physical process (process control), a machine tool (machine control), or machines with some humanlike work capabilities (robots).

Manufacturing execution systems (MES) are performance monitoring information systems for factory floor operations. They monitor, track and control the five essential components involved in a production process: materials, equipment, personnel, instructions and specifications, and production facilities. MES includes shop floor scheduling and control, machine control, robotics control and process control systems. These manufacturing systems monitor, report and adjust the status and performance of production components to help a company achieve a flexible, high-quality manufacturing process.

Collaborative manufacturing networks

Manufacturing processes like computer-aided engineering and design, production control, production scheduling and procurement management typically involve a collaborative process. Increasingly, this involves using the Internet, intranets, extranets and other networks to link the workstations of engineers and other specialists with their colleagues at other sites. These collaborative manufacturing networks may link employees within a company, or include representatives from a company's suppliers or customers wherever they may be located.

For example, Johnson Controls uses the Internet, intranets and other networks to link the workstations of employees at their Automative Systems Group with their counterparts at Ford and Chrysler and other companies worldwide. The engineers and other specialists use these computer networks to collaborate on a range of assignments, including car seat design, production issues and delivery schedules.

Process control

Process control is the use of computers to control an ongoing physical process. Process control computers control physical processes in petroleum refineries, cement plants, steel mills, chemical plants, food product manufacturing plants, pulp and paper mills, electric power plants and so on. Many process control computers are special-purpose minicomputer systems. A process control computer system requires the use of special sensing devices that measure physical phenomena such as temperature or pressure changes. These continuous physical measurements are converted to digital form by analogue-to-digital converters and relayed to computers for processing.

Process control software uses mathematical models to analyse the data generated by the ongoing process and compare them to standards or forecasts of required results. Then the computer directs the control of the process by adjusting control devices such as thermostats, valves, switches and so on. The process control system also provides messages and displays about the status of the process so a human operator can take appropriate measures to control the process.

Machine control

Machine control is the use of a computer to control the actions of a machine. This is also popularly called *numerical control*. The control of machine tools in factories is a typical numerical control application, though it also refers to the control of typesetting machines, weaving machines and other industrial machinery.

Numerical control computer programs for machine tools convert geometric data from engineering drawings and machining instructions from process planning into a numerical code of commands that control the actions of a machine tool. Machine control may involve the use of special-purpose microcomputers called programmable logic controllers (PLCs). These devices operate one or more machines according to the directions of a numerical control program. Manufacturing engineers use computers to develop numerical control programs, analyse production data furnished by PLCs and fine-tune machine tool performance.

Robotics

An important development in machine control and computer-aided manufacturing is the creation of smart machines and robots. These devices directly control their own activities with the aid of microcomputers. Robotics is the technology of building and using machines (robots) with computer intelligence and computer-controlled humanlike physical capabilities (dexterity, movement, vision, etc.). Robotics has also become a major thrust of research and development efforts in the field of artificial intelligence.

Robots are used as 'steel-collar workers' to increase productivity and cut costs. For example, a robot might assemble compressor valves with 12 parts at the rate of 320 units per hour, which is 10 times the rate of human workers. Robots are also particularly valuable for hazardous areas or work activities. Robots follow programs distributed by servers and loaded into separate or on-board special-purpose microcomputers. Input is received from visual and/or tactile sensors, processed by the microcomputer and translated into movements of the robot. Typically, this involves moving its arms and hands to pick up and load items or perform some other work assignment such as painting, drilling or welding. Robotics developments are expected to make robots more intelligent, flexible and mobile by improving their computing, visual, tactile and navigational capabilities.

Computer-aided engineering

Manufacturing engineers use computer-aided engineering (CAE) to simulate, analyse and evaluate the models of product designs they have developed using computer-aided design (CAD) methods. Networks of powerful engineering workstations with enhanced graphics and computational capabilities and CAD software help them analyse and design products and manufacturing processes and facilities. CAD packages refine an engineer's initial drawings and provide three-dimensional computer graphics that can be rotated to display all sides of the object being designed. The engineer can zoom in for close-up views of a specific part and even make parts of the product appear to move as they would in normal operation. The design can then be converted into a finished mathematical model of the product. This is used as the basis for production specifications and machine tool programs.

Manufacturing engineers design products according to product specifications determined in cooperation with the product design efforts of marketing research, product development and customer management specialists. One of the final outputs of this design process is the bill of materials (specification of all required materials) used by the MRP application. In addition, manufacturing engineers use CAD systems to design the production processes needed to manufacture products they have developed (computer-aided process planning).

Human resource information systems

The human resource management (HRM) function involves the recruitment, placement, evaluation, compensation and development of the employees of an organization. The goal of human resource management is the effective and efficient use of the human resources of a company. Thus, human resource information systems are designed to support (1) planning to meet the personnel needs of the business, (2) development of employees to their full potential and (3) control of all personnel policies and programmes. Originally, businesses used computer-based information systems to (1) produce paycheques and payroll reports, (2) maintain personnel records and (3) analyse the use of personnel in business operations. Many firms have gone beyond these traditional *personnel management* functions and have developed human resource information systems (HRIS) that also support (1) recruitment, selection and hiring, (2) job placement, (3) performance appraisals, (4) employee benefits analysis, (5) training and development and (6) health, safety and security (Figure 9.6).

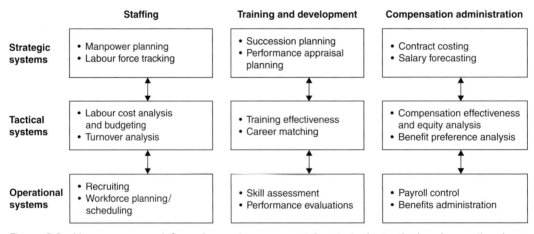

Figure 9.6   Human resource information systems support the strategic, tactical and operational use of the human resources of an organization.

HRM and the Internet

The Internet has become a major force for change in human resource management. For example, online HRM systems may involve recruiting for employees through recruitment sections of corporate websites. Companies are also using commercial recruiting services and databases on the World Wide Web, posting messages in selected Internet newsgroups and communicating with job applicants by Internet e-mail.

The Internet has a wealth of information and contacts for both employers and job hunters. For example, take the home page of Top Jobs on the Net, found at www.topjobs.com. This website is full of reports, statistics and other useful HRM information, such as an international job report by industry, or a listing of the top recruiting markets in various countries by industry and profession. Of course, you may also want to access the job listings and resource database of commercial recruiting services on the Web. [...]

HRM and the corporate intranet

Intranet technologies allow companies to process most common HRM applications over their corporate intranets. Intranets allow the HRM department to provide around-the-clock services to their customers – the employees. They can also disseminate valuable information faster than through previous company channels. Intranets can collect information online from employees for input to their HRM files and they can enable employees to perform HRM tasks with little intervention by the HRM department.

For example, *employee self-service* (ESS) intranet applications allow employees to view benefits, enter travel and expense reports, verify employment and salary information, access and update their personal information and enter data that have a time constraint to them. Through this completely electronic process, employees can use their Web browsers to look up individual payroll and benefits information online, right from their desktop PCs, mobile computers, or intranet kiosks located around a worksite.

Another benefit of the intranet is that it can serve as a superior training tool. Employees can easily download instructions and processes to get the information or education they need. In addition, employees using new technology can view training videos over the intranet on demand. Thus, the intranet eliminates the need to loan out and track training videos. Employees can also use their corporate intranets to produce automated paysheets, the online alternative to timecards. These electronic forms have made viewing, entering and adjusting payroll information easy for both employees and HRM professionals.

Staffing the organization

The staffing function must be supported by information systems that record and track human resources within a company to maximize their use. For example, a personnel record-keeping system keeps track of additions, deletions and other changes to the records in a personnel database. Changes in job assignments and compensation, or hirings and terminations, are examples of information that would be used to update the personnel database. Another example is an employee skills inventory system that uses the employee skills data from a personnel database to locate employees within a company who have the skills required for specific assignments and projects.

A final example involves forecasting personnel requirements to assure a business an adequate supply of high-quality human resources. This application provides forecasts of personnel requirements in each major job category for various company departments or for new projects and other ventures being planned by management. Such long-range planning may use a computer-based simulation model to evaluate alternative plans for recruitment, reassignment, or retraining programmes.

Training and development

Information systems help human resource managers plan and monitor employee recruitment, training and development programmes by analysing the success history of present programmes. They also analyse the career development status of each employee to determine whether development methods such as training programmes and periodic performance appraisals of employee job performance are available to help support this area of human resource management.

Compensation analysis

Information systems can help analyse the range and distribution of employee compensation (wages, salaries, incentive payments and fringe benefits) within a company and make comparisons with compensation paid by similar firms or with various economic indicators. This information is useful for planning changes in compensation, especially if negotiations with labour unions are involved. It helps keep the compensation of a company competitive and equitable, while controlling compensation costs.

Governmental reporting

Nowadays, reporting to government agencies is a major responsibility of human resource management. So organizations use computer-based information systems to keep track of the statistics and produce reports required by a variety of government laws and regulations. For example, in the USA, statistics on employee recruitment and hiring must be collected for possible use in Equal Employment Opportunity Commission (EEOC) hearings; statistics for employee health, workplace hazards, accidents, and safety procedures must be reported to the Occupational Safety and Health Administration (OSHA); and statistics on the use of hazardous materials must be reported to the Environmental Protection Agency (EPA). Software packages to collect and report such statistics are available from a variety of software vendors.

Accounting information systems

Accounting information systems are the oldest and most widely used information systems in business. They record and report business transactions and other economic events. Accounting information systems are based on the double-entry bookkeeping concept, which is hundreds of years old, and other, more recent accounting concepts such as responsibility accounting and activity-based costing. Computer-based accounting systems record and report the flow of funds through an organization on a historical basis and produce important financial statements such as balance sheets and income statements. Such systems also produce forecasts of future conditions such as projected financial statements and financial budgets. A firm's financial performance is measured against such forecasts by other analytical accounting reports.

Operational accounting systems emphasize legal and historical record-keeping and the production of accurate financial statements. Typically, these systems include transaction processing systems such as order processing, inventory control, accounts receivable, accounts payable, payroll and general ledger systems. Management accounting systems focus on the planning and control of business operations. They emphasize cost accounting reports comparing actual to forecasted performance.

Figure 9.7 illustrates the interrelationships of several important accounting information systems commonly computerized by both large and small businesses. Many accounting software packages are available for these applications. Let us briefly review how several of these systems support the operations and management of a business firm. Table 9.3 summarizes the purpose of six common, but important, accounting information systems.

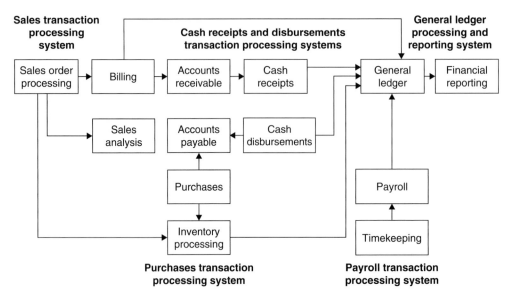

Figure 9.7   Important accounting information systems for transaction processing and financial reporting. Note how they are related to each other in terms of input and output flows.
Source: Adapted from Wilkinson, J.W. and Cerullo, M.J. *Accounting Information Systems: Essential Concepts and Applications*, 3rd edn, p.10. Copyright © 1997 by John Wiley & Sons, Inc.

Table 9.3   A summary of six widely used accounting information systems

Order processing
Captures and processes customer orders and produces data for inventory control and accounts receivable

Inventory control
Processes data reflecting changes in inventory and provides shipping and reorder information

Accounts receivable
Records amounts owed by customers and produces customer invoices, monthly customer statements and credit management reports

Accounts payable
Records purchases from, amounts owed to and payments to suppliers and produces cash management reports

Payroll
Records employee work and compensation data and produces paycheques and other payroll documents and reports

General ledger
Consolidates data from other accounting systems and produces the periodic financial statements and reports of the business

Online accounting systems

It should come as no surprise that the accounting information systems illustrated in Figure 9.7 and Table 9.3 are being affected by Internet and client/server technologies. Using the Internet, intranets, extranets and other networks changes how accounting information systems monitor and track business activity. The online, interactive nature of such networks calls for new forms of transaction documents, procedures and controls. This particularly applies to systems like order processing, inventory control, accounts receivable and accounts payable. These systems are directly involved in the processing of transactions between a business and its customers and suppliers. So naturally, many companies are using or developing network links to these trading partners for such applications, using the Internet or other networks.

Order processing

Order processing, or sales order processing, is an important transaction processing system that captures and processes customer orders and produces data needed for sales analysis and inventory control. In many firms, it also keeps track of the status of customer orders until goods are delivered. Computer-based sales order processing systems provide a fast, accurate and efficient method of recording and screening customer orders and sales transactions. They also provide inventory control systems with information on accepted orders so they can be filled as quickly as possible.

Inventory control

Inventory control systems process data reflecting changes to items in inventory. Once data about customer orders are received from an order processing system, a computer-based inventory control system records changes to inventory levels and prepares appropriate shipping documents. Then it may notify managers about items that need reordering and provide them with a variety of inventory status reports. Computer-based inventory control systems thus help a business provide high-quality service to customers while minimizing investment in inventory and inventory carrying costs.

Accounts receivable

Accounts receivable systems keep records of amounts owed by customers from data generated by customer purchases and payments. They produce invoices to customers, monthly customer statements and credit management reports. Computer-based accounts receivable systems stimulate prompt customer payments by preparing accurate and timely invoices and monthly statements to credit customers. They provide managers with reports to help them control the amount of credit extended and the collection of money owed. This activity helps to maximize profitable credit sales while minimizing losses from bad debts.

Accounts payable

Accounts payable systems keep track of data concerning purchases from and payments to suppliers. They prepare cheques in payment of outstanding invoices and produce cash management reports. Computer-based accounts payable systems help ensure prompt and accurate payment of suppliers to maintain good relationships, ensure a good credit standing and secure any discounts offered for prompt payment. They provide tight financial control over all cash disbursements of the business. They also provide management with information needed for the analysis of payments, expenses, purchases, employee expense accounts and cash requirements.

Payroll

Payroll systems receive and maintain data from employee time cards and other work records. They produce paycheques and other documents such as earning statements, payroll reports and labour analysis reports. Other reports are also prepared for management and government agencies. Computer-based payroll systems help businesses make prompt and accurate payments to their employees, as well as reports to management, employees and government agencies concerning earnings, taxes and other deductions. They may also provide management with reports analysing labour costs and productivity.

General ledger

General ledger systems consolidate data received from accounts receivable, accounts payable, payroll and other accounting information systems. At the end of each accounting period, they close the books of a business and produce the general ledger trial balance, the income statement and balance sheet of the firm and various income and expense reports for management. Computer-based general ledger systems help businesses accomplish these accounting tasks in an accurate and timely manner. They typically provide better financial controls and management reports and involve fewer personnel and lower costs than manual accounting methods.

Financial management systems

Computer-based financial management systems support financial managers in decisions concerning (1) the financing of a business and (2) the allocation and control of financial resources within a business. Major financial

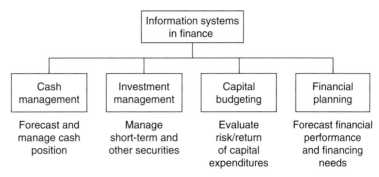

Figure 9.8   Examples of important financial management systems

management system categories include cash and investment management, capital budgeting, financial forecasting and financial planning (Figure 9.8).

Cash management

Cash management systems collect information on all cash receipts and disbursements within a company on a realtime or periodic basis. Such information allows businesses to deposit or invest excess funds more quickly and thus increase the income generated by deposited or invested funds. These systems also produce daily, weekly or monthly forecasts of cash receipts or disbursements (cash flow forecasts) that are used to spot future cash deficits or surpluses. Mathematical models frequently can determine optimal cash collection programs and determine alternative financing or investment strategies for dealing with forecasted cash deficits or surpluses.

Capital budgeting

The capital budgeting process involves evaluating the profitability and financial impact of proposed capital expenditures. Long-term expenditure proposals for plants and equipment can be analysed using a variety of techniques. This application makes heavy use of spreadsheet models that incorporate present value analysis of expected cash flows and probability analysis of risk to determine the optimum mix of capital projects for a business.

Financial forecasting and planning

Financial analysts typically use electronic spreadsheets and other financial planning software to evaluate the present and projected financial performance of a business. They also help determine the financing needs of a business and analyse alternative methods of financing. Financial analysts use financial forecasts concerning the economic situation, business operations, types of financing available, interest rates and stock and bond prices to develop an optimal financing plan for the business. Electronic spreadsheet packages, DSS software and web-based groupware can be used to build and manipulate financial models. Answers to what-if and goal-seeking questions can be explored as financial analysts and managers evaluate their financing and investment alternatives. [...]

Summary

- *IS in business.* Business information systems support the functional areas of business (marketing, production/operations, accounting, finance and human resource management) through a wide variety of computer-based operational and management information systems.

- *Marketing.* Marketing information systems provide information for the management of the marketing function. Thus, marketing information systems assist marketing managers in market research, product development and pricing decisions, as well as in planning advertising and sales promotion strategies and expenditures, forecasting the market potential for new and present products and determining channels of distribution. Major types of marketing information systems include interactive marketing, sales force automation, sales management, product management, advertising and promotion, targeted marketing, sales forecasting and market research. Interactive marketing on the Internet and other networks is changing marketing to a more customer-driven interactive process.

- *Manufacturing.* Computer-based manufacturing information systems help a company achieve computer-integrated manufacturing (CIM) and thus simplify, automate and integrate many of the activities needed to produce quickly high-quality products to meet changing customer demands. For example, computer-aided design (CAD) using collaborative manufacturing networks helps engineers collaborate on the design of new products and processes. Then material requirements planning (MRP) systems help plan the types of material needed in the production process. Finally, manufacturing execution systems monitor and control the manufacture of products on the factory floor through shop floor scheduling and control systems, controlling a physical process (process control), a machine tool (numerical control), or machines with some humanlike work capabilities (robotics).

- *Human resource management.* Human resource information systems support human resource management in organizations. They include information systems for staffing the organization, training and development, compensation administration and governmental reporting. HRM websites on the Internet or corporate intranets have become important tools for providing HR services to present and prospective employees.

- *Accounting and finance.* Accounting information systems record and report business transactions and events for business firms and other organizations. Operational accounting systems emphasize legal and historical record-keeping and the production of accurate financial statements. Management accounting systems focus on the planning and control of business operations. Common operational accounting information systems include order processing, inventory control, accounts receivable, accounts payable, payroll and general ledger systems.

- *Electronic commerce.* Electronic commerce encompasses the entire online process of developing, marketing, selling, delivering, servicing and paying for products and services. The Internet's Web browser and client/server architecture and networks of hypermedia databases on the World Wide Web, serve as the technology platform for electronic commerce among Internet-worked communities of customers and business partners.

- *Electronic commerce applications.* The Internet encourages innovation and entrepreneurship, thus generating many business opportunities to serve a global audience of both business and consumer customers. Successful retailing and wholesaling on the World Wide Web depend on factors such as efficient performance and service, personalization and socialization of the shopping experience, the look and feel of the website, incentives offered and the security and reliability of business transactions. Business-to-business applications of electronic commerce support the processes of supply chain management through a variety of Internet and website services and network applications like electronic data interchange.

- *Online transaction processing.* Online transaction processing systems play a vital role in electronic commerce. Transaction processing involves the basic activities of (1) data entry, (2) transaction processing, (3) database maintenance, (4) document and report generation and (5) enquiry processing. Many firms are using the Internet, intranets, extranets and other networks for online transaction processing to provide superior service to their customers and suppliers.

- *Electronic payment and security.* The electronic payment process presents a vital and complex challenge to business and financial institutions to develop efficient, flexible and secure payment systems for electronic commerce. A variety of payment systems have evolved for electronic funds transfers, including several major ways to provide security for transactions and payments over the Internet.

References

Halper, M. (1997) Meet the new middlemen. *Computerworld Commerce*, 28 April.

Keen, P. and Ballance, C. (1997) *Online Profits: a manager's guide to electronic commerce*, Harvard Business School Press.

Source: Adapted from O'Brien, J. (2000) *Introduction to Information Systems: essentials for the internetworked enterprise*, Irwin/McGraw-Hill Education.

Chapter 10

Distributed systems, EDI and the organization

Graham Curtis and David Cobham

Major developments over the last 30 years have been achieved in information technology. It is not uncommon to view this purely as the advent and development of computer systems. This, though, ignores the significant impact that improvements and innovations in telecommunications have had as an enabling technology for information systems.

This chapter begins with a consideration of the way in which centralized and distributed systems can be seen as alternatives for handling information provision. The impact of a distributed system on the organization, its benefits and its acceptability are analysed. [...] Finally the impact of electronic data interchange (EDI) and its effect on the competitive position of the firm within the market is assessed.

Networks and distributed systems

In the last decade many organizations have adopted the policy of installing several geographically distinct computers within their organizations and linking these with telecommunications. The computers may be microcomputers linked together locally within one site or even one office. Or it might be the linking of minicomputers or mainframe computers across large geographical distances. The issues involved in this distribution of computing power and the linking networks are the subject of this [chapter].

It used to be believed that computing benefited from economies of scale. This is enshrined in *Grosch's law* stating that the computational and data processing power of a computer increases with the square of its cost. It therefore made financial sense for an organization to centralize its computer systems in order to get the most power for its money. Under centralization an organization that is located on several geographically distant sites would then incur a large communication cost. Terminals at each site needed to interchange data constantly with the centralized central processing unit.

With the development of much cheaper computing hardware and, in particular, the development of the microchip, Grosch's law has broken down. There are no longer the same economies of scale to be gained by centralization. Local computers can carry out local processing needs and the necessity to communicate between different sites in an organization is reduced to those occasions where data held at one location are needed at another. This is called *distributed computing*.

An example of a distributed system is shown in Figure 10.1. A tyre and car battery manufacturer purchases materials and produces goods for sale throughout the country. The headquarters, factory and a warehouse are located at one site. In order to cut distribution costs and satisfy retail outlet orders quickly, the organization maintains two other warehouses in different parts of the country to which the manufactured goods are distributed for storage prior to sale. The headquarters' mainframe computer takes care of centralized accounting, purchasing, production scheduling, wages and salaries, local stock control and local sales order processing. Each of the two warehouses has a small minicomputer to handle its own local stock control and local sales order processing. These two minicomputers are connected to the mainframe computer so that an enquiry can be made to the other warehouses for products not held in the local warehouse that are needed for local retail outlets.

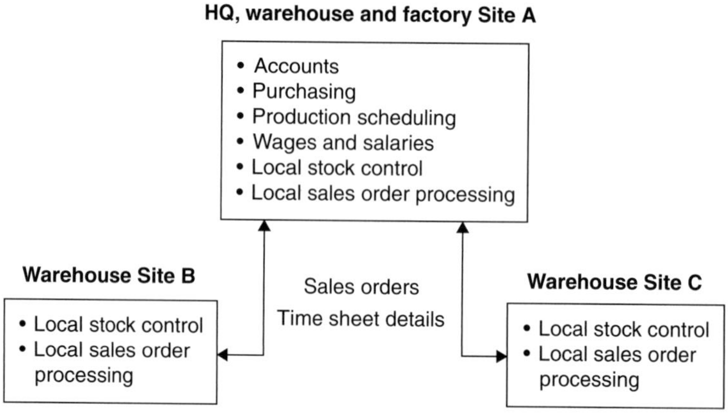

HQ, warehouse and factory Site A

- Accounts
- Purchasing
- Production scheduling
- Wages and salaries
- Local stock control
- Local sales order processing

Warehouse Site B

- Local stock control
- Local sales order processing

Sales orders
Time sheet details

Warehouse Site C

- Local stock control
- Local sales order processing

Figure 10.1   An example of functions in a hierarchical distributed system

Most of the stock control enquiries and updates will therefore be on the locally held data stores. On the occasions when the local warehouse cannot satisfy a customer demand interrogation is made of the data held at the other warehouses via the telecommunications links. As the accounting is carried out centrally, although the sales order processing is local, it is necessary to ensure that sales order and delivery details are exchanged between the local computers and the mainframe. As this is not required immediately on a sale then the data can be transferred at the end of each day in one transfer operation. Although accounting, wages and salaries are handled centrally in this organization, an organization with a different structure might grant greater independence to its branches. These functions would then be the responsibility of each site and headquarters would receive consolidated accounting reports.

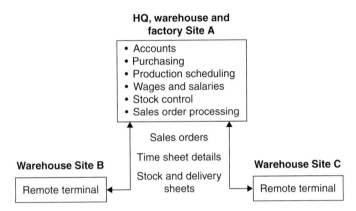

Figure 10.2   An example of functions in a centralized system

Compare this with a centralized system as shown in Figure 10.2. Here all the functions are carried out centrally at headquarters. Each time there is a need to access the data store or carry out any processing the interaction between the local sites and headquarters will involve a telecommunications link – even though the processing of data only concerns stock held at the local site. This involves a heavy telecommunications cost. Moreover, unless the links involve high-speed connections the response times in the interaction will be slow. At the headquarters the mainframe will need to be able to accept transactions from many sites and will need to give over some of its processing time to the maintenance and servicing of queues. This problem will be larger the greater the number of sites and the greater the traffic. In this scenario it is unlikely that computer centre personnel will reside at each of the sites. It would be more common to have a centralized team at the headquarters responsible for applications development and the day-to-day running of computer operations. It is easy for users at the local sites to feel isolated – particularly if help is required or difficulties are encountered with the operation of the system. As can be seen from the two treatments of essentially the same set of functions a distributed approach has much to commend it.

It would be simplistic, however, to suggest that there were only two possible approaches – distributed or centralized. In the above case there is a hybrid. In the 'distributed' version of the example certain functions are in fact centralized.

Within the 'distributed' version, the distribution of the stock control system, particularly that component dealing with the update of stock data relating to another warehouse held at another site, involves considerable technical complexity as the database itself is distributed. A variation on this is to hold copies centrally of the stock data on each of the sites. Downloading to each site of all the stock data on all of the sites occurs early in the morning. Local processing of data on stock held locally occurs during the day. However, information on stocks at other warehouses is obtained by interrogating the early morning copies received locally. These may be out of date – but only by a maximum of 24 hours. Requests for stock from other sites together with the end-of-day copy of the local stock data are transferred to the centralized mainframe at the end of the day. The central mainframe carries out overnight processing and produces up-to-date stock data for each site, which is downloaded the following morning. This escapes the complexity of requiring a truly distributed database at the expense of forfeiting the immediate update of all stock transactions.

It should be clear from the above that the simple idea of distributed versus centralized does not apply. Rather the question that is addressed nowadays is to what extent and how should the organization decentralize its functions and data? [...]

Organizational benefits of distributed systems

Distributed systems were first introduced in the 1970s and have become increasingly common in the 1980s and 1990s. This is partly because of technological advances in telecommunications, distributed databases and communications software, and partly because of the recognition of the benefits conferred on an organization by the use of such systems. This is one area in which IT developments have responded to user needs as well as being driven by them.

Organizational benefits are as follows:

- *Increased user satisfaction.* As stated above, users can feel remote from the computer centre, its expert staff and the development of applications if geographically separated from the source of the computing power. User needs are often not taken into account and assistance may be slow or at 'arm's length' through the computer terminal. Local computer centres serving local needs solve this problem by ensuring that users have greater autonomy. However, from a central organizational perspective, it is important that dispersed sites are connected with one another and the centre. This is not only for reasons of data sharing but also to ensure that, although autonomy may be welcomed, local sites act congruently with corporate goals. Distributed systems ensure that data transfer and connectivity with the centre occur while encouraging local autonomy and user satisfaction.

- *Flexibility of systems development.* An organization that is growing can add to its computer power incrementally in a distributed system by the purchase, installation and connection of new nodes to the network as the needs arise. With a centralized system flexibility is reduced by the inability to grow incrementally. Growth typically involves the overloading of the current system, which is then replaced by a more powerful computer. If further growth is planned this will need to be taken into account by building in redundant computing power in the current system to cope with a future growth in requirements. This is expensive.

- *Lower telecommunications costs.* In a distributed system it is usual for most of the local computing to take place locally. The network is accessed only when data or processing are required elsewhere. Telecommunications costs are reduced compared with a centralized system which requires transmission of local transactions for central processing.

- *Failsoft.* With a centralized system, if a breakdown occurs in the computer all computing functions within the organization come to a halt. This is an unacceptable state of affairs. Backup facilities, such as a duplicated computer or reciprocal agreements with other companies to use their computers in times of breakdown, are expensive and often not satisfactory. However, with a distributed system breakdowns will be limited to one computer at a time. The remaining machines in the network can continue functioning and perhaps also take over some of the work of the failed node. What can be achieved depends on the particular network topology and the communications software.

- *Transborder dataflows.* Many multinational corporations maintain separate computer systems in each country in which they operate. These are connected via networks. Only limited transborder dataflows may be allowed by legislation. Thus it is important to ensure local processing while retaining the possibility of transnational dataflows. Data protection legislation on the holding and processing of personal data (data on persons) is often different in different countries and this is particularly restrictive on transnational dataflows.

- *Lower data communications costs.* Processing relating to locally stored data and functions is carried out locally, rather than incurring the cost of data transfer to and from a centralized computer.

- *Response times.* Centralized systems can, at peak loading, give poor response time for users.

Persuasive though these organizational benefits may seem there are potential drawbacks and costs associated with distributed systems. These should be taken into account when assessing the overall systems strategy:

- *Loss of centralized standard-setting and control.* In a distributed system where processing, data storage and computing staff are located at many sites it is common for local practices to evolve, local alterations and 'patches' to software to be carried out to meet specific user needs and local adjustment to data representation and storage characteristics to occur. All these can lead to non-standardization across the organization and to difficulties in data communications and security.

- *Complex networking software is needed.* This controls data communications.

- *Possibility of replicated common data at several sites.* If the same portion of data is used by all sites it is common for the data to be held as copies at each of the several sites rather than be held once and accessed through the network when needed. This cuts down data communications cost and increases response times. However, it may lead to inconsistencies if the data are updated or changed.

- *Loss of career paths for computer centre personnel.* A large centralized computer centre provides more opportunities for staff development and promotion. Distributing staff leads to smaller numbers of personnel at each site.

Organizational levels and distributed systems

It is not usual within a distributed system for each node to be directly connected to each other node. Nor is it common, if data are to be distributed, that they are spread over all nodes within the distributed network. It is more likely that the structure for the distributed system reflects the organizational structure it is meant to serve.

A typical organization structure is shown in Figure 10.3. This is a traditional hierarchical structure, which exemplifies many large industrial and service organizations. There is a headquarters for the organization. The organization has several local plants or sites that carry out many of the functions of the organization itself at a local level. Examples are the functional departments of production, stock control and order processing. Within each functional department there are workgroups that reflect groupings of employees that perform much the same function within a department – an example might be customer enquiry handling within a sales order processing department. Then finally there are the individual employees who are the simplest 'processing unit' (i.e. unit that may require a computer for support) within the organization.

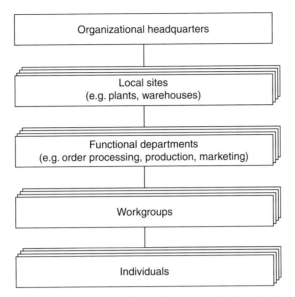

Figure 10.3   Typical hierarchical organizational structure

Where there are distributed systems within an organization one possible architecture for the distribution is to ensure that where data are distributed and computers are networked this occurs at the level reflecting the organizational structure. For example, within one workgroup the network ensures that connections and data needed by that group are spread over the entire group. The various levels will of course also be connected together and if required will effect data transfers.

The larger the organization the more likely it is to have large numbers of personal computers, minicomputers and mainframe computers. In this case it is also more important that the distributed architecture is planned to reflect the needs of the organization.

The extent of distribution

In the early 1980s one of the uppermost questions in the minds of those involved in long-term strategic planning of information systems was whether to employ distributed systems or whether to rely on centralized mainframes. The issue has now shifted to decisions on the extent to which the organization should embark on distributing its information systems for its future information provision.

There are technological determinants governing the distribution of data and computers, especially those to do with communications. However, technology is designed to support the organizational information requirements, not drive the development of information systems. Technological factors must be considered in deciding on the extent and nature of the distributed systems but other features are equally significant. Central among the other important characteristics are the following:

- *The corporate culture and employee behaviour.* Managerial assumptions about human behaviour will have implications for the amount of control that is exercised over employee activities. A traditional model characterizes attitudes in two distinct groupings. Theory X perspectives hold employees as inherently unwilling to work and needing to be controlled by incentives and discipline in order to ensure that their activities align with organizational goals. In contrast, Theory Y perspectives hold employees as self-motivated and willing to ensure that their activities are congruent with organizational objectives. In an organization where Theory X views are the dominant culture there will be an unwillingness to relinquish central power. This will be mirrored in a hierarchical organizational structure and a pressure towards centralization of information systems where standards and control are easier to implement. The local autonomy that accompanies distributed systems fits a managerial strategy of decentralization of control within a Theory Y culture.

- *The location of decision making.* Closely linked to the points raised above is the issue of who makes the key decisions. The further decision making is decentralized in an organization the more likely it is that the resources follow. Decentralization of resources and decisions over their commitment with respect to information technology is most compatible with a distributed system.

- *Interdependent activities.* Where one type of activity is very closely related to another it is more likely that processing associated with both will occur in one processing location. Distribution of processing between two activities tends to lead to a lack of connectivity, which should only be allowed if the activities are themselves not connected.

- *Homogeneous activities.* In some cases activities may be independent of one another but there is a case for centralized planning of distributed systems. For example, franchises may involve local franchisees in carrying out completely independent activities from each other. Yet their operations are so homogeneous that it makes sense that they each have the same type of system. This can only be achieved if there is centralized planning and control over the development and purchase of the information systems.

Electronic data interchange

Electronic data interchange (EDI) can be defined as:

the transfer of electronic data, from one organization's computer system to another's, the data being structured in a commonly agreed format so that they are directly usable by the receiving organization's computer system.

What distinguishes EDI from other electronic communications between organizations, such as fax, electronic mail, telephone and telex, is that in these latter cases the information is intended for consumption by a human being who needs to understand it before any action can be taken. With EDI the received electronic data can be immediately processed by the receiver's system without the necessity for human interpretation and translation before action.

An example

To see how EDI can be used in the context of significant in-house automation consider the following example. It is important for many manufacturing companies that assemble final products to be assured of the supply of components from their stock. When the stock of a particular kind of component runs low the manufacturer orders replacements from the supplier. The supplier then despatches these and invoices later.

The whole process can take a long time – particularly if the manufacturer's purchasing department needs to draw up a paper order that is posted to the supplier. At the supplier's end this needs to be processed by the accounts and the despatch department. The production of paperwork by the manufacturer and the supplier, together with the transfer of this between organizations can lead to costly delays and errors. It may be necessary for the manufacturing company to maintain larger stocks to take account of the lead time in ordering. This in itself will be a cost. Of course if the supplier is also low on stock of the component it may take several days for this to be notified to the manufacturer. This scenario can occur even if both organizations are fully computerized as far as their own internal transaction processing is concerned.

In the context of full automation and EDI this situation could be handled in the following way. As soon as the manufacturer's component stocks fall below a minimum level a computer-based list of possible suppliers is consulted and the most appropriate chosen. An electronic order is generated on the manufacturer's computer system. This is then transmitted to the supplier's computer system (EDI) where it is electronically matched against stock records of the item held. An instruction to despatch the goods with full delivery details is sent to the supplier's despatch department. An electronic acknowledgement of order satisfaction is transmitted to the manufacturer along with an electronic invoice which will await receipt of the goods before payment is made.

In the above EDI automated version there need be no paperwork exchanged at all. Human beings need only limited involvement – for instance, in the loading and distribution of the goods, or in the authorization of the placing of the purchase order by the manufacturer and agreement to satisfy the order by the supplier. These human authorizations can be by entry into the computer system, though it would be quite possible to automate the process of authorization entirely as well. The advantages for both companies are:

- the speed with which the order is satisfied

- the lack of paperwork involved

- the low cost of processing the transaction as the involvement of costly human labour on both sides is minimal

- the lack of human error.

There may be further organizational advantages if the respective trading relationship between the two companies is altered. [...] A typical configuration for EDI transfer is illustrated in Figure 10.4.

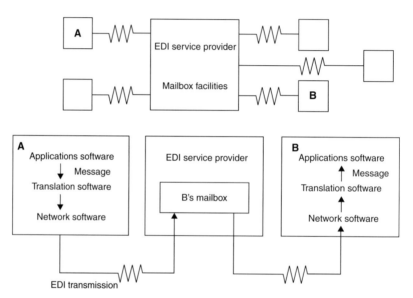

Figure 10.4   Electronic data interchange network

EDI – the method

EDI may be introduced where a group of organizations wish to ensure that electronic transactions are passed between one another. EDI groups require EDI services in order to effect the data exchanges. These are often provided by a third-party organization. The service provided by the third party is more than merely the transmission of the data. It is customary for added facilities, especially mailbox facilities, to be offered. An electronic mailbox for a client is an electronic storage location for messages or data that are sent to the client by other organizations. The client (addressee) can read the data or messages, which are usually held on an identified area of the service provider's disk space. By providing these services the third party adds value to the data transmission and is thus said to run a *value-added network*. [...]

The benefits of EDI

Some of the benefits of EDI are clear from the examples in previous sections. In particular, EDI ensures:

- The time with which an interorganizational transaction is processed is minimized.
- The paperwork involved in transaction processing is eliminated.
- The costs of transaction processing are reduced, as much of the need for human interpretation and processing is removed.
- Reduced human involvement reduces error.

These are benefits experienced by both sender and receiver in an EDI relationship. Of course there is a cost – the cost of purchase and installation of the technology. However, there are more strategic advantages associated with the introduction of EDI.

First, by increasing the speed of processing of transactions between an organization and its suppliers and between an organization and its customers it enables the supply chain to the customer to provide a faster service. This gives the companies in the supply chain a competitive advantage over other companies in the same sector.

Second, the speed of response to requests for component parts in the manufacturing process enables all participants in the supply chain to reduce their holding of buffer stocks. This reduces the need to tie up a company's assets in unproductive materials and is compatible with the organization of production on 'just-in-time' principles. The whole chain, therefore, gains a competitive advantage within the industry sector.

Finally, it is in the interests of an organization to 'tie in' both many suppliers and many customers through EDI. For example, a motor car production manufacturer will gain a significant competitive advantage by linking in many suppliers of substitutable component parts through EDI. While EDI benefits each supplier for the reasons stated above, its own position of dominance over the manufacturer in these circumstances is weakened by other suppliers participating in EDI. Similarly, it is in the interests of the supplier to link up with as many manufacturers through EDI as possible. The supplier's competitive position is then strengthened because it is no longer dependent on one customer manufacturer.

From the above it can be seen that the presence of EDI in the supply chain increases the competitive advantage of that chain over others in the sector. But, depending on the exact nature of the supplier–customer relationships, individual organizations in the chain may have their competitive advantage weakened or strengthened by EDI.

EDI – a case example

The American pharmaceuticals company, McKesson, began linking in its customer pharmacies in the USA through EDI by the installation of terminals. Pharmacies were then able to input orders for products directly. This saved McKesson the cost of employing sales personnel to take drug orders and reduced the number of paperwork errors. From the customer point of view the system, called ECONOMIST, enabled a speedy and error-free response to ordering stock, especially when late orders were required. McKesson could fill and deliver an order overnight, ensuring that the drugs would be on the shelves the following morning.

Stage two of the involvement occurred when McKesson also offered software through the terminals to assist pharmacists in the preparation of accounts and the improvement of shop layout. This provided an additional source of revenue for McKesson.

Finally, McKesson was then able to provide a service to pharmacists in processing the millions of medical insurance prescriptions put through pharmacists each year. This was achieved by electronically passing on the details to the identified medical insurance company. The effect was to save the pharmacist a great deal of time and expense. Once established it was difficult for a competitor pharmaceutical company to compete in the same arena.

Summary

[The 1990s] witnessed a dramatic increase in the use of distributed systems. [...]

The benefits of distributed systems include increased user satisfaction and autonomy – users do not need to rely on a remote computer centre for the satisfaction of their needs. Telecommunications costs are lower as local processing will not involve expensive remote links. Distributed computing also allows for flexible systems development in that computing power can be expanded incrementally to meet demand. Though there are substantial advantages, an organization needs to be aware that unbridled distribution may lead to problems of standard setting and loss of control. If data are distributed then duplication of data may lead to inconsistency.

Although technological features will be operative in determining the extent of the use of distributed systems, it is important to remember that other features are also significant. In particular the corporate culture and location of decision making need to be compatible with distribution which, by its nature, involves devolution of resources and power. The type of activities undertaken by the organization must also be considered – distribution is more likely to be recommended the less dependent computerized activities are on each other. [...]

Electronic data interchange (EDI) is one area where developments in telecommunications and networking are having an impact beyond that of merely passing messages between computer systems. EDI is understood as the exchange of formatted data capable of immediate computer processing. Various benefits derive from EDI including cost saving and speedy processing of transactions. In particular, though, EDI affects the nature of the trading relationships between organizations in a sector and, by way of influencing the supply chain, can considerably enhance the competitive advantage of a company.

Source: Adapted from Curtis, G., 'Distributed systems, EDI and the organization' in Hinton, M. (2006) *Introducing Information Management: a business approach*, Elsevier.

Strategy and change

Chapter 11

Strategy and information systems

Graham Curtis and David Cobham

The subject of this chapter is to expand on the relationship between strategy and information systems. Initially the need for a business strategy is explained together with a suggested overview of the business strategic planning process. The way in which this necessitates an information systems strategy is covered. There are many frameworks within which information systems strategy can be viewed. One framework is outlined and its various components are explained. Each emphasizes a different perspective on the issues that a firm may wish to take into account when formulating strategy. They all have one feature in common though – they acknowledge the need for an information systems strategy to be determined by the business needs of the organization, not by the functions of available technology.

The need for a business strategy

A business will function on a day-to-day basis without the obvious need for a business strategy. Orders will be taken from customers, goods dispatched, invoices sent and payments from customers acknowledged. Where stock runs low, purchase orders will be drafted and sent, goods will be received, stock stored and inventory records updated and when the invoices arrive from the suppliers these will be authorized for payment and payment made. Work will be scheduled and products manufactured. Payroll will produce payslips and instruct banks to make automated payment of wages and salaries at the end of the month. Sales reps' cars will be put into garages for maintenance, bills received and so on. This is the day-to-day functioning of business.

A business, or any other organization, may continue to function in this way for some period of time without reference to any strategy. However, a business under these conditions is analogous to a ship under way without a destination or without reference to the environment within which it is voyaging.

There needs to be a strategy and strategic planning for a business for several reasons:

1   The individual departments within an organization (subsystems within a system) may function well in terms of their own objectives but still not serve the objectives of the organization. This is because of a lack of coordination between departments, because departments themselves have specific objectives counter to those of the organization, or because subsystems optimization may on occasion lead to total systems suboptimization. It is therefore important that there be an agreed and communicated set of objectives for the organization and a plan on how to achieve these.

2   The organization will on occasion need to make major resource allocations, especially for the purchase and development of new plant, property and machines. Information systems will need expensive hardware and will incur design costs. They will need large resource allocations. These allocations can only be made against an agreed direction for the organization – a strategy for the future.

3   The organization will have responsibilities to a number of different groups. Included among these would be the owners, whether it be the shareholders or the public, the employees, the customers and those that provide finance such as banks. These parties will have a particular interest in the corporate strategy, as their interests will be served or otherwise by the extent to which the strategy takes into account their interests and the success of the organization in meeting these interests.

Business strategic planning

There is no *one* accepted method that a business should adopt in its strategic planning. There are, however, a number of different steps that would normally be taken in the development of a business strategy (Figure 11.1).

Most large organizations will already have strategies currently formulated. These strategies are often for a future period of five years. This is a convenient time horizon. If it were longer then future uncertainties would render the planning process for the later stages of little value; if it were shorter then many developments could not be planned through to fruition. (For some organizations the planning horizon will need to be significantly extended – national defence and the nuclear industry are two such examples.)

The business strategy is not frozen into the operations of the business but is evaluated and redrafted from time to time. This often occurs on a yearly basis when the strategy for the next five years will be decided. The business strategic planning process then yields a five-year rolling plan. Unless there

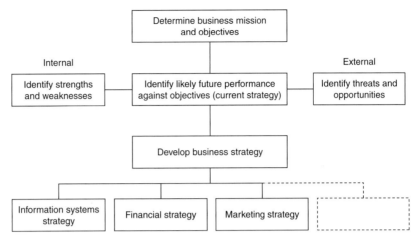

Figure 11.1   Developing a business strategy

are serious problems within the organization or it is undergoing major internal change it is likely that changes to strategy will be incremental. The following sections expand on Figure 11.1.

Determine the business mission and objectives

The mission of the organization will be a general statement of its overall purpose and aims. It often consists of a number of individual aims. Examples might be (for a chemical company) 'to become a major supplier of agrochemicals to the farming sector through the research and development of new and more effective fertilizer and pest controls' or (for a chain of hi-fi shops) 'to expand the number of retail outlets and diversify into the sale of all leisure electronic goods'.

The objectives, both medium and long term, should support the organization's overall mission. Each objective should have a measurable performance indicator, which can be used to determine the success of the organization in meeting the objective. In the above, an objective could well be 'to increase the number of retail outlets by 35 per cent within three years and the square metres of floor space devoted to sales by 50 per cent within the same period'.

Identify the likely future performance against objectives

The organization should be continuously monitoring and evaluating its performance against its current objectives. Part of this monitoring process will involve forecasts of future sales, cash flows, materials requirements and profitability, based on the current situation. In other words, when developing business strategy the current operations of the organization will have an implied future scenario, which can be compared with desired objectives.

As an input into the assessment of future performance it is common to identify internal and external factors that will have a significant impact. This *SWOT* (strengths, weaknesses, opportunities, threats) *analysis* will identify internal strengths, such as a highly trained and flexible workforce, and internal weaknesses, such as a poor internal information system, together with external opportunities, such as the opening up of trade through a common European Market, and external threats, such as the absence of low economic entry barriers to the industry.

Given the predictions and the identified strengths, weaknesses, opportunities and threats, it will be possible to estimate the extent of the gap between future objectives and forecast future performance. The business strategy should determine a series of measures and plans that will remove this gap.

Develop the business strategy

The business strategy will be the set of plans that the business will implement in order to achieve its stated objectives. These plans may involve new projects or the continued operation of existing activities.

Most businesses are modelled and managed in a functional way. Human resources, information systems, marketing, financial management, and production are examples of common functions. The business strategy will have as components a human resource strategy, an information systems strategy, a marketing strategy and so on. These strategies will support the business strategy and interact with one another. The information systems strategy is taking on a key role as more businesses rely increasingly heavily on their computerized information systems for all aspects of their business functions.

Business information systems strategy

The previous section identified, in broad terms, the steps taken in strategic planning. But it provides no insight into what specific factors should be taken into account in business information strategy development. In particular it does not give any framework within which to answer the questions as to which information systems should be developed and why. This section will be directed at these two issues.

First it is important to distinguish between a business information systems strategy and a business information technology strategy.

The *business information systems strategy* is focused on determining what information systems must be provided in order that the objectives of the business strategy are realized. The concentration is therefore on determining information needs and ensuring that the information systems strategy aligns with the business strategy.

The *business information technology strategy* is focused on determining what technology and technological systems development are needed in order that the business information systems strategy can be realized. The concentration is therefore on how to provide the information, not on what information is required. The strategy will also cover how the information resource and information systems development is to be managed.

There is a close interaction between the information systems strategy and the information technology strategy. The importance of distinguishing between them indicates that the emphasis on information systems is that strategy is led by the needs of the business, not by technology.

There has been a considerable debate as to how best to develop a strategy for information systems/information technology. The urgency of this debate has been fuelled by the speed with which information technology has changed and by a recognition that information technology is being used less in a support function within the business but is increasingly integral to the business operations and development itself.

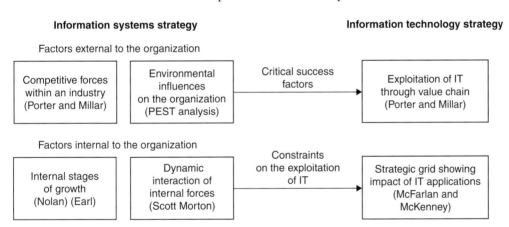

Figure 11.2   A framework for the interrelation of influences on information systems strategy and information technology strategy (adapted from source material by Susan Gasson, Warwick Business School)

Many models have been put forward to guide the strategist in formulation. An important selection is explained in the rest of this section. They have different approaches and objectives and cover different aspects of the strategy formulation process. The framework in Figure 11.2 indicates that some models address the area of information systems strategy whereas others can be seen as more relevant to information technology strategy. Within the former (information systems strategy) there is a division between those approaches which concentrate on internal aspects of the business compared with those that focus on areas within the environment of the organization.

Competitive forces within an industry – the five forces model

Modern technology is increasingly being used as part of an information systems strategy which yields competitive advantage for the organization. One way in which a business can gain a *competitive advantage* is by using information technology to change the structure of the industry within which it operates.

The five forces model (Porter and Millar, 1985) views a business, operating within an industry, as being subject to five main competitive forces. The way in which the business responds to these forces will determine its success. These forces are illustrated in Figure 11.3. Information technology can aid a business in using these competitive forces to its advantage. In this way information technology can be seen as a strategic competitive weapon.

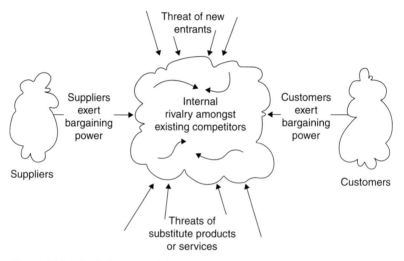

Figure 11.3   An industry and its competitive forces

Suppliers

The suppliers provide the necessary inputs of raw materials, machinery and manufactured components for the firm's production process. The suppliers to a business can exert their bargaining power on that business by pushing up the prices of inputs supplied using the threat of taking their supply goods elsewhere to a competitor business in the same industry. It is in the interests of the business to make alternative rival businesses who would purchase the supplier's goods seem less attractive to the supplier.

One way of achieving this is by creating good relationships with the supplier by using *electronic data interchange (EDI)*. EDI requires that there is an electronic connection between the business and its suppliers. When supplies are to be ordered this is accomplished by sending structured electronic messages to the supplier firm. The supplier firm's computer decodes these messages and acts appropriately. The advantage of this for both partners is:

- reduced delivery times
- reduced paperwork and associated labour costs
- increased accuracy of information.

For the business that is purchasing supplies, EDI can be part of its just-in-time approach to manufacturing. This yields benefits in terms of reduced warehousing costs.

Creating links with suppliers is becoming increasingly important in the manufacturing sector especially between car manufacturers and the suppliers of component parts.

Customers

Customers can exert power over a business by threatening to purchase the product or service from a competitor. This power is large if there are few customers and many competitors who are able to supply the product or service.

One way in which a business may reduce the ability of a customer to move to another competitor is by introducing switching costs. These are defined as costs, financial or otherwise, that a customer would incur by switching to another supplier. One way of achieving switching costs is to allow the customer to have online ordering facilities for the business's service or product. It is important that the customer gains a benefit from this or there is little incentive for the customer to put itself in a potentially weak bargaining position.

For instance, with electronic banking the belief is that once a customer has established a familiarity with one system, gaining advantage from it, there will be a learning disincentive to switch to another. Another example is American Hospital Supplies. It has improved its competitive position by allowing online terminals into customer hospitals. These allowed the swift order/delivery of supplies by using less skilled personnel compared with more expensive purchase agents. Once established it became very difficult for a hospital to change suppliers.

Substitute products

Substitute products or services are those that are within the industry but are differentiated in some way. There is always the danger that a business may lose a customer to the purchase of a substitute product from a rival business because that product meets the needs of the customer more closely. Information technology can prevent this happening in two ways. First it can be used to introduce switching costs as stated above. Or the technology may be used to provide differentiated products swiftly by the use of computer-aided design/computer-aided manufacturing (CAD/CAM). In this latter case the business produces the substitute product itself.

New entrants

Within any industry there is always the threat that a new company might enter and attract some of the existing demand for the products of that industry. This will reduce the revenue and profit of the current competitors. The traditional response has been for mature business within an industry to develop barriers to entry. These have been:

- exploiting economies of scale in production
- creating brand loyalty
- creating legal barriers to entry – for example patents
- using effective production methods involving large capital outlays.

Information technology can assist a business in developing these barriers. In as far as information technology makes a firm more productive, for instance by reducing labour costs or speeding up aspects of the production process, any firm attempting to enter the market place will be competitively disadvantaged without a similar investment in capital. If expensive CAD/CAM equipment is common for the production of differentiated products speedily then this will also act as a barrier to entry.

Competitor rivalry

Unless in a monopoly position, any business within an industry is subject to competition from other firms. This is perhaps the greatest competitive threat that the business experiences. Information technology can be used as part of the firm's competitive strategy against its rivals as illustrated in the preceding sections. Close linkages with suppliers and customers produce competitive forces against rivals, as does the investment in technology allowing product differentiation and cost reductions.

In some cases the investment in information technology will be necessary to pre-empt the competitiveness of other businesses. The major investment by the banks in automated teller machines is just one example of this.

Environmental influences on the organization – PEST analysis

Porter's five force model considers the industry sector within which the business operates. However, in formulating strategy there are other external factors which the strategist needs to take into account. This is the function of a PEST (political, economic, sociocultural, technological) analysis.

The questions to be asked are:

'Which environmental factors are currently affecting and are likely to affect the organization?'

'What is the relevant importance of these now and in the future?'

Examples of the areas to be covered under each heading are given below:

- *Political/legal.* Monopolies legislation, tax policy, employment law, environmental protection laws, regulations over international trade, government continuity and stability.

- *Economic.* Inflation, unemployment, money supply, cost of parts and energy, economic growth trends, the business cycle – national and international.

- *Sociocultural.* Population changes – age and geographical distribution, lifestyle changes, educational level, income distribution, attitudes to work/leisure/consumerism.

- *Technological.* New innovations and development, obsolescence, technology transfer, public/private investment in research.

At a minimal level the PEST analysis can be regarded as no more than a checklist of items to attend to when drawing up strategy. However, it can also be used to identify key environmental factors. These are factors that will have a long-term major influence on strategy and need special attention. For instance, included in the key environmental factors for a hospital will be demographic trends (increased percentage of older citizens in the population and decreased percentage of those who are of working age), increases in technological support, government policy on funding and preventative medicine. These key factors are ones that will have significant impact on strategy and must be taken into account.

PEST analysis may also be used to identify long-term drivers of change. For instance, globalization of a business may be driven by globalization of technology, of information, of the market and of the labour force.

In general a PEST analysis is used to focus on a range of environmental influences outside the organization and (perhaps) outside the industry, which are important to longer-term change and therefore strategy, but may be ignored in the day-to-day decisions of the business.

Internal stages of growth

The preceding two sections explain the way that factors external to the organization will need to be taken into account when developing an information systems strategy. However, factors internal to the organization will also need to be introduced into the strategy. The introduction, development and use of computing information systems cannot be achieved overnight. It requires the organization internally to undergo change and a learning process. This concerns not only the technological factors of information systems but also the planning, control, budgetary and user involvement aspects.

Over the last twenty years several influential approaches have been developed which look at the development of information systems within an organization as proceeding through several stages of growth. In the following sections two of these models will be considered.

The Nolan stage model

The earliest of these models, developed by Nolan, explains the extent and type of information systems used within an organization as being determined by the maturity of growth of information systems within that organization.

It was Nolan's original thesis that all organizations went through four stages of growth. This was later refined by adding two intermediate growth stages. The six-stage growth model (Nolan, 1979) was used to identify which stage of growth characterized an organization's information systems maturity. This, in turn, had further implications for successful planning to proceed to the next level of growth. The model has been used as the basis in over 200 consultancy studies within the USA and has been incorporated into IBM's information systems planning (Nolan, 1984). Before considering any planning implications of the model the stages will be briefly explained.

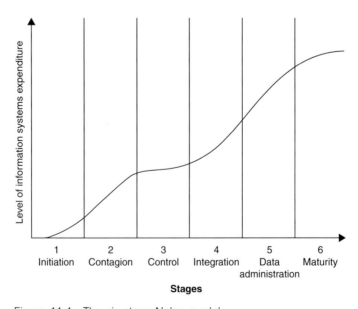

Figure 11.4   The six-stage Nolan model

The Nolan stage model purports to explain the evolution of an information system within an organization by consideration of various stages of growth. The model is based on empirical research on information systems in a wide range of organizations in the 1970s. Expenditure on IT increases with the stages (Figure 11.4).

Within each stage of growth four major growth processes must be planned, managed and coordinated:

- *Applications portfolio.* The set of applications which the information systems must support – for example financial planning, order processing, online customer enquiries.

- *DP organization.* The orientation of the data processing – for example as centralized technology driven, as management of data as a resource.

- *DP planning and control.* For example, degree of control, formalization of planning process, management of projects, extent of strategic planning.

- *User awareness.* The extent to which users are aware of and involved with the technology.

The stages have different characteristics (see Figure 11.4).

- *Stage 1 Initiation.* The computer system is used for low level transaction processing. Typically high volume data processing of accounting, payroll and billing data characterize the stage. There is little planning of information systems. Users are largely unaware of the technology. New applications are developed using traditional languages (such as COBOL). There is little systematic methodology in systems analysis and design.

- *Stage 2 Contagion.* The awareness of the possibilities of IT increases among users, but there is little real understanding of the benefits or limitations. Users become enthusiastic and require more applications development. IT is generally treated as an overhead within the organization and there is little check on user requests for more applications. Budgetary control over IT expenditure and general managerial control over the development of the information system are low. Technical problems with the development of programs appear. An increasing proportion of the programming effort is taken in maintenance of systems. This is a period of unplanned growth.

- *Stage 3 Control.* As continuing problems occur with the unbridled development of projects there is a growing awareness of the need to manage the information systems function. The data-processing department is reorganized. The DP manager becomes more accountable having to justify expenditure and activities in the same way as other major departments within the organization. The proliferation of projects is controlled by imposing changes on user departments for project development and the use of computer services. Users see little progress in the development of information systems. Pent-up demand and frustration occur within user departments.

- *Stage 4 Integration.* Having achieved the consolidation of Stage 3, the organizational data-processing function takes on a new direction. It becomes more orientated towards information provision. Concurrent with this and facilitating it, there is the introduction of interactive terminals in user departments, the development of a database and the introduction of data communications technologies. User departments, which have been significantly controlled in Stage 3 by budgetary and organizational controls, are now able to satisfy the pent-up demand for information support. There is a significant growth in the demand for application and a consequent large increase in the supply and expenditure to meet this demand. As the rapid growth occurs the reliance on computer-based controls becomes ineffective. In particular redundancy of data and duplication of data become a significant problem.

- *Stage 5 Data administration.* The response to the problems of Stage 4 is to introduce controls on the proper administration of data. The emphasis shifts from regarding data as the input to a process which produces information as an output, to the view that data are a resource within an organization. As such they must be properly planned and managed. This stage is characterized by the development of an integrated database serving organizational needs. Applications are developed relying on access to the database. Users become more accountable for the integrity and correct use of the information resource.

- *Stage 6 Maturity.* Stage 6 typifies the mature organization. The information system is integral to the functioning of the organization. The applications portfolio closely mirrors organizational activities. The data structure becomes a data model for the organization. There is a recognition of the strategic importance of information. Planning of the information system is coordinated and comprehensive. The manager of the information system takes on the same importance in the organizational hierarchy as the director of finance or the director of human resources.

The Nolan model – implications for strategic planning

The Nolan stage model was originally intended to be a descriptive/analytic model which gave an evolutionary explanation for information systems development within an organization. It identified a pattern of growth which an organization needed to go through in order to achieve maturity. Each stage involved a learning process. It was not possible to skip a stage in the growth process. As such the model became widely accepted. On the Nolan analysis most organizations will be at Stage 4 or Stage 5.

However, the model has also become used as part of a planning process. Applied this way, the organization identifies the stage it is currently occupying. This has implications for what has to be achieved in order to progress to the next stage. Planning can and should be achieved, it is argued, in the areas of the applications portfolio, the technology used, the planning and control structures and the level of user awareness and involvement. Managers should attend to planning which will speed the process of progression to the next stage and the accompanying organizational learning.

The Nolan model – critique

The model is based on empirical research in the 1970s. It cannot, therefore, incorporate recognition of the impact of the new technologies of the 1980s or 1990s. In particular its concentration on database technology ignores the fact that:

- the growth of microcomputers has significantly increased the extent to which users have been able to use information technology and to become autonomous of the computer centre

- there have been important developments in the area of communications and networks, especially local area networks linking microcomputers and other technologies together

- new software development tools and decision support tools have shifted the emphasis to the user as development agent.

Despite these limitations the Nolan stage model still provides a way of viewing the development of information systems within an organization by recognizing:

- that growth of information systems within an organization must be accompanied by an organizational learning process

- that there is an important interplay between the stimulation of growth involving the presence of slack resources together with the need for control

- that there is a shift of emphasis between the users and the computer centre in the process of growth

- that there is a move from concentration on processor technology to data management.

The Earl model

Earl (1989), along with others (e.g. Hirscheim et al., 1988; Galliers and Sutherland, 1991), takes seriously the idea of maturity through stages of growth. For Earl it is of particular importance to note that stages of growth apply to different technologies. The S-curve is still reflected for each technology with the relationship existing between the degree of organizational learning, the technology and time (Figure 11.5). It is also acknowledged that different parts of the organization may be at different points on the stages of growth.

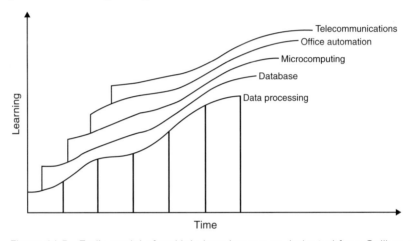

Figure 11.5   Earl's model of multiple learning curves (adapted from Galliers and Sutherland, 1983)

Earl's model concentrates not on the interplay between expenditure/control but rather on the task and objectives of planning at each stage. The view taken by Earl is that the early focus on information systems development is planned around the extent of IT coverage and the attempt to satisfy user demands. As the organization develops along the learning curve the orientation of planning changes. Senior managers recognize the need for information systems development to link to business objectives and so take a major role in the planning process. During the final stages of growth the planning of information systems takes on a strategic perspective with planning being carried out by teams consisting of senior management, users and information systems staff (Table 11.1).

Table 11.1   Earl's stage planning model (Galliers and Sutherland, 1991)

Factor	Stages					
	I	II	III	IV	V	VI
Task	Meeting demands	IS/IT audit	Business support	Detailed planning	Strategic advantage	Business-IT strategy linkage
Objective	Provide service	Limit demand	Agree priorities	Balance IS portfolio	Pursue opportunities	Integrate strategies
Driving force	IS reaction	IS led	Senior management led	User/IS partnership	IS/executive led: user involvement	Strategic coalitions
Method-ological emphasis	*Ad hoc*	Bottom-up survey	Top-down analysis	Two-way prototyping	Environmental scanning	Multiple methods
Context	User/IS inexperience	Inadequate IS resources	Inadequate business/IS plans	Complexity apparent	IS for competitive advantage	Maturity, collaboration
Focus	IS department		Organization-wide			Environment

Dynamic interaction of internal forces

Nolan and Earl were interested in the various internal stages of growth through which organizations progress in the use of information technology, together with the implications of this for strategic planning. The current section takes a different perspective in that it concentrates on internal organizational forces and how these must be acknowledged in the derivation of a business information systems strategy.

It has long been recognized that there is an internal organizational interaction between people, the tasks they perform, the technology they use to perform these and the structure of the organization in which they work. This drives from organizational psychology and has influenced strategy formulation and, among other areas, approaches to the analysis and design of information systems. [...]

Following this theme, an organization may be viewed as being subject to five internal forces in a state of dynamic equilibrium (as well as being subject to external influences and forces). This is illustrated in Figure 11.6. It is the central goal of the organization's management to control these forces and their interaction over time in order that the organization may meet its business objectives and its mission. Scott Morton (1991) takes this

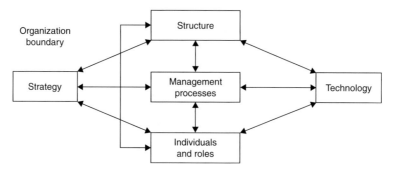

Figure 11.6   The dynamic interaction of internal forces

model as the basis for research into the likely impacts that changes in IT will have on organizations and to provide theories of management on how these changes may be steered to the benefit of the organizations concerned.

1   *Technology* will continue to change. The effect of this will be to cut down 'distance' within the organization as geographical separation is rendered less important. This will be aided through the development of telecommunications and will be evidenced by new applications such as e-mail, the intranet, video-conferencing and shared data resources. The organizational memory and access to it will be improved through more effective classification of data and its storage.

2   *Individuals and their roles* will change as information technology provides support for tasks and increases interconnection within the organization. This will require significant investment in training and the reclassification of roles. The nature of jobs will change as IT facilitates some roles, makes some redundant and has no effect on others.

3   The *structure* of the organization will change as roles vary. The greater interconnection brought about by information technology will lead to integration at the functional level.

4   *Management processes* will be assisted by the provision of easy access to fast, flexible, virtually costless, decision-relevant internal information. This will enable new approaches to operational planning and control within the organization.

5   The key to effective planning, and to the benefits of new information systems enabled by information technology, lies in the proper use of *strategy*. This will ensure that information systems/information technology developments are aligned with the business strategy.

Exploitation of IT through the value chain

Continuing developments in information technology, together with decreasing costs, have enabled businesses to exploit new opportunities to change the nature of competition. In a series of publications (Porter, 1980, 1985; Porter and Millar, 1985) Michael Porter has developed a model of business organization and its associated industry by focusing on the value chain and the competitive forces experienced (five forces model). This allows an understanding of the way competition affects strategy and the way information provision, in its turn, affects competition.

Central to Porter's analysis of the internal aspects of the business and the strategy for its exploitation of IT is the value chain. The *value chain* divides the firm's activities into those that it must carry out in order to function effectively (Figure 11.7). The value chain consists of nine *value activities*. Each of these activities adds value to the final product. In order to be competitively advantaged the business must carry out these activities at a lower cost than its competitors or must use these activities to create a product that is differentiated from those of its competitors and thereby be able to charge a premium price for the product. The nine activities are divided into two categories – *primary activities*, which are concerned with the direct generation of the organization's output to its customers, and *support activities*, which contribute to the operation of the primary activities.

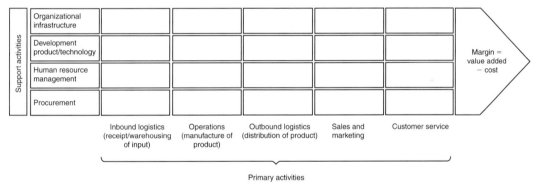

Figure 11.7   The value chain

- *Primary activities*
    - *inbound logistics*: activities which bring inputs into the organization such as receipt of goods, warehousing, inventory control
    - *operations*: activities which transform the product into its final form whether it be physical good or service
    - *outbound logistics*: activities which despatch products and distribute them to clients
    - *marketing and sales*: activities concerned with locating and attracting customers for the purchase of the product – for example advertising
    - *service*: activities which provide service and support to customers – for example maintenance, installation.
- *Support activities*
    - *firm infrastructure*: activities which support the whole value chain – for example general management, financial planning

– *human resource management*: activities concerned with training, recruitment and personnel resource planning
– *technology development*: activities which identify and develop ways in which machines and other kinds of technology can assist the firm's activities
– *procurement*: activities which locate sources of input and purchase these inputs.

As well as having a physical component, every value activity creates and uses information. The competitive advantage of the organization is enhanced by reducing costs in each activity compared with its competitors. Information technology is used to reduce the cost of the information component of each activity. For instance, inbound logistics activities use information technology to provide information on goods received and use this to update inventory records. Financial planning, an infrastructure activity, will use information technology to collect information provided by many of the firm's activities to generate forecasts on future performance. Information technology may also be used to increase product differentiation for specific customer needs. For instance, operations can use information technology to control the production process to generate tailor-made output for customers.

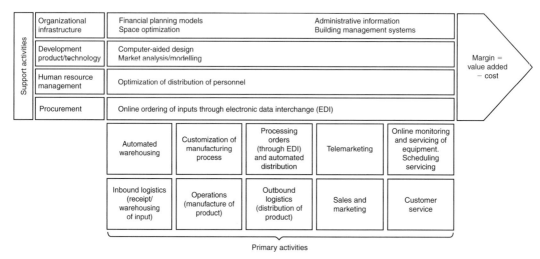

Figure 11.8   Information technology in the value chain

Where previously the organization relied on the manual production of information, it is now more common for information technology to permeate its entire value chain (Figure 11.8). The greater the extent to which this reduces costs or enables product differentiation the greater the competitive advantage conferred on the business.

The organization's value chain is composed of a set of interdependent activities that are linked to one another. These *linkages* need to be coordinated in order to ensure that the activities are carried out in the most effective way. Information is necessary to manage these linkages. One way this may occur is in *just-in-time (JIT) manufacturing*. JIT is an approach to production which requires the output of each stage of the production process to be fed into the following stage without undergoing an intermediate storage stage of indefinite length. The benefits of JIT are that it removes intermediate inventory storage costs for personnel and space and prevents the organization's working capital being tied up in goods waiting in the production process. JIT can also be extended outside the organization to include the purchase of inputs that are delivered just in time for the manufacturing process which, in turn, produces an output just in time to meet the specific needs of a customer. *Automated billing systems* or *electronic data interchange (EDI)* can be used for the external linkages. For JIT to work the effective management of linkages is imperative and it is here that information technology can provide the necessary information – accurately and on time. Hence cost reductions in the organization's value activities are achieved and the business can gain a competitive advantage.

In summary, information technology is at the basis of information systems within business which increase the competitive advantage of that business over its competitors by:

- reducing the cost of the information component of value activities

- allowing product differentiation

- providing information for the effective management of linkages.

The importance of this approach is that it views information not merely as a support for the tasks that a business undertakes but rather as permeating the entire set of business activities. As such its correct provision can give the organization a strategic competitive advantage over its rivals in the industry.

The strategic grid

The strategic grid (McFarlan and McKenney, 1983; McFarlan, 1984) assists the organization in determining within which of four categories it finds itself with respect to the impact of IT and its information systems (Figure 11.9).

The grid plots the extent to which the *existing* applications portfolio has a strategic impact against the likely strategic impact of the *planned* applications development. The four resulting possible positions are:

- *Support.* The role of the information system is to support the transaction processing requirements of the organization. The emphasis on information technology is on cost reduction and information is produced as a by-product of the process.

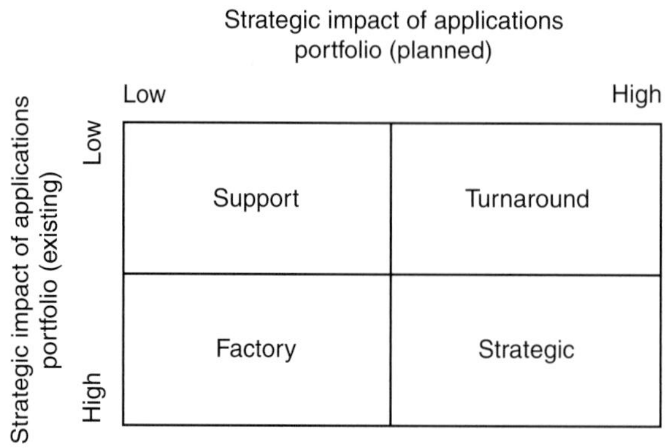

Strategic impact of applications
portfolio (planned)

Figure 11.9   The strategic grid (adapted from McFarlan and McKenney, 1983)

- *Factory.* The current information systems are an integral part of the strategic plan of the organization. Few strategic developments are planned and the focus of IT activity is on improving existing systems.

- *Turnaround.* This is a transitional phase. Organizations move from the 'support' category to this as a result of internal and external pressures. Internal pressures result from the confidence of management in the support systems together with the recognition of the strategic benefits of information technology as a competitive weapon. The external pressures come from improving technology acting as an enabler for development together with the increasing use of information technology by competitor firms within the same industry. If the firm continues with strategic innovation it will enter the 'strategic' category, otherwise it will revert to the 'factory' category.

- *Strategic.* This category requires a continuing development of information systems through the exploitation of information technology at a strategic level. It can only be accomplished with the commitment of senior management and the recognition of the integral part played by the information system within the entire fabric of the firm's activities.

These categories aid managers in identifying the role and importance of information technology within their business. It plots 'where we are now' rather than 'where we want to go' or 'how we get there'. This is not unimportant since each of the categories implies a strategy for the management of the information system. The 'support' and 'factory' positions are essentially static. They concern the more effective and efficient use of the existing applications portfolio and, as such, do not require an extensive senior management involvement. The 'turnaround' and 'strategic' categories imply a dynamic strategy which must, if it is to be successful, involve senior management in an active way in the implementation of strategy. An organization moving from one category to another should be prepared to adopt the appropriate involvement of senior management. [...]

Summary

There is a general recognition that businesses must strategically plan in order to ensure that individual operating units act in a coordinated way to support the business objectives of the organization, that those objectives are realizable given the internal resources within the business and the external environment and that current and future resource allocation is directed to the realization of these corporate objectives.

Although there is no one accepted method of strategic planning, central themes are commonly accepted. Specifically there must be a determination of business objectives, an identification of future performance against these objectives and the development of a plan to close any identified gap.

Businesses are commonly viewed as being composed of various functions. Each of these will require information in order to plan, operate and monitor performance. The function of the provision of information is thus key to an organization's success. The development of an information systems strategy to support this function recognizes the priority of information systems planning over information technology planning. The latter supports the former.

There are many frameworks within which one can develop an information systems strategy. The one provided in this chapter distinguishes the information systems strategy from the information technology strategy and within the former recognizes both the influence of factors external to the organization and those internal to it.

One of the factors external to the firm is the forces exerted on it depending on the structure of the industry within which it operates. These competitive forces may be exerted by suppliers, customers, existing competitors, new entrants or through differentiated products. An analysis of these forces can provide a guide to information systems strategy. A PEST analysis takes into account other political, economic, sociocultural and technological influences.

Emphasizing internal factors, the work of Nolan suggests that organizations undergo a series of several discrete stages of development in their evolution. By identifying the current stage an organization can plan the most effective and swift route to the next. Although this research was based largely on the evolution of mainframe systems, there are striking similarities with the development of microcomputers and local area networks. This approach has been extended by Earl. As well as the internal evolution of the information system within the organization and its connection with technological development, it is important to recognize that the technology will have an impact on the work of individuals and the roles they fulfil. Management control may be significantly affected along with the internal structure of the organization. This must be taken into account in the formulation of strategy.

The work of Porter and Millar views the firm as being composed of a linked value chain consisting of nine primary and supporting activities. If an organization is to be competitive then each of these must function at a cost advantage over similar functions within its competitors, or help to produce a differentiated product. The way in which information technology can be used as a competitive weapon and support these activities and coordinate their linkages was examined. The strategic grid of McFarlan and McKenney identifies the strategic impact of existing computer-supported applications compared with planned applications. The firm broadly falls into one of four categories – support, factory, turnaround and strategic. Different information systems strategies are suggested dependent on which category best fits an organization currently and which best fits its likely development. [...]

This [chapter] looks at a selection of the more influential approaches to information systems strategic planning. What has been emphasized is that business information needs should determine strategy, not the characteristics of the various technologies.

References

Earl, M. (1989) *Management Strategies for Information Management*, Prentice Hall.

Galliers, R. and Sutherland, A. (1991) Information systems management and strategy formulation: the 'stages of growth' model revisited. *Journal of Information Systems*, 1, 89–114.

Hirscheim, R., Earl, M., Feeny, D. and Lockett, M. (1988) An exploration into the management of the information systems function. *Proceedings Information Technology Management for Productivity and Strategic Advantage*, IFIP Conference, March 1988.

McFarlan, F.W. (1984) Information technology changes the way you compete. *Harvard Business Review*, May–June, pp. 98–103.

McFarlan, F.W. and McKenney, J.L. (1983) *Corporate Information Management: the issues facing senior management*, Dow-Jones-Irwin.

Nolan, R.L. (1979) Managing the crisis in data processing. *Harvard Business Review*, March–April, pp. 115–126.

Nolan, R. (1984) Managing the advanced stages of computer technology: key research issues. In *The Information Systems Research Challenge*, McFarlan F.W. ed., pp. 195–214, Harvard Business School Press.

Porter, M.E. (1980) *Competitive Strategy*, Free Press.

Porter, M.E. (1985) *Competitive Advantage*, Free Press.

Porter, M.E. and Millar, V.E. (1985) How information gives you competitive advantage. *Harvard Business Review*, July–August, pp. 149–160.

Scott Morton, M. (ed.) (1991) *The Corporation of the 90s: information technology and organizational transformation*, Oxford University Press.

Source: Adapted from Curtis, G. 'Strategy and information systems' in Hinton, M. (2006) *Introducing Information Management: a business approach*, Elsevier.

Chapter 12

The search for opportunity

Lynda M. Applegate, F. Warren McFarlan and James L. McKenney

Five key questions can be used to guide an assessment of the impact of IT on strategy.

Can IT build barriers to entry?

A successful entry barrier offers not only a new product or service that appeals to customers but also features that keep the customers 'hooked'. The harder the service is to emulate, the higher the barrier to entry. A large financial service firm sought to build an effective barrier to entry when it launched a unique and highly attractive financial product that depended on sophisticated software that was both costly and difficult to implement. The complexity of the IT-enabled product caught competitors off guard; it took several years for them to develop a similar product, which gave the initiating firm valuable time to establish a significant market position. During this time, the firm continued to innovate, enhancing the original product and adding value to the services. Competitors not only had to catch up, but had to catch a moving target.

The payoff from value-added features that increase both sales and market share is particularly strong in industries within which there are great economies of scale and where customers are extremely price sensitive. By being the first to move onto the learning curve, a company can gain a cost advantage that enables it to put great pressure on its competitors.

Systems that increase the effectiveness of the sales force represent another kind of entry barrier – a knowledge barrier. For example, several large insurance companies have implemented sophisticated, customer-oriented financial-planning support packages that have greatly expanded the ability of their agents to deal with the rapidly changing and increasingly complex knowledge requirements within the industry. By increasing the capabilities of the sales force (a key strategic resource of the firm), these insurance companies have created significant barriers to entry that are exceedingly difficult to emulate. With the advent of the Internet in the late 1990s, many companies are finding that knowledge barriers are among the most potent of competitive forces.

Can IT build in switching costs?

Are there ways to encourage reliance on IT-enabled products and services? Can industry participants be encouraged to embed these products and services into their operations in such a manner that the notion of switching to a competitor is extremely unattractive? Ideally, an IT system should be simple for the customer to adopt at the outset, but then, through a series of increasingly complex – yet very valuable – enhancements, the IT system becomes tightly intertwined with the customer's daily routine. Proponents of electronic home banking hope to capitalize on the potential of increasing switching costs. Indeed, many 'virtual' banks now exist that have no branches; their customers, having tightly integrated their financial records into the bank's IT systems, conduct all transactions electronically.

A manufacturer of heavy machines provides another example of how IT can add value to and support a company's basic product line while also increasing switching costs. The firm embedded into its product software that enables remote monitoring and, in some cases, correction of problems. In case of mechanical failure, the diagnostic device calls a computer at corporate headquarters, where software analyses, and if possible, solves the problem. If the problem cannot be solved remotely, the computer pages a mechanic and provides a complete record of the current problem and the maintenance history of the product. Availability of the parts required to fix the problem is also noted and technical documentation is provided. Now installed around the globe, the system has dramatically improved service quality and response time, significantly enhanced customer loyalty and decreased the tendency of customers to buy service contracts elsewhere.

The joint marketing programme of MCI, Citibank and American Airlines, through which customers can earn American Airlines frequent flyer miles whenever they use the telephone or their credit cards, is another example of how IT can support value-added services that enhance customer loyalty and increase switching costs.

Can IT change the basis of competition?

In some industries IT has enabled a firm to alter fundamentally the basis of competition within the industry. This occurs when a firm uses IT to change radically either its cost structure (cost advantage) or its product/service offerings (differentiation advantage).

For example, in the mid-1970s, a major distributor of magazines, a very cost-competitive industry segment, used IT to lower significantly its cost structure by developing cheaper methods of sorting and distributing magazines. By radically reducing both headcount and inventory, it was able to become the low-cost producer in the industry. Because buyers were extremely price sensitive, the distributor was able quickly to increase market share, but it did not stop there. Having attained significant cost advantage, the distributor differentiated its products and services. Recognizing that its customers were small, unsophisticated and unaware of their profit structures, the distributor used its internal records of weekly shipments and returns to create a new value-added product – a customized report that calculated profit per square foot for every magazine sold and then compared these data with aggregate information from comparable customers operating in similar neighbourhoods. The distributor could thus tell each customer how it could improve its product mix. In addition to distributing magazines, the company used IT and the information it generated to offer a valuable inventory-management service. In this example, the distributor initially used IT to change its competitive position within an industry; it then used IT to change fundamentally the basis of competition.

Dramatic cost reduction can significantly alter the old ground rules of competition, enabling companies to find strategic opportunity in the new cost-competitive environment. For example, there may be an opportunity for sharp cost reduction through staff reduction or the ability to grow without hiring staff, improved material use, increased machine efficiency through better scheduling or more cost-effective maintenance, or inventory reduction. In the drug wholesale industry, for example, from 1971 to 1996, the average operating cost/sales ratio of the major players dropped from 16 per cent to 2 per cent mostly through the use of IT and a fragmented industry of 1000 firms was consolidated to approximately 100, with the top five players controlling 80 per cent of the market.

Understanding when to take advantage of these competitive opportunities can be particularly difficult and troublesome. For example, few people now doubt that home banking is becoming important to financial services. The importance was less clear in the mid-1980s, when pioneering banks launched home banking services that failed miserably. The situation confronting libraries is another excellent example of the uncertain nature of competitive decisions. Drawing on over 1000 years of tradition in storing books made of parchment and paper, today's libraries are at a crossroads. Soaring materials costs, expansion of computer databases, networking, the Internet, and electronic links between libraries have made the research facility of today utterly unrecognizable from that of 1990. In many cases, the period of transition is relatively short, the investments high and the discontinuity with the past dramatic.

As managers consider opportunities to use IT to alter radically the basis of competition, it is often difficult, especially in the early stages, to distinguish the intriguing (but ephemeral) from the path-breaking innovations. The consequences of action (or inaction) can be devastating if managers misread the cues.

Can IT change the balance of power in supplier relationships?

The development of IT systems that link manufacturers and suppliers has been a powerful role for IT within the firm. For example, just-in-time inventory systems have dramatically reduced inventory costs and warehouse expenses, while also improving order fulfilment time. Traditionally, companies have used inventory to buffer uncertainty in their production processes. Large safety stocks of raw materials and supplies are kept on hand to allow operations to run smoothly. But inventory costs money; it ties up capital, it requires costly physical facilities for storage and it must be managed by people. Increasingly, companies are using IT to link suppliers and manufacturers; by improving information flow, they are able to decrease uncertainty, and, in the process, reduce inventory, cut the number of warehouses and decrease headcount while also streamlining the production process. In some cases, they have been able to pass inventory responsibility and its associated responsibilities from one player in an industry value chain to another.

A large retailer capitalized on these advantages by electronically linking its materials-ordering system to its suppliers' order-fulfilment systems. Now, when 100 sofas are needed for a particular region, the retailer's computer automatically checks the inventory status of its primary sofa suppliers; the one with the fastest availability and lowest cost gets the order.

Equally important, the retailer's computer continually monitors its suppliers' finished-goods inventories, factory scheduling and commitments against its schedule to make sure enough inventory will be available to meet unexpected demand. If a supplier's inventories are inadequate, the retailer alerts the supplier; if a supplier is unwilling to go along with this system, it may find its share of business dropping until it is replaced by others.
As a purely defensive investment, a major textile manufacturer recently undertook an $8 million IT project to build a new order-entry-and-fulfilment system: failure to do so would have meant the loss of its top three customers.

A major manufacturer proposed CAD-to-CAD links with a $100-million-a-year-in-sales pressed-powder metal parts manufacturer. Within 18 months, this system shortened the product design cycle from eight months to three.

Such interorganizational systems can redistribute power between buyer and supplier. In the case of [an aerospace manufacturer], CAD-to-CAD systems increased dependence on an individual supplier, making it hard for the company to replace the supplier and leaving it vulnerable to major price increases. The retailer, on the other hand, was in a much stronger position to dictate the terms of its relationship with its suppliers.

Can IT generate new products?

As described earlier, IT can lead to products with higher quality, faster delivery or less cost. Similarly, at little extra expense, existing products can be tailored to meet a customer's special needs. Some companies may be able to combine one or more of these advantages. In addition, at little additional cost, as in the case of the online diagnostic system for machine failure described earlier, electronic support services can increase the value of the total package in the consumer's eyes.

Indeed, mergers are currently being planned around those capabilities. For example, a catalogue company and a credit card company recently examined the possibility of combining their customer data files to facilitate cross-marketing and offer a new set of services.

In another example, credit card companies have become voracious consumers of delinquent accounts receivable data from other firms; indeed, there is a whole industry dedicated to the collection and organization of these data. Similarly, non-proprietary research data files often have significant value to third parties.

In some cases, a whole new industry has emerged. For example, a number of market research firms now purchase data from large supermarket chains, analyse it and then sell it back to the supermarkets in scrubbed and easily analysable form. The market research firm organizes these data by [postal] code into a research tool for retail chains, food suppliers and others interested in consumer activity.

Finally, the information content of products has increased markedly. For example, today's upscale cars have more than 100 microcomputers in them controlling everything from braking to temperature. Sewing machines use microcomputers to control everything from stitching pattern to complex thread shifts. Fighter aircraft and submarines have highly sophisticated automated control systems.

Analysing the value chain for IT opportunities

An effective way to search for potential IT opportunities is through a systematic analysis of a company's value chain – the series of interdependent activities that bring a product or service to the customer. [...] In different settings, IT can profoundly affect one or more of these value activities, sometimes simply by improving effectiveness, sometimes by fundamentally changing the activity and sometimes by altering the relationship between activities. In addition, the actions of one firm can significantly affect the value chain of key customers and suppliers.

Inbound logistics

In many settings IT has expedited procurements of materials. One major distribution company, for example, installed hundreds of personal computers on supplier premises to enable just-in-time, online ordering. The company required its suppliers to maintain adequate inventory and provide online access to stock levels so that they can appropriately plan orders. This system decreased the need for extensive warehousing of incoming materials and reduced disruptions due to inventory shortfalls. The need to maintain inventory safety stocks and the associated holding costs were reduced for both the supplier and the buyer.

A retail chain's direct linkage to its major textile suppliers not only improved delivery and enabled inventory reduction but also provided the flexibility to meet changing demand almost immediately. This, in turn, offset the impact of the lower price offered by foreign suppliers, thus enabling US textile manufacturers to gain share in this cost-sensitive, highly competitive, fast-response environment.

Operations and product definition

Information systems technologies can also influence a manufacturer's operations and product offerings. In 1989, a manufacturer of thin transparent film completed a $30 million investment in new computer-controlled manufacturing facilities for one of its major product lines. This change slashed order response time from 10 weeks to two days and improved quality levels significantly.

A financial services firm, having decided to go after more small private investors (with portfolios of about $25 000), introduced a flexible financial instrument that gave its investors immediate online ability to move their funds among stocks and other financial products, provided money market rates of idle funds and offered the same liquidity as a checking account. The company – the first to introduce this service – captured a huge initial market share, which it has maintained over the years by continued product enhancement. In the first two years, the company achieved six times the volume of its nearest competitor. Five years later it still retained a 70 per cent share of the market.

A major insurance company that defined its business as a provider of diversified financial services improved its services to policyholders by allowing immediate online access to information on the status of claims and claims processing. The company also provided online access to new services and products, including modelling packages that enabled corporate benefits officers to tailor various benefit packages, balancing cost and employee service. In response to client demand, it sold either software for claims processing or claims-processing services. The company credits these

IT-enabled product initiatives for its ability to maintain its position at the top of its industry despite tremendous competition from other diversified financial services companies.

Outbound logistics

IT can also influence the way services and products are delivered to customers. [The] reservation system, provided chiefly by United Airlines and American Airlines, has profoundly affected smaller airlines that do not furnish this service. Indeed, in December 1984, the Civil Aeronautics Board, believing that the systems strongly influenced purchasing behaviour, issued a cease-and-desist order that required that all carriers' flights be fairly represented. Automatic teller machines, as well as theatre-ticket and airline-ticket machines, allow cash and services to be rapidly and reliably delivered to customers where they work or shop. Today, the Internet has become an important retail channel for all types of physical and information-based products and services.

Marketing and sales

Marketing and sales, functional areas often neglected in the first three decades of IT, are now areas of high impact. In many firms, the sales force has been supplied with a wide array of personal portable technologies that enable firms to collect detailed customer and market data and then to package and deliver the data back to the sales force – and directly to customers.

A large pharmaceutical company offered online order entry for its products and those of its non-competitors. This service increased its market share and revenues. The companies excluded from the system threatened legal action because of damage to their market position.

An agricultural chemicals company developed a sophisticated online crop-planning service for its major agricultural customers. From a personal computer, using a standard telephone connection, farmers can access agricultural databases containing prices of various crops, necessary growing conditions and the costs of various chemicals to support different crops. They can then access various models and decision support systems, tailor them to their unique field requirements and examine the implications of various crop rotations and timing for planting. The model also helps the farmers to select fertilizer and chemical applications and to group their purchases to achieve maximum discounts. Finally, with a few keystrokes, farmers can place orders for future delivery. Similar services have been offered by a major seed company in coordination with a state agricultural extension service. To strengthen its marketing of agricultural loans, a major bank has offered a similar crop-planning service. This example shows how three companies in different industries are now offering the same software to the end consumer.

Over the past decade, a major food company has assembled a national database that keeps track of daily sales of each of its products in each of the 500 000 stores it services. This database is now totally accessible through a wide-area network to market planners in their 22 regional districts. Combined with market and competitor data from market research companies, this information has significantly increased the precision and sophistication of market planning and execution. Similarly, one of the store chains, using a customer loyalty card and the market data, can precisely identify which customers buy which brands of competing merchandise. This information is of extraordinary importance to suppliers as they focus their coupon efforts.

After-sales service

IT is also revolutionizing after-sales service; for example, on its new line of elevators, an elevator company has installed online diagnostic devices. These devices identify potential problems before the customer notices a difficulty, thus enabling the service representative to fix the elevator before it breaks down, reducing repair costs and increasing customer satisfaction. 'The best elevator is an unnoticed elevator' in the words of their CEO.

A large manufacturer of industrial machinery has installed an expert system on its home-office computer to support product maintenance. When a machine failure occurs on a customer's premises, the machine is connected over a telephone line to the manufacturer's computer, which performs an analysis of the problem and issues instructions to the machine operator. Service visits have decreased by 50 per cent, while customer satisfaction has significantly improved.

Corporate infrastructure

A large travel agency has electronically connected via satellite small outlying offices located near big corporate customers to enable access to the full support capabilities of the home office. These network capabilities have transformed the organizational structure from one large central corporate office to many small full-service offices, resulting in a 27 per cent growth in sales.

Management control

A major financial services firm used to pay a sales commission on each product sold by its sales force; thus, the sales force had maximum incentive to make the initial sale and no incentive to ensure customer satisfaction and retention. Using its new integrated customer database, the company implemented a new commission structure that rewarded both the initial sales and customer retention. This approach, made possible by new technology, aligned the company's strategy and its sales incentive system much more effectively.

In some instances, IT has dramatically enhanced coordination by providing greater access to a more widely connected network using fairly simple but powerful tools such as voice mail, electronic mail, groupware and video-conferencing. New networked 'workflow' systems are also enabling tighter coordination of operation. For example, due to high capital costs and operating expense, every major US air carrier uses a network to monitor the precise location of all its aircraft. It knows each airplane's location, the passengers on-board, their planned connections and the connection schedules. It can instantaneously make decisions about speeding up late flights or delaying connecting departures. The opportunities for controlling fuel costs and preventing revenue loss amount to tens of millions of dollars a year. Trucking companies and railroads use similar methods to track cargoes and optimize schedules.

Human resources

Human resources management has also changed. For example, to facilitate important personnel decisions, an oil company has given personal computers to all its corporate management committee members, thus giving full online access to the detailed personnel files of the 400 most senior members in the corporation. These files contain data on five-year performance appraisals, photographs and lists of positions for which each person is a backup candidate. The company believes this capability has facilitated its important personnel decisions. Additionally, special government compliance auditing, which used to take months to complete, can now be done in hours.

Technology development

To guide its drilling decisions, a large oil company processes vast amounts of data gathered from an overhead satellite. The company uses this information to support oil field bidding and drilling decisions. Similarly, CAD/CAM (computer-aided design and manufacturing) technology has fundamentally changed the quality and speed with which the company can manufacture its drilling platforms.

A seed company considers its single most important technology expenditure to be computer support for research. Modern genetic planning involves managing a global database of millions of pieces of germ plasm. These database planning and molecular simulation models – the keys to their future – are not possible without large-scale computing capacity. Repeatedly, their detailed data files have allowed them to find a germ plasm thousands of miles away in Africa to solve a problem in an Iowa cornfield.

Procurement

Procurement activities are also being transformed. For example, with a series of online electronic bulletin boards that make the latest spot prices instantly available around the country, a manufacturing company directs its nationwide purchasing effort. The boards have led to a tremendous improvement in purchasing price effectiveness, both in discovering and in implementing new quantity pricing discount data, as well as ensuring that the lowest prices are being achieved.

A retailer, by virtue of its large size, has succeeded in its demand for an online access to the inventory files and production schedules of its suppliers. This access has permitted the company to manage its inventories more tightly and to exert pressure on suppliers to lower price and improve product availability.

New market opportunities also abound. For example, an entrepreneurial start-up provides desktop software to allow traders and others with intense needs for fast-breaking information to pull relevant material from over 400 continuous news feeds (e.g. Reuters, Dow Jones), analyse the information and deliver it to end users. The firm's revenues – $40 million in 1997 – are growing rapidly.

In summary, a systematic examination of a company's value chain is an effective way to search for profitable IT applications. This analysis requires keen administrative insight, awareness of industry structure and familiarity with the rules of competition in the particular setting. Companies need to understand their own value chains as well as those of key customers and suppliers in order to uncover potential new service areas. Similarly, understanding competitors' value chains provides insight on potential competitive moves. Careful thought is needed to identify potential new entrants to an industry – those companies whose current business could be enhanced by an IT-enabled product or service.

Reference

Jelassi, T. (1994) *European Casebook on Competing through Information Technology,* Prentice Hall.

Source: Adapted from Applegate, L.M., McFarlan, F.W. and McKenney, J.L., 'The search for opportunity' in Hinton, M. (2006) *Introducing Information Management*, Elsevier.

Chapter 13

Using information systems to rethink business processes

David Boddy, Albert Boonstra and Graham Kennedy

Redon

Redon is a city council in a western country and has approximately 200,000 inhabitants. In this country, city councils are responsible for local economic policy, attracting companies, parts of the infrastructure and for services directed to local residents and companies, such as licences and permits. Municipalities are partly funded by the central government but also collect local taxes from residents and companies. Some services are standardised and simple (e.g. car licences) while others are complicated (attracting companies to settle). Redon is vertically organised, which means that 20 rather isolated departments provide services.

The Redon tax administration is responsible for collecting local taxes, which add about €100m to the revenues of the municipality, mainly through a property tax. It has about 120 employees who work in a highly computerised environment. The organisation structure includes main departments such as valuations, levy, collection and remissions and support departments such as finance, HRM and IS.

Some years ago, management realised that changes were needed and they had to use IS more effectively. The city council wanted better information while the tax unit itself faced internal problems:

- contacts with local taxpayers were not effective – they saw the system as bureaucratic and frustrating
- there was a large backlog of assessments and objections
- it made mistakes because of using incorrect data
- the process for dealing with each customer involved many departments – valuations estimated building values, another department assessed the tax, a third collected the tax and yet another arranged payments and remissions.

The information systems were designed to serve internal needs, such as recording historical data. Every department had its own IS policy, though the IS department had connected some systems to enable them to use each other's data.

An external consultancy analysed the organisation and identified the following problems:

- the functional structure was oriented towards procedures rather than customers
- taxpayers were all treated in the same way in spite of their differing needs
- the functional structure and rigid rules led to complex procedures even in simple cases
- the information systems were not integrated, which led to unreliable data and too many mistakes
- there were no clear standards against which to measure the administration's performance.

This chapter discusses how problems such as those faced by Redon can be dealt with by taking a new view of operational processes and by using IS to support those processes. Later in this chapter there is an interview with one of the directors and a description of how staff in the organisation responded to the problems.

Introduction

Early information systems supported separate business functions. These often worked well for the function concerned, and encouraged managers to apply computer-based systems more widely. However, these independent systems produced inconsistent and often unreliable data. The next step was to link the systems with one joint database. This included (ideally) consistent data about all the separate functional areas and often led to more efficient, reliable and accessible information systems – but management was still using the technology to support existing business processes. The way of doing business and organising work did not fundamentally change.

Developments in information systems technology, and some prominent experiments by new companies using this technology, led others to think more radically. They saw that modern information systems could enable business to work in a fundamentally different way (Galliers and Baets, 1997; Grover and Malhotra, 1997; Sauer and Yetton, 1997). In the management literature, people such as Hammer (1990) and Davenport (1993) also advocated a completely new approach. They called this 'business process re-engineering' or 'business process redesign'. Other terms representing similar ideas for linking separate aspects of a business include enterprise resource planning (ERP) systems and customer relationship management (CRM) systems.

This chapter elaborates this perspective, showing how people can use information systems to organise processes more effectively. This includes inter-organisational as well as internal processes, since the Internet and other networks make it easier to link all the processes within a value chain. This may blur the boundaries between organisations and changes the value chain of a business. Figure 13.1 illustrates these stages.

The chapter case is about a local authority tax department that has begun to make changes in the direction shown in the figure. It used to have many isolated processes and unconnected systems – which led to a wasteful system that provided a poor service to local residents. It then tried to work in a more customer-centred way by redesigning its processes and supporting them with modern information systems. That experience illustrates many of the themes in the chapter.

The first main section defines the topic more precisely, while the next section describes some approaches to innovating business processes. We then explain how IS can play an important role in process innovation. Next, we consider the managerial and organisational aspects, and the chapter concludes by discussing some management dilemmas in process innovation. The overall aim is to understand the managerial issues when people use information systems to change business processes in and between organisations.

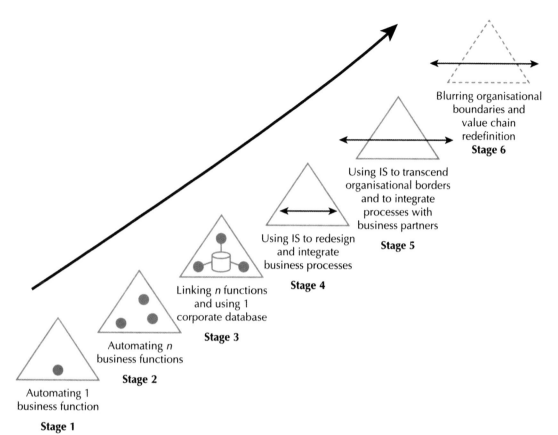

Figure 13.1   Evolution of information systems in organisations

Rethinking and innovating business processes

Day-to-day pressure and the force of habit mean that the established way of doing things becomes the only way. It is hard to think about these processes with an open mind. People in an established department, say purchasing, see themselves as specialised, experienced and knowledgeable. Purchasing is their job. Suppose that someone suggests that production operators could, with the assistance of modern information systems, order the materials that they use. Purchasing staff are likely to resist the suggestions instinctively whatever the possible merits. This illustrates a central challenge of rethinking and innovating business processes – an independent position, an open mind and a critical attitude to things that people take for granted are all needed.

What is a business process? Teng et al. (1994) define it as 'a set of logically related tasks performed to achieve a defined business outcome'. A business outcome is a product or service which is delivered to a customer (internal or external). The business process is the chain of tasks from purchasing to manufacturing to selling and delivering.

Different functional departments usually perform these linked tasks. They specialise in one step, such as design or purchasing, and design internal systems to make that part of the process efficient. The difficulties arise at the boundaries as the product or service moves between departments. This can become a source of trouble and wasted time which Goldratt and Cox (1992) illustrate in an amusing way. Boundary troubles lead to misunderstandings and time-consuming meetings since nobody fully owns the complete process or takes responsibility for it. Departments optimise their partial responsibility. Purchasing tries to buy goods under optimal delivery conditions. Manufacturing focuses on an optimal use of production facilities. Sales tries to meet all the expectations of its customers. The result will often be a slow process, full of mistakes and with more attention to internal procedures than to customer value. It is also very difficult to connect the different information systems.

These problems led to the argument that people should manage organisations from a process view rather than a functional view. This would lead to customer-directed processes that would improve quality and lower costs, supported by information technology. One of the earliest advocates of process innovation (Hammer, 1990) said: 'we should re-"reengineer" our businesses: use the power of modern information technology to radically redesign our business processes in order to achieve dramatic improvements in their performance'. Similarly Teng et al. (1994) wrote: 'redesign or reengineering is the critical analysis and radical redesign of existing business processes to achieve breakthrough improvements in performance measures'. What these authors emphasise is the notion of discontinuous thinking. They advocate recognising, and breaking away from, the historical rules and assumptions that underlie current operations.

Information technology is important in process innovation, but it is not the only place to start. Critical evaluation of business practice and creative thinking can also lead to process innovations as the ITEC example shows.

MIS in practice ITEC

ITEC, a company which repairs and maintains computers in printing companies, provides an example of process innovation without using IT. When there is a fault, someone in the printing office calls the company. An engineer comes to diagnose the problem and estimates the time needed to do the repair and the costs. If the customer accepts the estimate the engineer orders the parts and repairs the computer. ITEC later sends an invoice for payment. The whole process is often time-consuming and leads to many complaints. The company therefore analysed the breakdowns. They found they could speed up the process by selling customers a pack of the spare parts most likely to be needed. Customers who bought such a pack got an immediate repair in 90 per cent of all cases. This simple process redesign improved efficiency and satisfied customers.

However, computer-based systems such as enterprise resource planning (ERP) systems can strengthen the case for radical process change. They make possible what was previously impossible, and the Internet has opened up yet more possibilities.

Managers usually make process innovations by combining separate processes and designing the remaining ones to be more efficient. They often find that most of the time in a process is taken up waiting for the next process to start – a sure sign that it involves too many departments.

MIS in practice Port of Rotterdam

The Port of Rotterdam (www.portofrotterdam.com) controls approximately 100 km of waterway. This process starts at sea as each ship reports its approach to the harbour. That information is used for traffic control, tariffs and special arrangements for dangerous cargoes. Not long ago the harbour had 126 departments, each with its own IT systems, and used more than 100 applications. 'That became unmanageable,' says Chris van de Weerd, IT manager at the Traffic Management department.

At the start of this year we moved from a departmental structure to a process-based organisation. This move also led to an IT audit and a redesign of our information systems architecture. Now we only have a few information systems which support the arrival and departure of any ship. One of these systems is a knowledge system which helps to analyse all relevant data and to determine whether a ship needs a pilot to enter the harbour.

While the principles are easy to understand, the practice is more difficult, since process innovation involves significant changes in responsibilities and a more explicit orientation towards the customer. The changes also need to be aligned with broader strategy. They might involve closer cooperation with suppliers and customers as there are further benefits in innovating processes between, as well as within, organisations. Finally, new information systems will support the new processes. They are challenging projects to manage, and the failure rate is high.

Summary

- Changing environments and new IT generate ideas for process redesign.
- IT enables a process orientation (as opposed to functional ways of organising).
- Process changes potentially affect all aspects of the organisation, including IS.

Approaches to innovating processes

Consultants and researchers have developed principles and methods for innovating business processes.

Organising process innovation

Process innovation usually takes place as a project within an established organisation, with staff seconded from several units to work with external consultants. Figure 13.2 shows a common sequence of activities.

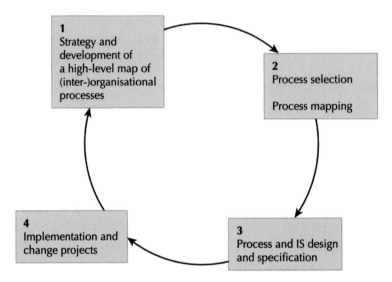

Figure 13.2   Phases of process innovation

Most authorities take the view that a company should start with a view of the organisation (or business unit) as a whole and a clear strategic vision of the business and the environment. Business processes should not be (re) designed in isolation, so, first, a high-level map of the (inter-) organisational processes has to be constructed. From that map, particular processes or subprocesses can be prioritised for innovation.

Common criteria are:

*   the health of the process (unhealthy processes are dysfunctional and prone to error, with extensive information exchange, redundancy of work and iteration of tasks)
*   the criticality of the process (processes can be ranked in order of importance relative to the competences and the performance of the organisation. Which processes have the greatest potential for improvement?)
*   the feasibility of innovation (it is more feasible to change some processes than others, either on technical grounds, e.g. a new software package, or organisational, e.g. readiness to change).

Then the process innovation can be designed, specified and implemented.

Systematic design or clean sheet?

Within this view on the organisation of process innovation there are two different methods (Peppard and Rowland, 1995):

- systematic design: identify and analyse existing processes, evaluate them critically and plan major improvements

- clean sheet approach: fundamentally rethink the way that the product or service is delivered and design new processes from scratch.

The first approach will probably get more support from staff who are actively involved in processes and may lead to certain improvements more quickly. The danger is that starting from the current situation may limit radical thinking. The second approach is more fundamental but can probably be carried out only with the help of external advisers because of the bias of staff inside a company.

Systematic approach

If a company decides to follow a systematic design approach, Peppard and Rowland (1995) suggest asking four questions:

1   Is it possible to eliminate process steps? Many processes contain unnecessary steps and consequently cause unnecessary waiting times. For example, insurance claims move between departments and have a waiting time in each one. Every stage of transport, and each activity, takes time and effort. Managing and monitoring each of these steps is also time-consuming.

2   Is it possible to simplify process steps? Often, unnecessary forms and too many procedures are used. Nowadays many firms use the Internet to enable the customer to key in necessary data to start a process that is an example of simplification.

3   Is it possible to integrate process steps? Some tasks which are separated and executed by different people or different departments can easily be done by one. This often makes it easier to manage a process and divide responsibilities more clearly.

4   Is it possible to automate process steps? For example, can dangerous or boring work be eliminated, and is there scope for eliminating duplication in capturing and transferring data?

Process mapping and modelling

Kim (1995) developed an approach that models a process and then uses this model to analyse the process (see Figure 13.3). This method can be used for both the systematic design and clean sheet approaches. Kim distinguishes three constructs:

1   Event: a perceived change of status at one point in time that is of interest to the organisation.

2   Process: an activity or series of activities performed by the customer or between the customer and organisation over time, often as a response to the triggering events.

MIS in practice

John Smith arrives at the hospital with stomach ache at 1.30 p.m. He has to go to the reception desk first to register. He has to fill in a form, verify his insurance status, wait his turn and pay the doctor's fee in advance (as required by this particular healthcare scheme). After receiving a consultation slip from the reception desk, he has to go to the internal medicine department on the second floor. It is now 2 p.m.

At the second floor reception, John gives his form to a nurse and waits for his turn. This is normally at least an hour even when he has an appointment. Consultation with the doctor lasts about fifteen minutes. The doctor diagnoses food poisoning and prescribes some medicine. John takes the prescription to the cashier's desk in reception, pays the bill and goes down to the pharmacy in the basement. After waiting another half an hour, he receives his medicine.

By the time he leaves the hospital, it is already 4 p.m., too late to return to work. John wonders if anything can be done to speed up this slow process.

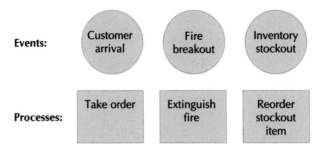

Figure 13.3   Symbols in modelling process change

3   Wait: a significant average delay before the start of an event or a process due to a queue or other unfavourable conditions of the organisation.

In the hospital example below, the approach will be explained by describing the old process and the design of a new one.

Figure 13.4 models this process in a diagram, which helps us to analyse the process flow. We can use the model to give an accurate picture of the present situation and to identify how it can be improved. We also need to consider whether those improvements should be made radically or incrementally.

Each process (boxes P1–P3) can be divided in subprocesses – Figure 13.4 only shows the broad picture. The challenge is to improve the process by cutting lead times and reducing the number of people involved without

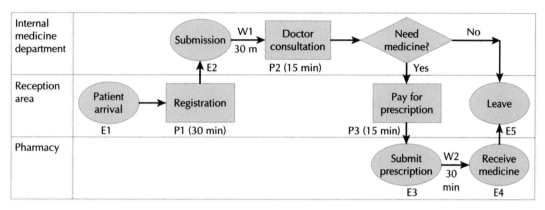

Figure 13.4   Old process at hospital

causing quality problems. Kim mentions the following principles for designing processes:

1   Start with the most critical process.
2   Reduce the number of process steps by eliminating unnecessary ones.
3   Transform processes into events. In Figure 13.4 the registration process can turn into an event by issuing each patient with a smart card containing personal health and bank account information.
4   Minimise the travel distance. When the chain moves up and down a 'red flag' is raised. The number of involved parties should be as small as possible.
5   Make processes and events parallel. In Figure 13.4, process P1 and process P3 can be done simultaneously while event E3 can be done by the doctor during the consultation.
6   Reduce the waiting time before process but eliminate it before event. Events take hardly any time and it is irritating and often unnecessary to have to wait.

To illustrate what can be done, Figure 13.5 shows the improved process.

These suggestions are derived from Teng's process-modelling approach. He suggests that a process has to be as short as possible (less time) and as narrow as possible (fewer people). Comparing the old and the new processes we can see that IS (card readers, smart cards, networks and databases) make it possible to:

• change the registration process (old P1) into an event (new E2)

• remove the wait (old W2) into an event (new E3)

• remove the payment process (old P3) by integrating it in the receipt event (new E3).

This illustrates how computer-based information systems open many opportunities to rethink a process and bring significant reductions in process steps and waits.

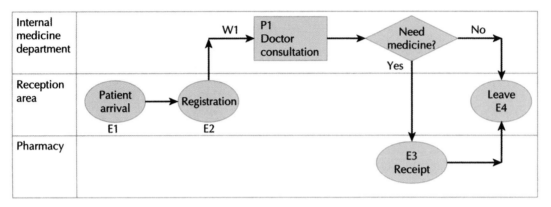

Figure 13.5 New process at hospital

This method can stimulate discussions about 'old' and 'new' processes. A clear scheme of the old situation shows how things really are and how much time and how many steps they take. A danger is that it is close to 'systematic design': it improves the situation without designing a fundamentally new process, disconnected from the old situation. However, in designing processes, a clear scheme of a proposed alternative makes a good discussion possible.

Summary

- Process innovation can take place by analysing the old processes or by designing a new process from scratch; both have advantages and disadvantages.

- In doing a systematic design, asking 'can we eliminate, simplify, integrate or automate' can help to stimulate ideas.

- Modelling and analysing old and new processes (e.g. with Kim's modelling approach) can help in making new designs.

The role of IS in process change

Information systems and process change provide a further illustration of the interaction model. One perspective is that managers should first redesign their processes and then implement IS to support them – as in Figure 13.6(a).

The alternative view is that rapidly developing information technologies are themselves often driving business process change. Davenport (1993) gives examples of computer-based information systems – what he calls a 'disruptive technology' – enabling new processes. He suggests that the power of information systems is to set new 'rules', which enable change in the way people and organisations work – as shown in Table 13.1.

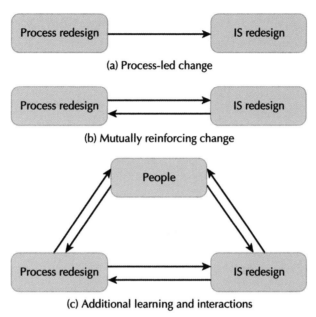

Figure 13.6 Interaction between processes, information systems and people

Table 13.1 How information systems can change to rules

Old rule	Disruptive technology	New rule
Information can appear in only one place at one time	Shared databases	Information can appear simultaneously in as many places as it is needed
Only experts can perform complex work	Expert systems	A generalist can do the work of an expert
Managers make all decisions	Decision support tools	Decision-making is part of everyone's job
Field staff need offices where they can receive, store, retrieve and transmit information	Wireless data communication and portable computers	Field personnel can send and receive information wherever they are
You have to find out where things are	Automatic identification and tracking technology	Things tell you where they are

Source: Based on Davenport (1993)

The Internet is the driving force behind many of the electronic marketplaces that are changing purchasing processes so radically. As these markets develop, people need to update their processes – and they need more advanced systems to support these new processes. So process change and IS are becoming mutually reinforcing factors – as shown in Figure 13.6(b).

A further interaction, of great practical significance, is that, as people use information systems to improve their processes, they learn what is possible. This helps them to become more confident in breaking out of the old mindset. They are more willing to abandon the traditional ways of thinking which, as we remarked at the outset, can block attempts at process change. They can see new possibilities of process change – which will require further new systems.

The continuing chapter case illustrates the interaction between information systems and business process and organisational change at the tax administration.

The case illustrates how IS enables process innovation and strategic change. It reduces the number of steps, departments and people involved, and supports individuals by helping them to access data and make well-informed decisions quickly. The information systems are built around points of contact with customers instead of around functions that are just a small part of a process. Information systems follow from the chosen organisational design and become increasingly cross functional and inter-organisational. In this case, the information systems have enabled these new ways of organising. That does not always happen, and depends on management decisions on each of these elements.

Davenport (1993) suggests that there are many opportunities to use information systems to support fundamental process changes. He distinguishes nine categories of impacts, which are shown in Table 13.2.

This table illustrates that IS enables organisations to work on a wider geographic scale and in a more consistent, controlled and reliable manner. Customers can be anywhere (Internet), employees can be anywhere (groupware, Internet, portable systems) and processes can be controlled more effectively (workflow management systems, expert systems).

Table 13.2 How information systems can support business process change

Category	Description	Example
Integrative	Coordinating and integrating tasks and processes	With all the relevant information easily available at one time and place, bank staff can help customers with different needs
Geographical	Transferring information over long distances	Using the Internet, businesses can perceive the whole (connected) world as their marketplace, rather than a limited region
Automational	Eliminating or reducing human labour	In the retail industry, many inventories are connected electronically with suppliers in order to automate the stock control completely
Analytical	Support decision-making by better analysis of information	Decision support systems help users to develop different scenarios and make better decisions`
Informational	Providing information in right amounts at the right time	Information systems can be helpful in providing managers with information in the form of, e.g. exception reporting
Sequential	Changing the process sequences or enabling parallelism	Because information is available at many places at the same time, people can work simultaneously on the processing of an order
Intellectual	Capturing and distributing intellectual assets	Expert systems, for instance in financial services, can distribute corporate knowledge to financial advisers
Tracking Disintermediation	Monitoring processes Eliminating intermediaries	Point-of-sale systems to constantly monitor inventory levels IT can replace the information previously supplied by the intermediary (e.g. wholesalers)

Source: Davenport (1993)

Clearly Table 13.2 identifies links between process innovation and broader strategy and choices for companies about whether to perform certain processes themselves or outsource them, supported by information systems.

Lockamy and Smith (1997) suggest two principles in using information systems to innovate business processes:

• systems must facilitate easy access to process information across functional boundaries

• the assessment of IS for use in process design must be conducted within the context of the wider IS strategy.

These two principles suggest that information systems enable the innovation of processes based on a strategic vision of the organisation. IS can bring that vision to life. The next section illustrates this by describing three examples of process change enabled by IS: ERP, e-commerce and Internet procurement.

Redon: continued

To overcome their problems, the administration started to define their products, services, markets and customers. They learned that groups of taxpayers have different needs and expectations. Companies expect a more personalised approach – such as an account manager at the tax administration with whom they can discuss their tax position. They expect that person to be able to give advice. Taxpayers expect a simpler form, and the possibility of sending it via the Internet. They also appreciate a call centre they can phone to get answers to tax questions.

Managers used this idea to restructure the organisation around customer groups. There are line departments, each dealing with one group of customers – big companies, medium/small companies or local residents. Within the company departments, staff deal with particular companies. Work processes and information systems reflect these differences.

The local residents department deals with large numbers, and needs to be reliable and timely. A workflow management system helps managers to control the speed and reliability of customer contacts. There is also a call centre (with an e-mail option) to answer taxpayers' questions quickly. The system is easy to use and supports staff by including a feature which suggests the questions they should ask the citizen. An interactive website allows people to submit their tax forms and check progress electronically which saves time for everyone.

The company-directed departments needed an advanced 'company information system' to record relevant company data in an orderly manner. External systems, such as that at the chamber of commerce, had to feed into this system, so it was connected to the Internet. The account managers had very specific demands in terms of screen layouts and drilldown features, so an expert system was provided that helps them deal more consistently with complex tax problems.

Company account managers, call centre agents and people who deal with local residents were trained to be effective, efficient and customer-oriented. Many had to be re-educated from being a tax expert to being a customer-directed account manager.

Summary

- IS will often support or drive process change.
- IS can (among other things) be used to facilitate easy access to process information across functional boundaries.
- A management issue is to relate IS used to support process design to the overall IS strategy.

Examples of IS-enabled process change

Enterprise resource planning

Many companies now use information systems for enterprise resource planning (ERP). An ERP system helps coordinate all facets of business, including planning, manufacturing, sales and finance (Laudon and Laudon, 2004). ERP systems eliminate expensive links between isolated IT systems in different business functions. Within an ERP system, sales representatives can easily enter online orders from customers and verify inventory levels. Manufacturing and purchasing files are automatically updated. If the system has a link to the Internet, customers can check the progress of an order.

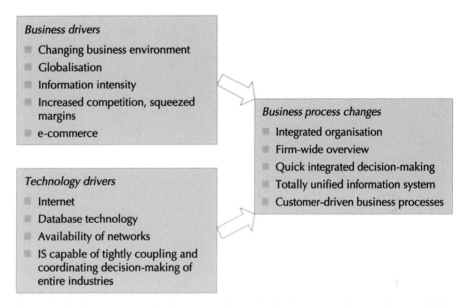

Figure 13.7   Business and technology drivers behind process change through ERP systems

Implementing an ERP system implies changing processes. Vendors advise changing these radically before putting such a system in place. Information flows cross functional borders and different units can access the same data. Enterprise systems are usually implemented in stages, with the most essential modules first (often finance, purchasing, manufacturing and marketing). Many organisations choose to extend their system to suppliers and customers (often using the Internet) so that it becomes an inter-organisational system. In this 'extended enterprise' borders become unclear and several partners use the same database and information systems.

Figure 13.7 shows business and technology drivers that lie behind the wide acceptance of ERP. They lead to an integrated business from an information flow point of view. Customers trigger a chain of activities (a business process) when they make a transaction. People in companies who share responsibility for a process have an overview and can make decisions more confidently. Technology, as mentioned in the figure, makes this possible. But, people and procedures are also part of the system and their response will affect the outcomes of process innovation.

The following example illustrates the implementation of an ERP system at Elf Atochem and shows the strong relation between strategy, process change and IS.

While ERP has many advantages, there are also disadvantages. These include possible inflexibility and the difficulty of securing a fit between the system and the characteristics of the business. Many managers say that they have to adapt their business to the ERP system rather than vice versa to make the system work. The system forces the company to organise its processes in a prescribed way – which may lose a distinct advantage.

MIS in practice ERP at Elf Atochem

Elf Atochem North America is a chemicals subsidiary of the French company Elf Aquitaine. Following a series of mergers in the early 1990s, managers were hampered by the fragmentation of critical information systems among its 12 business units. Ordering systems were not integrated with production systems: sales forecasts were not tied to budgeting systems or to performance measurement systems. Each unit was tracking and reporting its financial data independently. As a result of the many incompatible systems, operating data were not flowing smoothly through the organisation and senior management was not getting the information needed to make sound and timely business decisions.

The company's executives saw that an enterprise system would be the best way to integrate the data flows. Looking beyond the technology, the executives saw that the real source of Elf Atochem's difficulties was not the fragmentation of its systems but the fragmentation of its organisation. Although the 12 business units shared many of the same customers, each unit was managed autonomously.

Management decided to focus on four processes: materials management, production planning, order management and financial reporting. These cross-unit processes were the ones most distorted by the fragmented organisational structure. Moreover, they had the greatest impact on the company's ability to manage its customer relationships in a way that would both enhance customer satisfaction and improve corporate profitability.

Elf Atochem also made fundamental changes to its organisational structure. In the financial area, for example, accounts receivable and credit departments were combined into one. This enabled the system to consolidate a customer's orders into a single account and issue a single invoice. It also allowed managers to monitor overall customer profitability – something that had been impossible to do when orders were fragmented across units.

Source: Based on Davenport (1998)

This brings us to a more general point: IS can also constrain real process innovation. Information systems that are expensive legacies of the past are difficult to adapt and limit the ability of organisations to change their processes radically. New systems, such as ERP, can urge organisations to arrange their processes in a specific way without leaving enough space for creativity and for doing things differently. Managers who are aware of these dangers can, however, ensure that they try to obtain the benefits of such systems, without the limitations.

Using the internet for e-commerce

Another example of IS-enabled process change is the use of the Internet. This opens up enormous possibilities for the transformation of processes. Most organisations now have an Internet presence through their website, which has to reflect a strategic vision about how the business will use the Internet. If the site is going to manage transactions with customers, reliable methods for handling them need to be organised. This implies a new design of that core business process.

When organisations decide to use the Internet, they also have to decide between combining it with non-Internet activities or transferring all their operations to the Internet. The companies taking the former (multi-channel) route have to combine processes consistently and clearly for their customers (see Figure 13.8)

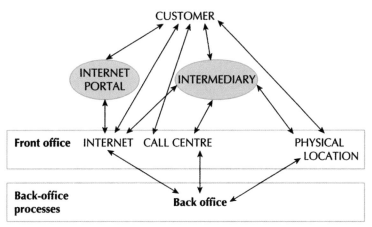

Figure 13.8   Multi-channel approach: customers choose their own channel for every transaction

Organising such complicated processes in order to have an efficient and reliable fulfilment is a major focal point for many project managers. An important concern for companies that move (a part of) their processes to the Internet has been to ensure they can handle the associated physical processes, such as handling orders, arranging shipment, receiving payment and dealing with after-sales service. This gives an advantage to traditional retailers who can support their websites with existing fulfilment processes. Effective B2B applications require that the business processes between customers and suppliers fit with each other. This has been a bigger task than many expected.

Due to the advent of mobile phones (so-called m-commerce) and other devices, the number of channels that people may use to contact companies and place orders is growing. This means that the forefront of customer contact increases in variety and options, while back-office systems are needed to collect all relevant information and make it available to all front-office contact points, such as call centres and branches.

Procurement refers to all activities involved with obtaining items from a supplier; this includes not only purchasing, but also inbound logistics such as transportation, goods-in and warehousing before the item is used (Chaffey, 2002). Since the advent of the Internet, procurement is increasingly perceived as a business process that can be used to achieve significant savings and other benefits. A traditional procurement process includes activities and process steps such as:

- search for goods
- fill in paper request
- send to buyer
- into buyer's in-tray
- buyer enters order number
- buyer authorises order
- buyer prints order
- order copied to supplier and goods-in
- delivery from supplier
- order copy to accounts
- three-way invoice match
- cheque payment.

This process can be characterised by a long cycle time and by many process steps that all lead to a slow, expensive flow of activities open to errors. Hammer (2001, p. 84) says about traditional procurement processes:

> It's the mirror image of your supplier's order-fulfillment process, with many of the same tasks and information requirements. When your purchasing agent fills out a requisition form, for instance, she is performing essentially the same work that the supplier's order entry clerk performs when he takes the order. Yet there's probably little or no coordination between the two processes.

Information systems can be used to reduce the number of steps and to reduce the number of people involved (e-procurement is the electronic integration and management of all procurement activities). An important driver for e-procurement is of course cost reduction; in many cases the cost of ordering exceed the value of the products purchased. Direct cost reductions are achieved through efficiencies in the process that may result in less staff time spent in searching and ordering but also in reduction of inventory costs by lower cycle times. Other advantages include: improved budget control, quality improvement and elimination of errors, increased buyer productivity (now they can concentrate on more strategic issues), lower prices through company-wide standardisation and control and better management information (Turban et al. 2000).

A typical e-procurement process may include the following process steps:

- search for goods
- order on the Internet
- deliver from supplier
- receive invoice
- cheque payment.

These steps can be automated, however, if company systems are integrated with supplier systems.

There are a number of organisational risks and impacts related to e-procurement. One issue is that the integration of company systems with those of suppliers demands trust and a long-term partnership with the supplier. Building up such a relationship may take years and will not always be perceived as desirable, since system integration with a supplier may lead to dependency.

Another internal issue is that e-procurement has huge implications for the procurement staff; it may for instance lead to redundancies or redeployment. When e-procurement process is operational, procurement staff have to focus on more strategic activities, such as contract management. An implication for other employees is that they may all get authorisations for procurement, which may lead to a dispersion of tasks and responsibilities. It may also create a number of complicated security issues, since many people become involved in this process.

MIS in practice e-procurement at IBM

An IBM purchasing manager reported about the company's e-procurement system:

[Our Internet procurement system] has eliminated a lot of transactional activity – raising orders, printing orders, fax, paper trails all over. Previously most suppliers were receiving purchase orders by paper. They would then look at what we wanted, write that on the paper and send it back to us, and we would key it into our system – a lot of manual activity. That is now completely automated – an order goes electronically to the supplier ... they send back an electronic message saying they can deliver. We receive the goods into the system, and there is a match between the physical and the electronic, which triggers the payment process.

Source: Personal communication.

Summary

- Implementing an ERP system is an example of IS-based process change because it integrates information resources and redesign processes. Managers should think carefully about which modules of

ERP will be implemented, given the strengths and limitations of such systems.

- Doing business over the Internet by electronic commerce is another example of (inter-organisational) process change. Implementing such a change has huge implications and demands a new process design.

- The Internet can also be used to enable electronic procurement. This may lead to ongoing improvements in the buying process. The organisational issues are associated with dependency on suppliers, the reorganisation of the procurement function and the involvement of other members of the organisation with the e-procurement process.

Managing process innovation

Many authors on process innovation emphasise the radical organisational change with information technology. They suggest a strong reduction of process steps and lead times by making fewer people responsible for the process. Critics argue that this approach is too narrow and fails to address important issues, particularly those concerning organisational change and politics. Process innovation projects usually have wide-consequences (Willcocks and Smith, 1995):

- work units change, from functional departments to process teams

- jobs change, from simple tasks to multi-dimensional work

- people's roles change, from controlled to empowered

- focus of performance shifts, from activity to results

- values change, from protective to productive.

If such changes are not managed carefully and consciously, problems may arise, going from indifference and passivity to stronger forms of resistance. A potential danger is that the focus of the project team is on the development or adaptation of the IS behind the process change and the design mechanics of the new process. Human issues can easily be ignored, which may lead to problems during implementation and operations.

The chapter case interview below with one of the directors of the Redon tax administration unit provides an illustration of the view of a manager on process innovation. The interview suggests that business process change is a challenging activity – mainly because of the need to manage the interactions between the various organisational elements. Markus (1994) researched the organisational issues that surround process innovation by interviewing more than 50 management consultants. The objective was to identify which process innovation projects have a good chance of succeeding. From the interviews various positive and negative starting points arose. These are summarised in Table 13.3.

Table 13.3   Positive and negative starting points for process change

Positive starting point for process innovation	Negative starting point for process innovation
Senior management support	No sponsor or wrong sponsor
Realistic expectations	Technical focus
Independent and cooperative staff	Low-level support
Project directed to growth and development rather than cost reduction and savings	Too many changes at the same time
Joint vision and mission	Project leader without authority
Continuing communications	Poor financial conditions
Full-time project team with competent members	Fear and lack of optimism
Resources	Animosity to IT

Source: Markus (1994)

Redon: Interview with a director

Why did you decide to reorganise the processes of your administration?
When I started as a director in this unit, I was confronted with an organisation which received an enormous amount of written objections to tax assessments (more than 15 per cent of all the assessments resulted in a formal objection). Many of these objections were the result of mistakes on our side. Another problem was that we did not differentiate between types of customers: big companies were treated in the same way as individuals. Such a working procedure results in annoyances and other problems.

Can you describe your ideals with respect to your organisation?
My ideal is a customer-directed and efficient organisation. Customers have to be treated in an appropriate way; there are big companies, small companies, different kinds of individuals (e.g. prosperous people, students, immigrants) and they all need to be treated suitably. Employees have to manage themselves and take responsibility for their work and their errors. They have to deal with taxpayers and cooperate proactively with colleagues.

Customer-focus in a tax administration?
Yes. Our starting point is compliance: this is a strategy where those subject to tax (customers) are treated in a just and careful way in order to create a relationship beneficial to the customers as well as to us. By treating customers well, they become more cooperative in paying tax.

How can you realise customer focus?
We try to shorten lead times, to increase accessibility by phone, to set up websites, to have account managers and to create help-desks to assist people with their forms. People are more willing to pay taxes (though as little as legally possible) when we treat them in a friendly and efficient way.

Is this only a matter of culture?
No, it is not only a matter of culture. The structure of the organisation, the working processes and the automated systems also have to contribute to such a change. An integrated approach is needed; this is much more important than simply changing cultural aspects, parts of the structure or the IT system. The complexity of such a change is that organisational issues, human issues and technological issues all play an important role. To manage these aspects similarly makes such change rather difficult, but also challenging.

So this is a far-reaching renovation?
Yes, it can be compared with a house. When the circumstances and the needs of the residents change they have to renovate the house. In many cases, an outsider sees the need before the residents. They live there and have dealt with the problems for years. Translate this to an organisation: from time to time it is necessary to change the functions and processes to make the organisation more customer-directed. This is because the needs of the customers change or because there are new possibilities (for example IS) or organising things in more effective ways.

Markus concludes that if there are more negative than positive starting points, it is better to improve these conditions rather than to start IT-enabled process innovation. The chapter case shows how the context of change influences the outcome.

Redon: continued

The account of the tax administration of Redon shows how some units of the municipality are changing their processes, using IS and the Internet to make it possible. Some are now well advanced in using the Internet to improve their services – the tax administration is one. Other departments only have a 'brochure ware' website or no website at all. The municipality lacks an overall vision of how to transform and use IT including the Internet to become more efficient and more customer-focused.

The home page of Redon's website makes policy documents and reports available and provides information and links to department websites. It is also possible to submit specific questions, e.g. about policies and procedures, by the Internet, but the response is slow because there is no clear procedure on how to deal with them. This often leads to complaints.

Another possible problem for Redon is that many employees have a quite bureaucratic department-centred attitude and find it difficult to collaborate effectively with other departments and to perceive the services from the local residents' point of view.

Summary

- Process design projects are broad projects where different dimensions demand explicit attention. These dimensions include: IS, politics, people and financial resources.

- The human side especially demands a lot of attention because of the implications it may have for people: their work units and their jobs may change.

- This implies that process design projects need to take account of the challenging task of managing not only the technical aspects but also the interactions between the many organisational elements.

Conclusions

In this chapter we have outlined the idea of process innovation and how it is being enabled by developments in computer-based information systems. Some advocates of process redesign take a mechanistic approach: they perceive the design of a process as an engineering task rather than as a socio-technical problem. Such a focus on information technology and the mechanics of the process design, while important, can easily be overemphasised. The cases and other material presented in this chapter show that real organisational innovations involve people, jobs, skills and structures as well as the latest software.

The central theme of this chapter has been interaction. This was introduced at the start, showing the mutual interaction between IS and process innovation. We then extended it to include people's interaction with both of the other elements, and later brought in wider issues of strategy and culture. The evidence is clear: effective use of information systems to innovate processes depends on managing a range of interactions; it is not a narrow technical project.

Many process innovators believe that such projects must be conducted from the top down, but this opinion can be challenged. The detailed understanding of process design and customers often resides with the people who do the work. In many cases resistance to new work designs has occurred when people do not want their jobs defined by someone else. There is growing empirical support for the view that changes with more of a bottom-up character may be more successful, besides which such major changes will have a strong political element as vested interests try to shape the direction of the project.

A related issue is whether process change should be conducted as a radical one-off approach or a continuous and incremental activity. How managers resolve this dilemma will depend on factors such as the urgency of the problem and the readiness of the organisation for radical change. Some will stress the urgency of pressures from the market, while others will want to take time to ensure the commitment and support of influential stakeholders. Whichever approach is taken, those implementing it will confront some challenges – not dissimilar from those experienced by the managers in the tax administration.

References

Chaffey, D. (2002) *E-Business and E-Commerce Management*, Financial Times/Prentice Hall, Harlow.

Davenport, T.H. (1993) *Process Innovation: reengineering work through information technology*, Harvard Business School Press, Boston, Mass.

Davenport, T.H. (1998) Putting the enterprise into the enterprise system. *Harvard Business Review*, 76, 4, 121–132.

Galliers, R.D. and Baets, W.R.J. (1997) *Information Technology and Organizational Transformation: innovation for the 21st century organization*, Wiley, Chichester.

Goldratt, E.M. and Cox, J. (1992) *The Goal: a process of ongoing improvement*, Gower, Aldershot.

Grover, V. and Malhotra, J.K. (1997) Business process reengineering: a tutorial on the concept, evolution, method, technology and application. *Journal of Operations Management*, 15, 3, 193–213.

Hammer, M. (1990) Reengineering work: don't automate, obliterate. *Harvard Business Review*, 68, 4, 104–128.

Hammer, M. (2001) The superefficient company. *Harvard Business Review*, 79, 9, 82–91.

Kim, Y.G. (1995) Process modelling for BPR: event process chain approach. *Proceedings of the 16ᵗʰ International Conference on Information Systems*, NorthHolland, Amsterdam.

Laudon, K.C. and Laudon, J.P. (2004) *Management Information Systems: organization and technology in the networked enterprise*, Prentice Hall, Englewood Cliffs, NJ.

Lockamy, A. and Smith, W.I. (1997) A strategic alignment approach for effective business process reengineering: linking strategy, processes and customers for competitive advantage. *International Journal of Production Economics*, 50, 2/3, 141–153.

Markus, M.L. (1994) Preconditions for BPR success. *Information Systems Management*, 11, 2, 7–14.

Peppard, J. and Rowland, P. (1995) *The Essence of Business Process Reengineering*, Prentice Hall, Englewood Cliffs, NJ.

Sauer, C. and Yetton, P. (1997) *Steps to the Future: fresh thinking on the management of IT-based organizational transformation*, Jossey-Bass, San Francisco.

Teng, J.T.C., Grover, V. and Fiedler, K.D. (1994) Business process reengineering: charting a strategic path for the information age. *California Management Review*, 36, 3, Spring, 9–31.

Turban, E., Lee, J., Chung, H. (2000) *Electronic Commerce: a managerial perspective*, Prentice Hall, Upper Saddle River, NJ.

Willcocks, L. and Smith, G. (1995) IT enabled business process reengineering: organizational and human resource dimension. *Strategic Information Systems*, 4, 3, 279–301.

Source: Adapted from Boddy, D., Boonstra, A. and Kennedy, G. (2008) *Managing Information Systems: strategy and organisation*, Financial Times/Prentice Hall.

Chapter 14

Frameworks for e-business

Jennifer Rowley

Introduction

Most introductions to e-business open with a history of the growth of the Internet, and predictions for the growth of e-commerce and e-business. Even historical statistics are difficult to interpret, and predictions communicate even less about the real impact that e-business is likely to have on the world in which we live. For those who have a predilection for such statistics, some websites that give up-to-date versions of these figures are listed at the end of this chapter.

Nevertheless, there is no denying that there is considerable excitement and media interest around the concept of e-business (or cybermarketing), e-commerce, online communities, v-business, World Wide Web marketing (or Internet business). Even the terms used to describe the e-business revolution inject a sense of novelty and excitement. Add to this media enthusiasm for reporting new initiatives in e-business, the extent of promotion of e-business ventures through all media, and the concern of governments about the potential impact of the Internet on societies and economies, there can be no doubt about the level of interest in e-business. Yet, how can a few messages on a small screen in our homes or offices have any real impact on our lives and the way in which we do business? After all, we can choose to use the PC, we choose what websites we visit and what Internet service we use. It would appear that the Internet, accessed through PCs, mobile technologies, kiosks and other routes is an engaging communication channel that many of us cannot resist.

Some definitions

The terms e-business and e-commerce are both used in this book and, whilst they are closely related concepts, the distinction is important.

e-commerce is doing business electronically across the extended enterprise. It covers any form of business or administrative transaction or information exchange that is executed using any information and communications technology. Morath (2000) views e-commerce as often taking a narrow perspective limited to specific initiatives, such as sales via the Internet, electronic procurement, or electronic payment.

e-business is a wider concept that embraces all aspects of the use of information technology in business. It includes not only buying and selling, but also servicing customers and collaborating with business partners, and often involves integration across business processes and communication within the organisation.

The model proposed in Table 14.1 is essentially a model for e-commerce in that it focuses on the 'transaction' or service interface with the customer. e-business embraces such interfaces, but it is also concerned with business processes that are necessary to support the promise that lies behind the interface. Once organisations enter into the final two stages of the model, they can no longer treat Internet commerce as a separate entity, and need to develop integrated solutions to the use of information technologies across the business. e-commerce continues to be important at the customer interface, but without the more pervasive approach inherent in the concept of e-business it will have limited success.

Developing e-commerce

Table 14.1 proposes a four-stage model of the development of e-commerce that underpins the structure and approach of the remainder of this chapter. Early developments are in the first stage, Contact. In this mode the Internet is simply an additional channel through which marketing communication can be delivered. Typically such sites display basic company and possibly product information; they often extend to only a few pages. Such sites are described as '**brochureware**', since they are essentially an electronic version of a publicity brochure. All organisations need some visibility in e-space, but not all organisations need to progress to the other three stages. In further development of Internet activities, organisations need to understand the types of relationships that they are seeking to establish with customers and partners, and to develop models that match those objectives.

Stage 2, Interact, is concerned with enhanced information exchange with customers and trading partners. Web pages will provide links to facilitate communication and, on the basis of that communication, it may be possible to start to target marketing efforts. Some sites in this category may run to hundreds of thousands of pages, and interaction may take the form of searching for information within the website, using search engines and other search tools.

In Stage 3, Transact, the functionality that offers order placement and other transactions is made available. Many e-shopping applications are currently in this stage of development. Financial service institutions are focusing on the opportunity to execute online transactions, but because trust and confidentiality are important prerequisites in successful financial services businesses, they need to consider moving to Stage 4 applications.

In Stage 4 two-way relationships are established, with full integration of Internet capability into the business. In consumer markets this may mean allowing consumers access to organisational databases that show stock level, order tracking, prices and discounting schemes, and other product details. In an organisation-to-organisation relationship suppliers and other partners may have access to significant elements of the organisation's databases, including valuable product and customer-profile information, through the organisation's extranets. All such information can be regarded as marketing communication, since perceptions and relationships will be influenced by:

• which information a partner is permitted to access, and

• what that information communicates about the company (which may include bad news as well as good).

Table 14.1   Stages of e-commerce service development

Stage	Characteristics	Website functionality
1 Contact	Promote corporate image Publish corporate information Offer contact information	Content
2 Interact	Embed information exchange Targeted marketing effort	Communication
3 Transact	Online transactions Catalogue order/fulfilment Interaction with trading partners	Commerce
4 Relate	Two-way customer relationships Full integration of Internet capability into the business Service interface integration with delivery and other business operations	Community

Careful attention needs to be given to the development of appropriate knowledge access, security, privacy and confidentiality policies and their implementation, because these all communicate something about the nature of the organisation's relationship with its customers and suppliers. Access to organisational information raises issues of trust and commitment. The challenge is, through these arrangements, to demonstrate the organisation's commitment to the relationship, to inculcate trust in the partner and, where possible, to engage customers as active co-producers.

Figure 14.1 shows the information that is exchanged as part of a two-way relationship based on an order transaction. Some of these processes, such as those that generate order-confirmation notification (probably by e-mail) and order-tracking information can be automatic. State-of-the-art systems software allows organisations to configure this interaction in terms of language, currency, stages of interaction (such as whether automatic order confirmation is offered or whether a credit limit is checked) and product details shown (such as stock levels).

Business	Customer
Product/catalogue details	
Price details	
Business process details	
Brand values and messages	
	Order details
	Customer details
	Bill to and ship to address
	Order placement confirmation

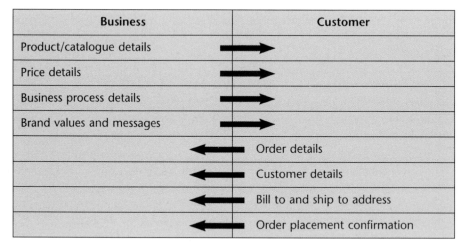

Figure 14.1   Stage 4 of e-commerce service development: integration of internet capability

The final column in Table 14.1 identifies the focus of website functionality associated with each stage of development. Content, communication, commerce, and community are widely cited as the essential prerequisites of a successful website. As businesses develop their websites through the stages they add functionality, starting with content and adding communication, commerce and, finally, community. In addition, as the website functionality increases and the extent of engagement in e-business evolves towards the Relate stage, content and communication tools are likely to become more sophisticated.

The model is a generalisation and the order of these four stages of development may vary depending on the type of company. Quelch and Klein (1996), for example, distinguish between existing major companies and Internet start-up companies. They propose that Internet start-ups are likely to introduce transaction facilities earlier than existing companies, because this is the essence of their revenue stream. Existing companies venturing into Internet activity have other established revenue streams and can afford to gain experience of the e-business environment through promotional activities, and using a website to communicate with, and offer customer service to, customers prior to launching a transaction-based service.

Organisations will have a variety of different types of engagement with Internet marketing and e-business. This will impact upon their approach to website design, customer relationships, customer service, community and business strategy. In addition the marketplace in which the business operates (consumer or business) and the role that the organisation plays in that marketplace will influence priorities.

Drivers for e-business

The media are inclined to colourful tales of the impact that e-business will have on traditional marketplaces and retailers. Dot.com companies such as Amazon and PlanetRX are cited as the upstarts that are models for businesses that will totally undermine retailing through existing channels, in surprisingly short periods of time. Such stories would encourage the more insecure managers to look over their shoulders for e-business-based competitors and drive them to contemplate how they might steal the march on any potential competitors and forge ahead in e-business. Others, including customers, managers and academics, have been immunised against media hype by long exposure and are sceptical that e-business can really have any significant impact on their life or their business. Customers ask: 'Is it secure?', 'Is it really more convenient?' and 'Is it really cheaper?'. Business sceptics prefer to believe that their customers could not possibly desert them for an arid and demanding e-business environment. The reality is that e-business will affect businesses on many different levels. e-business is challenging existing business models and is creating a climate in which established consumer behaviour, attitudes and relationships may all be subject to re-evaluation and change. Change will probably be slower than the enthusiasts would like us to believe, and its rate and nature will be different in different organisational and business sectors. e-business offers an opportunity to rethink a whole range of assumptions about how businesses operate, how they relate to their customers and suppliers, and their role and positioning in the wider marketplace.

This section summarises some of the oft-quoted drivers for e-business. These can be divided into threats and opportunities. The threats mostly arise from the need to respond to change and to remember that if an organisation does not rise to the challenge then 'the competition is only a click away'. Opportunities arise from the redefining of traditional business models, business sectors and customer loyalties.

Threats

1 *Increasing customer expectations about choice*, especially in relation to a wide product range, the opportunity to undertake comparison shopping, and 24-hour availability.

2 *Pressure on product margins*. In markets which already have pressure on product margins, additional pressures will arise from an additional channel of delivery.

3 *Barriers to entry are minimal*. It takes only a relatively short period of time to implement Web presence and thereby to launch a new e-business. This is likely to lead to increased and different competition, with different business models.

4 *Size does not matter and, indeed*, small to medium-sized enterprises may be more flexible and able to adapt.

5 *Disintermediation* may lead to the removal of retailers and closer direct relationships between manufacturers and customers in some sectors. (Peterson, 1997)

Opportunities

1 *The opportunity to choose a business model*. Some organisations – such as Prudential Assurance with Egg and the Co-operative Bank with Smile – have launched separate Internet businesses, and have taken the opportunity to establish a new brand which might be more representative of their vision for the future of the business, than stale long-standing brands. For other organisations, the marketing communication may be undifferentiated between delivery channels, but differentiation may take place at the operations level. For example, whilst Tesco has chosen to deliver from existing stores, Sainsbury's and Asda have differentiated their e-commerce delivery activities by building dedicated picking centres from which deliveries will be made.

2   *Redefinition of business relationships*. For example, Compaq, in coming to an agreement with the developers of the Millennium Dome for e-ticketing facilities, did not simply offer a transaction based on the provision and maintenance of a computing capability, but rather opted to be paid on the basis of ticket receipts. This means that they have a continuing relationship with their customer and, perhaps more significantly, they share the risk.

3   *Cost savings on transactions can be considerable*, because the customer takes responsibility for a large element of the service transaction. Optimum cost savings will only be achieved if the customer interface, and business processes are fully integrated.

4   *e-commerce also presents an opportunity to redefine the relationship with customers*. Routine service transactions are under the customer's control. The customer is encouraged to learn the script (for example, the process associated with placing an order); this learning increases the barriers to switching. It is supported by Frequently Asked Questions menus (FAQs). Human service agents are engaged to provide a higher level of expertise, and to give tailored customer care when required, from a call centre setting (Dawes and Rowley, 1998).

5   *Access to new global markets* (Peterson, 1997). Although, especially in niche markets, access to such global markets has provided welcome opportunities for small businesses, entering global markets also poses its challenges. There is a need to deal with issues of culture (styles of business, delivery options expected by customers), currency and delivery.

6   *Customer knowledge*. As discussed above, e-commerce transactions embed the collection of customer contact data. Customers are known by name and various addresses. It is also possible to profile customers by tracking what they order. Banks, in particular, are in a strong position to collect such transaction data. This data can form the basis of targeted marketing strategies, more effective segmentation, and targeted marketing spend. Ultimately, provided customers do not resent the manipulation and intrusion that they might perceive to be implied through such an approach, there is the potential for increased levels of customer loyalty and benefits.

Table 14.2   Features of e-commerce

Key feature	Implication
Availability	24/7 and immediate access
Ubiquity	It can be assumed that all organisations and customers will soon have Internet access
Global	Leaving delivery on one side, our mental map of near and far will radically change
Local	Internet is also a good medium to reinforce local physical presence and local person-to-person business relationships
Digitisation	Business will increasingly be happening in information space. This will lead to: • Convergence of telecommunications, broadcasting and other information industries • Different economic laws operating, with increasing rather than decreasing returns to scale
Multimedia	Provides new opportunities for information provision during buying and selling and provides new opportunities in consultancy, design and entertainment
Interactivity	An opportunity to improve customer service at an affordable price
One-to-one	Using data processing and customer profiling, one-to-one marketing is a natural consequence of doing business on the Internet. It may also be a necessity to overcome the anonymity of Internet business relationships
Network effects and network externalities	Low cost and fast growth in the number of relationships enable business models that require a significant number of parties in the network and whose benefits increase faster with a growing number of parties – that is, these business models exhibit network effects and/or network externalities
Integration	The value of combined information across steps of the value chain is more than the sum of its parts. The Internet now provides at least part of the technology for value-chain functional and information integration. Advanced electronic commerce companies show how to exploit the added value

Source: Based on Timmers (1999)

Consumer and organisational e-marketplaces

It is important to understand that whilst there may be some characteristics of e-commerce and e-business that impact across any different sectors, there are also significant differences between organisational and consumer markets, and the impact of e-business on specific market sectors. In organisational markets there is a history of e-business based on EDI. The difference between electronic data interchange (EDI) and the Web is the ubiquitous platform that removes the technological constraints that tied organisations to a set of specified suppliers. In organisational contexts in particular, e-business also embraces knowledge management within the organisation in support of effective business processes, and learning. Table 14.3 summarises some of the key differences between organisational and consumer e-commerce. In organisational markets there are typically fewer, but more high-value, customers, and there are established relationships with those customers.

In consumer markets the impact and penetration of e-business varies between sectors. In particular, the relative sources of competitive advantage of e-business, as compared with traditional retailing, are unique to specific sectors. So, for example, in gambling, the source of competitive advantage was initially associated with the avoidance of UK gambling taxes, which leads to larger winnings and larger profits. For air-travel booking, lower transaction costs have been passed on to customers in the form of lower fares. For banks, lower transaction costs strengthen the banks' competitive position by allowing them to offer higher interest rates for investors. Supermarkets, on the other hand, are seeking differentiation on the basis of a more personalised service and the convenience of remote ordering and home delivery, and expect to be able to charge customers for this service.

Table 14.3   Comparing organisational and consumer markets

Organisational markets	Consumer markets
Fewer customers and known customers	Lots of customers necessary for success
Fewer transactions	Large number of transactions
Each transaction of larger value	Relatively low-value transactions
Net worth of key customers is high	Cannot predict growth rate
Regular transactions	Less regular transactions with individual customers
Credit rating known	Credit rating often not known

Table 14.4 is one list of the most-visited e-commerce sites. The ranking is not important, and has probably changed since the data was compiled, but it does give a view of the kinds of activities that consumers are performing online, and some of the significant online brands. Note that the list of sites is quite different for the different countries listed, although the activities are comparable. Table 14.5 gives examples of a few e-marketplaces and portals for B2B e-commerce.

Table 14.4   Most-visited e-commerce sites

United Kingdom	Germany	United States
Streetsonline.co.uk *Music, literature*	Amazon.de *Music, literature*	Amazon.com *Music, literature*
Amazon.co.uk *Music, literature*	Comdirect.de *Broking, finance*	Priceline.com *Marketplace*
Egg.com *Banking, mortgage, insurance*	Bahn.de *Transport*	Disney.com *Entertainment*
Lastminute.com *Travel and tourism*	t-versand.de *Telecommunication*	Shopnow.com *Mall*
Amazon.com *Music, literature*	Primus-online.de *Mall*	Webshots.com *Photography*
Jungle.com *Computer hardware*	Bol.de *Music, literature*	Pch.com *Mall*
Barclays.co.uk *Banking, mortgage, insurance*	Consors.de *Broking, finance*	Expedia.com *Travel and tourism*
Tesco.co.uk *Supermarket*	Adobe.de *Software*	Barnesandnoble.com *Music, literature*
Ugo.com *Games*	Dig-online.de *Computer hardware*	Nestcard.com *Banking, mortgage, insurance*
Expedia.com *Travel and tourism*	Deutsche-bank-24.de *Banking, mortgage, insurance*	Travelocity.com *Travel and tourism*

Source: Based on Connectis (November 2000), pp. 6–7

Table 14.5 B2B e-marketplaces and portals

www.paperx.com	PaperX brings together Europe's paper manufacturers, merchants, publishers and printers. Buyers respond to offers posted on the site by sellers. The London-based B2B marketplace checks that the traders are authorised to buy and sell paper, and handles payment and credit verification. Sellers are charged a transaction fee
www.buyingpower.com	Buyingpower is an independent Irish energy broker that targets small and medium-sized enterprises in the UK. Businesses register with the site and submit requirements for gas and electricity. The site pools businesses from the same region into 'powergroups' and invites suppliers to bid for their energy requirements. The supplier with the lowest bid wins
www.bizdirect.pt	Bizdirect is aimed at small and medium-sized businesses wishing to buy or sell office equipment, consumables and services. The site is a joint venture between Sonae, a Portuguese telecommunications and Internet services provider, Aitec, a Portuguese Internet business accelerator, and Banco Portugues de Investimento, the Portuguese bank
www.constructeo.com	Constructeo is an Internet portal launched by French construction company Vinci-GTM in partnership with purchasing specialists Masai and Eyrolles. Site features include industry news, online catalogues, and e-procurement services, financial market trends and technical information. The site also hosts extranets or private networks for sharing correspondence, inspection certificates, blueprints and engineering documents
www.comdaq.net	Comdaq is a London-based commodities exchange for trading sugar, coffee and cocoa. Because of price fluctuations, only Category A members (that is, established producers and consumers) are allowed to take part in instant trade. Category B members must contract with each other after trading to reconfirm transactions

New channel?

The sceptics in both business and academia declare that the Internet is 'just another channel' or, in other words, just another way of doing business. They assert that customer benefits and the value of the customer to the business remain the platforms for successful business. Customer satisfaction will continue to derive from quality services and products and these can only be created through effective partnerships and alliances, and an understanding and leverage of the business processes inherent in specific industries.

May (2000) identifies two uses of the word **channel**, and suggests that e-commerce is subtly blending these together. These two uses emerge from different prior professional and academic groups, each of which has previously been able to own and define the concept for its own purposes. Commerce is forcing a reconsideration of such fundamental concepts. May suggests that:

- In the *media world*, a channel is a branded carrier of entertainment or information to an audience; the purpose of the channel is to send content to an audience.

- In the *marketing world*, channel means any permanent route to a group of customers. Channels are conduits for a company's products and services with consuming populations fitted at their outlets.

In the traditional media world there is a differentiation between those who provide primary content for the channel (such as television) and those who use it to send commercial messages. For marketers, content generates audiences for commercial messages and can help to deliver suitable demographics. Authors and producers tend to regard advertising as a layer superimposed on the chief purpose of the channel in order to contribute to commercial viability. Marketers also deal with various channels that are purely commercial in orientation, such as publicity and mail-order catalogues.

The website must combine a mix of these functions. It must be a route to a market, but at the same time it is an information and entertainment medium. The Web is a place where stories are told, dialogues are initiated and information is discovered. Further, it is largely text-based and users are readers and often writers. The development of the Web as a channel requires an understanding of the way in which information, entertainment and commerce can be melded together.

In using the Web to communicate, consumer response to business offerings will be crucial. Consumers will place themselves along a spectrum, which at one end involves the engagement and fostering of intimate relationships with a business over a period of time and at the other end involves 'rational decision-making behaviour' in which they will seek the best economic value from each individual transaction. Tools exist to support either of these approaches. Table 14.6 summarises some of the characteristics of each of these opposing poles. Ultimately customers in both organisational and consumer markets will decide where they sit on this spectrum, in respect of the different products and services that they acquire. For some products, customers will tend to cluster at one or the other end of the spectrum, but for others the customer group will be more widely spread through the spectrum.

Table 14.6   Consumer economic behaviour

Loyal customer relationships	Customers pursue best value
More likely in B2B, although improved information on alternative trading partners may undermine existing relationships	More likely in B2C, but search cost might outweigh perceived benefits and lead to inertia and apparent loyalty
Businesses need to understand the unique glue for relationships in their sector	Search tools need to be efficient and effective to encourage evaluation and comparison of offerings
Important for transactions in which trust and confidence are factors	Suitable for commodity marketplaces
Customisation based on customer profiles gathered over the period of a relationship	Standard product, offered at a competitive price. Auctions and shopping agents are tools that support identification and selection of product for purchase
Community encourages tighter identification with the business and the customers that form its community	Transaction-focused with little development or learning and customer satisfaction based on individual transactions
Differentiation on the basis of relationship	Cost leadership

E-business models

There has been much discussion of new business models for the digital economy. Timmers (1999) defines a business model thus:

> An architecture for product, service and information flows, including a description of the various business actors and their roles, a description of the potential benefits for the various business actors, and a description of the sources of revenue.

Embracing both consumer and business marketplaces and covering a wide range of business sectors, there is a wide range of different models available to e-businesses. Most of the business models that exist in other business contexts are mirrored in the e-business context. However, the digital environment is likely to have two effects:

- Fundamental impact on the significance, role in the marketplace and operation of a given business model. It may also impact on the success of a specific business model for a business, but the overall range of business models remains relatively stable. For example, there remains a role for financial service intermediaries or advisers, but the execution of this role may be informed by a much more powerful knowledge base, and customisation of communication between the adviser and the customer may be possible on a much larger scale than previously.

- Businesses may need continually to re-evaluate the business model that is most effective for them, and to consider some of the remodelled approaches presented by the Web, such as portalling, auctions, and communities.

Since the e-marketplace is so diverse it is challenging to categorise the business models available, and there are many approaches to the categorisation of business models on the Internet. Table 14.7 shows one such model proposed by Hanson (2000). Hanson views business models from the perspective of the benefits to be accrued to the business. He embraces the category of revenue-generating business models, discussed by May (2000) (as summarised in Table 14.8), and also recognises the benefits to be derived from business improvement. These arise from enhancement to existing brands and products and services, increases in efficiency and increases in effectiveness, particularly in relation to communication with suppliers, dealers and retailers, and customers. To experience the benefits in this second category a business does not need to engage in e-commerce. Many of these benefits are achieved through a holistic approach to the penetration of e-business through the organisation. In addition, some of these benefits may be particularly appropriate to public-sector organisations, in which enhanced service and information provision is often a more important performance indicator than success with revenue generation.

Table 14.7   Web business benefits

Improvement-based business models	Revenue-based business models
Enhancement, including brand building, category building and quality *Efficiency* – cost reduction *Effectiveness* – dealer support, supplier support, information collection	*Provider pays* – sponsorship, alliance, advertising, prospect fees, sales commissions *User pays* – product sales, per use (for information and access services), subscriptions, bundle sales

Source: Based on Hanson (2000)

Table 14.8 Revenue-generating business models

Revenue-generating model	Description
Additive channel	Sell more of our traditional lines to new markets
New offer channel	Invent a new product or service for the e-commerce channel
Subscription	Charge for access to content
Advertising	Sell advertising space on the site
Sponsorship	Apply a brand to a content offering
Licensing	Restrict a channel to paying carriers
Portalling	Charge destinations for sending users there
Commission	Take a percentage on transactions effected through the channel
Tolling	Take a percentage on transactions effected through your mechanism

Source: Based on May (2000)

Table 14.9 offers an alternative categorisation of business models on the basis of the function or role played by businesses in the e-marketplace. This is useful in offering perspectives on the type of activity in this marketplace. It also identifies some of the business functions that are new, or at least have been significantly redefined in the e-marketplace. Most of these roles can be fulfilled by '**pure play** Internet business' or by existing businesses, which in the retailing sector are often described as '**bricks-and-mortar**' stores. E-commerce is associated with most of these options, but many roles can on occasion be performed with motives other than direct revenue generation. This second categorisation aims to emphasise the value added by the business to the marketplace, whereas categorisation on the basis of a revenue-generating model indicates how businesses can draw value or revenue from the marketplace. These are two complementary perspectives.

Table 14.9   Business function-based business models

Business model	Comment
Digital information delivery	Digital information can be easily customised and delivered without delay. Production and distribution have become much more tightly coupled. Businesses involved with the creation and distribution of music, electronic magazines, information and advice, e-books, video and radio have been significantly affected and face a real challenge in finding the most effective business model. Issues of intellectual property and control of copying are fundamental to continued business opportunities
e-service delivery	Concerned with the delivery of a service over the Internet. Typical sectors in this group include financial services, estate agency, banking, gambling, travel agency and theatre bookings. These are often information-based services, in which transactions are conducted and a record of those transactions maintained. In some cases the Internet just provides ticketing or contracting (for example, travel agency) and the actual service (flights and accommodation) is separated from the ticketing operation. Transactions are typically much cheaper than through traditional channels
Retailing	Retailing also embraces a service element, but the primary concern is the sale of a product or a service (but not its delivery). Typical industry sectors include toys, CDs and printed books, computer hardware, supermarkets, flowers and clothes. Retailers may have access to more geographically scattered markets and customers can compare offerings from several outlets
Intermediaries or aggregators	Intermediaries add value in the chain between the manufacturer and the consumer. Retailers are a special kind of intermediary. Others include third-party marketplaces (that support e-procurement), sourcing operations that provide information about business performance, portals, shopping malls, and cybermediaries
Infrastructure support providers	Infrastructure support providers are businesses that offer the hardware and software, and telecommunications platforms that underpin e-business. They include businesses such as Dell, Microsoft, IBM, many of the Internet service providers and telecommunication systems providers. This group stands to gain the most through growth in e-business. The more businesses participate and invest, the higher the revenues to this sector
Marketing communications agencies	Media and communications agencies have a major role to play in supporting business communication on the Internet, and about e-business offerings in other media. In addition to the traditional skills exercised by, for instance, advertising and promotions agencies, services are offered in website design, placement and design of banner advertisements, networking and registering with search engines

Chapter summary

This chapter has explored the nature of e-business and e-commerce from a variety of different angles. After encouraging reflection on definitions, the four-stage model of e-commerce development was introduced to emphasise that not all e-business activity involves transactions. Websites can also be used for content, communication, and community building. Drivers towards engagement in e-business can be seen in terms of threats and opportunities. Although it is possible to identify key features of the Internet that can provide businesses with market advantage, these features impact differentially in different sectors. One major distinction is between consumer and organisational, or business, marketplaces. In consumer marketplaces the concept of the Internet as a channel provides a useful perspective. Consumer economic behaviour is an important factor in business success. There are a number of different categorisations of business models. Together these emphasise the diversity of e-business ventures and activity.

References

Cram, C.M. (2001) *E-commerce Concepts*, Thomson Learning, Boston.

Dawes, J. and Rowley, J. (1998) Enhancing the customer experience: contributions from information technology. *Management Decision*, 36, 5, 350–357.

Financial Times, Connectis, November 2000, pp. 6–7.

Hanson, W. (2000) *Principles of Internet Marketing*, South-Western College Publishing, Cincinnati, Ohio.

May, P. (2000) *The Business of Ecommerce: from corporate strategy to technology*, Cambridge University Press, Cambridge.

Morath, P. (2000) *Success @ E-business*, McGraw-Hill, London.

Peterson, R.A. (1997) *Electronic Marketing and the Consumer*, Sage Publications, Thousand Oaks, London.

Quelch, J. and Klein, L. (1996) The Internet and international marketing. *Sloan Management Review*, Spring, 61–75.

Timmers, P. (1999) *Electronic Commerce: strategies and models for business-to-business trading*, Wiley, Chichester.

Web statistics

www.commerce.net/research/stats/stats.html (Internet demographics and e-commerce statistics)

www.webreference.com/internet/statistics.html

www.nua.ie/surveys/index.cgi (Internet surveys)

www.forrester.com (Forrester research)

Source: Adapted from Rowley, J. (2002) *E-Business Principles and Practice*, Palgrave.

Chapter 15

Assessing the costs and benefits of information systems

David Boddy, Albert Boonstra and Graham Kennedy

Evaluating IS at a utilities company

In 1981 a state-owned utilities company became a public limited company. It faced competition for the first time, and needed to become more efficient and responsive to customers. To support these changes the company invested heavily in IS throughout the 1980s and developed a more commercial management structure and culture. The value of managing information as a resource was identified for the first time. One consequence was that senior management challenged the business value and contribution of the company's IS.

The company has relied on evaluation processes that were cost-focused and used accounting frameworks. Managers identified many shortcomings in these including:

- they used only financial measures, especially costs
- the process treated projects in isolation from other current developments
- they ignored the human or organisational implications of projects
- the standards for formulating a business case varied between divisions
- there were no mechanisms to monitor and track the expected benefits.

Between 1989 and 1996 senior managers introduced evaluation techniques and processes that would address these problems. Methods were developed that included both the tangible and intangible benefits of IS proposals, and linked these to strategic objectives. Managers were made accountable for the delivery of the project objectives and responsible for delivering the benefits. The method for tracking benefits had to be included in any proposal. Tools were developed to assist managers to make realistic estimates of costs, benefits and risks, and to standardise the building of business cases.

These new evaluation processes had limited success. They moved the company in the direction of treating IS as an asset and promoted the notion of business/IS coordination. It helped the organisation to make a cultural shift from a public bureaucracy to an entrepreneurial business.

On the other hand, the new methods were not universally adopted and many stakeholder groups rejected their credibility. Even when the new methods were introduced they were often quickly superseded by yet more proposals. The problem was not one of ideas, but of application.

The chapter examines the problem which all companies face in using conventional, financially based IS project evaluation methods. It also examines various alternative techniques that some propose, which may be used to complement earlier methods.

Source: Based on Serafeimidis and Smithson (2000)

Introduction

People in organisations are rarely short of ideas and proposals that promise to enhance their information systems. Suppliers of hardware, software and communications systems vie with each other in promising that their systems will dramatically enhance performance, usually implying that doubters will become extinct. From business process re-engineering (BPR) to enterprise resource planning (ERP) to customer relationship management (CRM), the conveyor belt of three-letter acronyms presents managers with the challenge of deciding between competing IS investment proposals. They will probably base this choice on estimates of what the project is likely to cost and potential benefits to the organisation. This is simple to say, but difficult to put into practice.

The costs and benefits of IS projects are notoriously difficult to determine accurately:

- The cost of the Libra project to provide a national system for 385 courts in the UK had soared from £146m to £390m. Despite spending more than twice what they expected, the court service still did not have a working system (*Computer Weekly*, 11 November 2003).

- Over 50 per cent of systems projects fail to meet their expected rate of return due to fundamental flaws in predicting initial costs (*Financial Times IT*, July/August 1999, p. 10)

- A study of 365 executives revealed that as many as half of all IS projects exhibited significant cost and schedule overruns. In 1995, American companies spent an estimated $59 billion in cost overruns on such 'runaway' projects and another $81 billion on cancelled software projects (Johnson, 1995).

What went wrong with these projects? Why are the costs and benefits of information system projects so difficult to predict and control? This chapter reviews the most common reasons.

People have many motives for evaluating project proposals. It is a means of making objective decisions about competing proposals. It also helps to establish the value of information systems to the organisation and its growth (Farbey et al., 1993; Willcocks, 1994), and to rank alternatives (Hawgood and Land, 1988; Clemons, 1991) when formulating an IS strategy (Peters, 1994; Baker, 1995).

These are not the only uses. Hirschheim and Smithson (1987) pointed out that formally appraising a project proposal can serve as the first stage in a feedback function that assists organisational learning. It can also be part of the political game – a way of gaining legitimacy for a project which promoters desire for other reasons. If the culture of the organisation is one that values rationality, people need to support their proposals with apparently rational information, to give an appearance of playing by the rules (Gregory and Jackson, 1992; Powell, 1992; Farbey et al., 1995).

A radical view is that the issues are so complex that it is simply impossible to quantify the costs and benefits of IS projects accurately. Attempting to do so merely gives a comforting delusion of predictability in a fundamentally unpredictable world. Those who take this approach suggest that managers should instead focus on other criteria that demonstrate the overall value to the organisation (Bannister and Remenyi, 2000).

The chapter case traces the evolution of IS evaluation in an energy company as it moved from being a state-run business to one operating in a competitive market. It shows how managers developed alternative ways of assessing IS proposals and how others within the business reacted to these changes.

The chapter begins by outlining the elements of the formal-rational evaluation techniques. This appears simple – until we describe the problems with the approach. The following section details the wider considerations required when estimating the costs and benefits of information systems. Several alternative evaluation methods are described that take a more holistic approach to evaluation by incorporating human and organisational perspectives. Finally, we consider some organisation design issues that influence the effectiveness of IS projects. The aim is to identify the factors that influence the evaluation of information systems and what that means for those managing such projects.

Formal-rational methods for evaluating IS proposals

Traditional methods of project evaluation express the idea that the costs of an investment need to be related to the benefits which the investment brings. The costs tend to be incurred now, while the benefits come later. So the calculation needs to take account of the timing as well as the amounts of costs and benefits. The longer the delay in receiving the financial benefits, the greater the risk – which also needs to be included. Having made those calculations for the projects under consideration, managers then have an apparently rational basis upon which to decide between them. The more the estimated payback from the investment in a project appears to be, the more likely managers are to approve it. To illustrate the principles involved some common techniques for making these calculations are outlined below; Laudon and Laudon (2004) includes a much fuller discussion.

Payback period

This method calculates the number of years required before the cumulative financial returns equal the initial investment. If a company invests £10m, and expects to receive returns of £2m each year, the payback period is 5 years. A shorter payback period is more attractive as it means the investment is at risk for less time. The difficulty is that this ignores the fact that some investments will produce returns for longer periods than others.

Return on investment

This method calculates the return on the investment (ROI) by estimating the annual benefits to be achieved over the life of the project, and dividing that number by the amount invested. The annual benefit is calculated as the expected cost savings, additional revenue or whatever other benefits people expect. In the example above, the annual benefit of £2m would give an ROI of 20 per cent.

Discounted cash flow

Payback and ROI are simple and easy to understand. The difficulty is that neither takes account of the timing of the costs and benefits. A project which brings immediate benefits is worth more than one in which the benefits occur much later – but ROI calculations would not show this. Similarly a project with a short payback period would be preferred over one in which the benefits took longer to repay the investment. This ignores the fact that the second project, while slow to deliver, may produce benefits for a much longer period.

To overcome these problems, accountants have developed more sophisticated appraisal methods, which take account of the fact that money itself has a value. In the discounted cash flow (DCF) method, costs and returns are calculated over the expected whole life of the project, but then adjusted for the fact that distant returns are worth less than those that are received soon.

All methods depend on identifying and estimating the costs and benefits of the project, and the major elements of these are outlined in the next section.

The costs of information systems

People make different interpretations of the cost of IS. Those in the finance function tend to consider the purchase invoice. Those in the IS department will think more about support and maintenance costs. Users will look at training and business process costs. Organisations have great difficulty establishing the true cost of their information systems. Viewing IS as a product that can be purchased, plugged in and forgotten fails to capture the cost impact of all but the most simple stand-alone applications. The complex and costly systems being implemented today – many of which transcend organisational boundaries – require a rigorous approach to cost estimation.

One method is to calculate the total cost of ownership (TCO) of an information system, rather than the more obvious purchase price. TCO refers to the activity of taking a holistic view of costs over the lifetime of an investment, rather than viewing the purchase price in isolation. This is difficult but essential. Knowing exactly what a system costs to buy and run is the first step on the road to reducing those costs.

The manager preparing a project proposal needs a checklist of the likely costs. This needs to include both the costs of initial purchase and the longer-term costs of implementation, ownership and change. The following pages indicate costs that people may overlook, but which add to TCO.

Cost of purchase

For most information systems the acquisition cost consists mainly of hardware and software. These costs dominate formal-rational evaluation techniques but become a smaller part of the true costs as systems become more integrated into organisation processes.

Hardware costs

- The front end – user interfaces and peripherals (monitors, keyboards, control equipment, printers, scanners, etc.).
- The middleware – networking equipment (cabling, routers, switching devices, encryption devices and other communication linkages).
- The back end – processing equipment (servers, mainframes, desktops PC units, etc.).

When considering the total cost of a large project, it may also be worth separately considering any elements of the new system that could be described as infrastructure. These are elements that can be used by more than one system. For example, a national cable network for a bank's automated teller machines (ATMs) might also be used for a future communications system such as intranet or video-conferencing links. The desktop computers given to office workers for word-processing could also be used for e-mail. Logically the infrastructure costs would be shared across such other projects, and so affect relative costs and benefits.

Software costs

- Developments costs if built in-house, package and licence costs if bought-in
- Operating system software
- Application development tools
- Security and encryption packages
- Networking and communications software
- Systems management software
- Database and database management software
- Front-end packages such as office applications (e.g. word-processing, spread sheets), data analysis packages, presentational software, management information systems, browsers.

Implementation ownership and change

Information systems inevitably interact with other aspects of the organisation. This brings with it a variety of implementation costs which, while significant, are hard to measure. They include:

- Re-engineering current business processes
- Decommissioning and disposing of existing systems
- Staff communication and training
- Customer communication and training
- Costs of parallel running during the rollout period
- Error correction and compensation for quality 'dip' during initial use of the new system.

Those proposing and approving projects frequently ignore or underestimate these costs. Doing so puts an extra burden on staff during implementation – which adds yet further cost elements.

Having purchased and implemented a new system, managers must understand the cost of maintaining and supporting it throughout its active life cycle. Costs of ownership will include.

- **Support**: Help-desk functions – user manuals, retraining staff.
- **Disaster recovery**: Duplication of facilities at alternative sites to ensure continuity of operation in the event of major problems at the main site.
- **Staff**: Recruiting development staff, training developers, maintainers and users.
- **Maintenance**: Hardware and software incur costs of minor enhancements, bug-fixes and requests for change. Is the product high-quality/low-maintenance, or low-quality/high-maintenance?

Availability and cost of spare parts? For how long? Availability and cost of suitably skilled technicians and help-desk staff?

- **Obsolescence**: Does the product comply with an industry standard with an established history and foreseeable life? If not, the product may soon be impossible to maintain or upgrade.

- **Upgrade**: Both hardware and software are likely to need upgrading – to meet new communication standards, regulatory changes, new market requirements, expanded applications or new processes. Having bought a particular software package, it is hard to avoid paying for successive upgrades. This in turn may require additional hardware capacity.

In times when markets, technologies and regulatory requirements change rapidly change itself becomes a major, if rarely considered, cost category. How rapidly will the IS department be able to adapt the information system to changes that were impossible to forecast when it was designed? Some points to consider are:

- Interoperability of hardware: Can the proposed hardware platform operate with other platforms, operating systems, networks, peripheral equipment? Flexibility in this area allows future merging of systems, changes of operating platform, software applications, etc.

- Openness of software: Can the software be easily and cheaply modified, or linked to other systems? Open, modular, object-oriented software is normally preferable to a single-platform, specialised one-use system architecture.

Summary

- The true cost of a new IT system extends well beyond the purchase costs of the hardware and software, covering the costs of implementation, ownership, change and infrastructure.

- Costs associated with the impact of the new system on staff, customers, suppliers and other stakeholders must be considered.

- Long-term costs are difficult to foresee, but choices in the design of the system influence their scale.

The benefits of information systems

No useful business case can be based on cost alone. Often the more important issue is not what is spent, but what is received in return and when it will appear. When working out the benefits of an investment, the project manager needs first to consider what business benefits senior managers or the project sponsor are expecting to achieve from the investment. Ideally these will derive from, or at least contribute to, the wider strategy.

Managers with high growth targets will be most interested in systems that increase sales capability, while those fighting for survival in a competitive market may prefer one that cuts costs.

Having established the benefits that managers expect from a new system, they need to be quantified if policy requires a formal-rational assessment of the proposal. However, while staff can estimate immediate costs reasonably accurately, benefits are a different matter. These will arrive in the future and will be affected by factors beyond the control of the project team. Even more than with costs, people make subjective judgements about the benefits of a system. They will inevitably make different judgements based on their interpretation of the future course of the business or their position in relation to the project. Those most in favour will naturally be most optimistic about the potential benefits both tangible (directly quantifiable) and intangible (difficult to quantify).

Tangible benefits

Direct cost savings

Often, the most obvious benefit is that an information system can save costs by automating processes and so replace people. More accurate and timely distribution of work (e.g. using document imaging or telephone call routing systems) can decrease operator waiting time and lead to efficiency-based cost reductions. Fewer staff can mean lower property costs. In practice these are usually less than expected owing to:

- agreements with trade unions preventing job losses
- staff time saving may be spread over several locations, limiting the ability to reduce staffing at any one location
- time saved only counts as a benefit once people have moved to other profitable work.

Quality improvements

A major benefit is the ability of a computer-based system to reduce errors when it replaces a manual system. While people can provide a personal and flexible service, they can also make mistakes and act inconsistently. Customers became annoyed if they are treated differently each time they use a service or see others receiving more favourable treatment. Errors are also expensive since they need additional effort to find and correct, and may result in compensation payments or lost business.

Other aspects of quality include:

- Which customers see benefits from consistent, standardised processing?
- What reduction in reworking and compensation costs will be achieved?
- What revenue may accrue if we reduce the number of customers lost?
- How much less money will be spent in servicing warranty agreements?

Avoiding cost increases

A modern information system can save an organisation from a future increase in costs. Like a car, an ageing system will incur high maintenance costs just to keep it going. Breakdowns disrupt operations and annoy customers – and spares become harder to find. Most organisations replace their PCs after about five years, as maintenance costs then rise sharply. If a new system will avoid these costs, this should be in the evaluation.

Revenue increases

Those advocating a new system will emphasise the prospects of increased sales through offering new services, delivery channels, promotional activities or market penetration. These can be real benefits – but are likely to be optimistic. They are also notoriously difficult to validate, since any change in sales is usually the result of a variety of factors, not necessarily connected in the new system.

MIS in practice RBS Manufacturing Division – using IS to reduce costs

---

The Royal Bank of Scotland (RBS) Group Manufacturing Division is responsible for the operational areas of the Bank that support the income-generating business areas. It has three functional areas: Technology (IT operations and development), Operations (account management, lending, telephony, payments) and Services (purchasing, property, other support units). As the primary back-office 'engine room' for the World's 5th largest bank, Manufacturing provides operational services to over 20 branches serving 20 million customers across a variety of delivery channels (branches, Internet, ATMs, telephone, etc.).

Since 1999, RBS income has increased by an average of 14 per cent a year. During this period the number of people employed in Manufacturing has remained static (about 20,000) or even decreased when transfers from other divisions are taken into account.

How has Manufacturing driven such significant cost reductions at a time of growth?

One way has been by basing its IS strategy on the idea of 'build once use many times'. This means developing a single IT platform to support the many different financial brands and delivery channels across RBS. By building the newly acquired business areas, and the growing needs of existing businesses, into the same IT platform, Manufacturing has established a very large system with big economies of scale. By developing common processes for the different brands, this large platform operates very efficiently while meeting the different demands of businesses.

Manufacturing's scale has allowed it to develop large information processing centres specialising in account management, lending, telephony, payments or credit cards and handling large volumes of transactions from low-cost buildings. Using integrated information systems to drive efficient processes, Manufacturing staff are dramatically increasing their productivity. In one year (2002–03) staff in payments centres handled a 30 per cent increase in payments per head. Furthermore, these increases in productivity are being achieved while RBS employee opinion surveys indicate one of the highest rates of staff moral in the industry.

In its report to market analysts in October 2003, Manufacturing promised to continue increasing efficiency. Initiatives under way include the introduction of Image and Workflow technology, improved customer query management systems, improved fraud detection, simplified account-opening processes and further consolidation of the IT platform.

Source: Information from managers and staff in Manufacturing

Staying in business

Sometimes introducing a new system is simply essential if the organisation is to continue. In a highly regulated environment, it may be necessary to be able to operate in a certain manner just to be allowed to continue to provide the service. Suppliers to Wal-Mart and many other retail chains have had to implement new information systems to manage their relationship with the customer, or lose the business. Major engineering companies require their suppliers to be able to receive drawings and specifications electronically. Those unable to do so have to merge with those who can.

Research summary Benefits of being early

The companies that in the mid-1970s invested in automatic and electronically controlled machine tools were well positioned to explore the microprocessor-based revolution in capabilities that hit during the early 1980s. Because operators, maintenance personnel and process engineers were already comfortable with electronic technology, it was relatively simple to retrofit existing machines with powerful microelectronics. Companies that had earlier deferred investment in electronically controlled machine tools fell behind: they had acquired no option on these new process technologies.

Source: Kaplan (1986)

Intangible benefits

The tangible benefits can be quantified to some degree, but still with a wide margin for interpretation. Other benefits, the intangible ones, are those which people cannot usually quantity. Table 15.1 lists some of these.

Brynjolfsson and Hitt (2000) propose that a large part of the benefits of IS investments come from intangible benefits such as variety, convenience and service – which are hard to measure quantitatively. Nevertheless, these lead ultimately to an economic contribution substantially greater than the initial investment costs.

Table 15.1   Some intangible benefits of information systems

Possible improvements	Description
Communications	Between staff and suppliers, customer or investors
Staff morale	Staff may see improvements in their role or working environment
Customer satisfaction	Brings repeat business and reduces the costs of sales
Reputation	New systems may send positive signals to the market about commitment to innovation
Customer management	Using customer data in advanced information systems may improve reaction to customers' needs

Possible improvements	Description
Value chain management	Building direct systems links between partners in the value chain can improve responsiveness and reduce costs
Flexibility	IS often enable an organisation to react more quickly and easily to changes in the marketplace
Organisational learning	IS enable lessons from current practices to spread more widely; staff can also learn about external events, and be better placed to take advantage of new developments
Differentiation	An important strategic use of IS is differentiation; it is hard to quantify the benefits, as we cannot know how soon competitors will match it

Summary

- Information systems have a wide-ranging set of tangible and intangible benefits that need to be carefully considered from an organisational perspective.

- Overemphasis on costs (which tend to be immediate and certain) and underemphasis on benefits (which tend to be in the future and uncertain) would lead to overly conservative decisions.

Creating a balanced portfolio of project types

Large organisations typically undertake several related projects at once so they need to evaluate individual projects as part of a wider programme. The programme will contain projects representing different types of activity, such as:

- Upgrading a network connecting different locations to a more modern platform that will provide capacity for new applications across all business areas.

- Building a new web-based system for presenting product features to customers, collecting order and payment details and passing them to the operational area to complete the transaction.

While both projects provide vital functions, they have different types of costs and benefits. Building a new network will have specific costs, but the benefits are intangible as they are not related directly to customer sales.

Organisations typically support a portfolio of projects like this – some of them help to build the infrastructure. They develop the ability of the organisation to perform effectively and efficiently, but viewed in isolation deliver no tangible benefits. Nonetheless, shareholders will need reassurance that the investment is sound.

A simple approach is to categorise certain types of projects as 'enablers', making no attempt to determine benefits as they are hard to quantify in isolation. Instead managers justify them on the basis that they cannot implement other specified projects without the prior implementation of the enable project. It makes sense to accept the proposal if its costs, added to those of the projects it enables, are covered by the benefits of the latter. The portfolio, or programme, of projects has a positive business case, being a balance of enabler and enabled projects.

Ross and Beath (2002) describe a more detailed approach to viewing IS investments across the organisation and suggest four categories of IS investment that make up the 'framework for IT investment' shown in Figure 15.1.

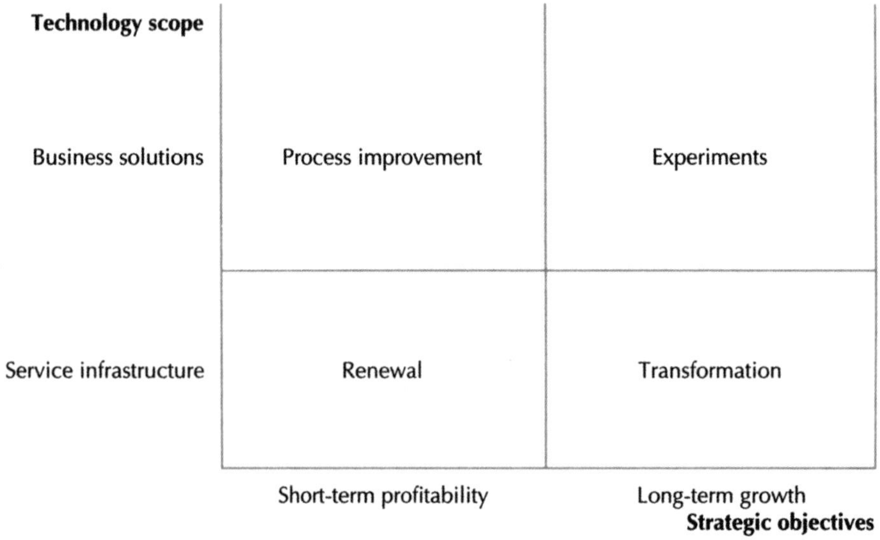

Technology scope		
Business solutions	Process improvement	Experiments
Service infrastructure	Renewal	Transformation
	Short-term profitability	Long-term growth
		Strategic objectives

Figure 15.1   A framework for IT investment
Source: Laudon and Laudon (2004), p. 53

By balancing short- and long-term projects on the strategy scale, and infrastructural and business solutions on the scope scale, organisations can achieve an effective mix of IS investments.

Summary

- Often, IS projects cannot be justified on a formal-rational basis in isolation, but must be viewed in the context of the other IS investments taking place at that time.

- Some IS projects must be justified on the basis of the benefits received from other projects that they 'enable'.

- Organisations often must achieve an effective mix of different IS investments – short- and long-term, infrastructural and business-specific.

Problems of formal-rational evaluation

Formal-rational techniques depend on the assumption that the costs incurred in purchasing the system, and the benefits obtained from it, can be identified and accurately estimated. This applies to both the values and their timing. This assumption is rarely met in the fast-changing world of information systems. Technology changes during the course of the project – and will continue to do so during the expected life of the system. This plays havoc with the approach.

Table 15.2   Reasons often given for information system projects failing to meet investment appraisal targets

Reason	Description
Overemphasis on purchase costs	When planning an IT investment, the most obvious costs are those related directly to the purchase of the necessary equipment and software. However, studies of existing systems show that these initial purchase costs are only a part, and often the lesser part, of the overall system costs
Over-ambitious rates of return	In setting rates of return in DCF calculations, figures of 12 per cent and even 15 per cent are not uncommon. However, studies of the real cost of capital upon which these return rates should be based (e.g. Kaplan, 1986) indicate that a figure of 8.5 per cent per annum is a much more realistic target
Underestimation of implementation time and costs	The project is not finished when the system is purchased or built. It then has to be rolled out to the operational areas of the organisation and start delivering the anticipated benefits. The time and costs incurred in this implementation stage are frequently misunderstood
Poor communication with users and customers	Misunderstandings over the functions and uses of a new system add to costs. Alienating staff can make them reluctant to use the system. Both of these problems are caused by a lack of effective communication with staff. Further problems can be incurred when customers have not been kept informed and experience problems when they use the new system for the first time

Reason	Description
Unrealistic benefit predictions	Enthusiastic project managers overestimate the expected benefits. Careful analysis of the likelihood of achieving them can reveal significant overstatements
Unexpected demand levels	When introducing a new system that customers access directly, such as a call centre or a website, it is difficult to anticipate early demand. Providing too much capacity is as costly as providing too little and losing business
Not learning from past experiences	Most organisations fail to learn from their experiences with previous projects and so repeat mistakes. Formal post-implementation reviews are not popular with busy project teams but can bring huge learning benefits

Table 15.2 lists the commonly quoted reasons for information system projects failing to meet their investment appraisal targets. These testify to the complexities surrounding such projects and limiting the ability of the formal-rational techniques to predict adequately the value of a project.

A common error in formal-rational investment appraisal is to overemphasise the costs, which tend to be easier to quantify, and underemphasise the benefits, which are less certain and harder to justify. This inevitably has a detrimental effect on the attractiveness of the project. It is also common for decisions to be biased towards those IS projects whose benefits are easy to identify, such as cost reduction through automation. This limits the success chances of revenue-generating projects and can lead to the late adoption of critical infrastructure investments. Research by Bensaou and Earl (1998) shows this to be a cultural factor, not a force of nature – see the box below.

Research summary Western and Japanese approaches to investment

---

A study by Bensaou and Earl (1998) of the differences between western and Japanese IS investment decision-making revealed an important difference in approach.

In Japanese corporations, IT [sic] projects are not assessed primarily by financial metrics; audits and formal approval for investments are rare instead, because operational performance goals drive most investments, the traditional metric is performance improvement, not value for money. (p. 123)

This was not an excuse for poorly defined benefit values. The Japanese companies in the study had very firm views on the performance improvements that were expected from a new system and accurately tracked these before and after implementation.

Many of the benefits of information systems are qualitative in nature and do not lend themselves easily to the strictly quantitative approach of the formal-rational techniques. There is nothing new about this. In her study of twenty companies implementing CAD/CAM systems, Currie (1989) found that managers were routinely fabricating cost-benefit cases to pass formal-rational appraisal hurdles in order to gain the qualitative benefits which they knew were essential for the success of their departments. She later found that 85 per cent of managers believe that qualitative benefits are as important as the financial ones, but only 53 per cent attempt to quantify them because of their vague nature (Currie, 1995). Ignoring such intangible benefits, as Kaplan (1986) noted, is a common folly.

Any evaluation process requires us to consider the size and timing of costs and benefits. Formal-rational techniques do this, but the depth to which information systems integrate themselves within organisations and the impact of human factors require a holistic, organisation-wide view of the costs and benefits. As we argue throughout this book, information systems integrate themselves deeply into an organisation. They affect not just the processes to which they are applied, but the whole job design of the users and resources, plus the broader spectrum of stakeholders such as support staff, customers, suppliers, managers, investors and so on. They are central to the strategic direction of the organisation, they cross divisional brand and geographic boundaries, they affect the culture and staff behaviours, they alter the distribution of power. The organisation changes alongside the new information system, which should also be reflected in the appraisal process.

Summary

- The quantitative approach of traditional formal-rational evaluation techniques does not fit well with the complexity of information system projects.
- Information systems integrate themselves deeply into organisations. Their value therefore requires consideration of a wide range of factors beyond the system itself.

Wider criteria for evaluating IS

Given the difficulties we have described with formal-rational methods for evaluating IS proposals, it is no surprise that people have attempted to address the need for an evaluation method that takes account of a wider set of factors. For example, Doherty et al. (2003) list a set of measures for information systems success as shown in Table 15.3, only one of which covers the costs and benefits.

Saarinen (1996) describes a four-dimensional model of IS success measurement, illustrated in Figure 15.2. The first dimension, Development process, considers the success of the development of the system. This incorporates adherence to the allocated budget (costs) and time schedule, and the efficient use of development resources. The second dimension, Use process, covers the effectiveness and efficiency of service delivery to the users of the system. Together, these define the process success of the system and relate to the costs of both build and ownership.

Table 15.3   Measures for system success

Measure	Description
Systems quality	Reliability, features and functions, response time
Information quality	Clarity, completeness, usefulness and accuracy of information provided
Information use	Regularity of use, number of enquiries, duration of use, frequency of report requests
User satisfaction	Overall satisfaction, enjoyment, no difference between information needed and received software satisfaction
Individual impact	Problem identification, correctness of decision, decision effectiveness, time taken to take decision, improved individual productivity
Organisational impact	Contribution to achieving goals, cost-benefit ratio, return on investment, service effectiveness

Source: Doherty et al. (2003)

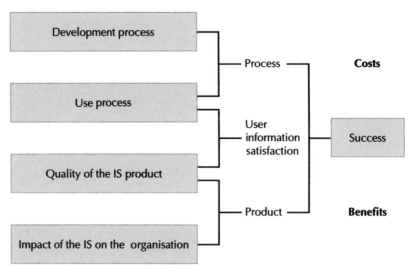

Figure 15.2   Main dimensions of IS success
Source: Saarinen (1996)

The third dimension described by Saarinen, Quality of the IS product, relates to system factors such as reliability, accuracy, robustness, usability and flexibility to change. The fourth dimension, Impact of the IS on the organisation, covers the extent to which the system contributes to cost savings, productivity improvements, increased market share, competitive advantage, etc. (i.e. the benefits). Together, these latter two dimensions define the success of the system as a product.

Strassman (1999) goes further by saying that there is no relation between a company's investment in IT and its profitability. The benefits of an effective system come from improvements in competitive advantage, strategic positioning and management style and quality – which merely investing in IT does not deliver. The benefits come from reshaping the organisational factors, not from spending on IT. A company that spends wisely – even if sparsely – on IT and makes the appropriate organisational changes will see its performance enhanced. A company that spends indiscriminately on IT will see its performance diminished, because IT will merely amplify its poor business practices.

Many companies have used the Balanced Scorecard technique (Kaplan and Norton, 1992) to measure performance against strategic objectives. This technique seeks to develop an organisation-wide view of performance based on an appropriate balance of four measures: financial, internal effectiveness, customers and innovation/learning.

Kaplan and Norton developed the technique to offer an alternative to the formal-rational techniques, for much the same reasons as we have discussed above. They wanted to offer a way of viewing information systems in a broader organisational and human perspective. Figure 15.3 shows the four elements of the scorecard.

Financial measures will obviously still be important, and a favourable impact of the new system on these measures will be critical. This is the area that has traditionally been given most attention in organisations and is most supported by the traditional formal-rational approach, so requires least explanation here. The important lesson from the Balanced Scorecard approach is that concentrating solely on financial measures can lead to a dangerously short-term perspective.

Customer measures will drive the organisation towards the way it wishes to be perceived by its customers. They can include such specific goals as time taken to fulfil orders, customer satisfaction levels and market share. Information systems can do all of these things, but their benefits are hard to quantify. The formal-rational method would therefore be biased against such projects, to the detriment of the company.

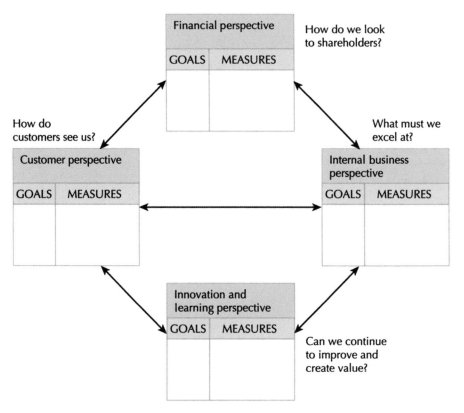

Figure 15.3   Components of the Balanced Scorecard
Source: Kaplan and Norton (1992)

Internal effectiveness measures define what the organisation must do internally to compete effectively. They can include productivity levels, error rates, safety records and staff skills. A new information system could be expected to impact on all these factors and so its value to the organisation should be assessed from all these perspectives.

Innovation/learning measures are intended to drive the organisation towards continuous improvement and the creation of ever greater value to customers and shareholders. These refer to such measures as percentage of revenue from new products and/or markets, research and development achievements, and improvements in operating efficiencies. Many of these measures are strongly influenced by the ways in which information systems improve performance and expand opportunities in organisations.

The example in the box below illustrates the use of the method.

MIS practice The Balanced Scorecard at WHC

Wayton Haulage Contractors Ltd (WHC) was considering implementing an Internet-based tracking and customer communication system. This system would create a website linked to a database of orders, items in transit, drivers, vehicles and customers. Head-office staff could access the database through a browser, entering new information and tracking progress with the movement of goods. Drivers could access the system through truck-mounted mobile network devices to enter progress with deliveries and to pick up new instructions. Customers could access information on progress with their deliveries through a secure extranet link.

To evaluate the system, WHC senior management applied the costs and benefits of the system to the measures in their existing Balanced Scorecard to ensure that a holistic view was taken, linked to their overall strategy.

Financial measures were considered first. Formal-rational techniques were applied to measure the rate of return on investment that could be achieved. This required some estimation of future costs and benefits that WHC knew could change due to the unpredictable nature of such initiatives. Nonetheless the measures suggested adequate financial performance.

Next, the WHC management thought about their customers. Theirs is a cut-throat market, with tight margins and low customer loyalty. Providing leading-edge, convenient service based on reliability and timeliness was a key strategic goal. The new system would provide customers with a convenient means of tracking the progress of their deliveries, leading to higher satisfaction and retention rates.

From an internal effectiveness perspective, the new system would have several advantages. Responding to customer enquiries traditionally took up a great deal of staff time, and giving customers access to their own information seemed like an ideal way of reducing back-office processing costs and lead times. Further efficiencies could be expected from improved utilisation of drivers and vehicles through coordinated job allocation processes.

Finally, WHC management recognised that the system would provide them with opportunities to understand their work patterns and customer requirements better by providing a means of tracking trends and outcomes. Their ability to innovate and learn from the system was therefore assured.

Using the four elements of the Balanced Scorecard, WHC was able to take a holistic and strategic view of the new system. This went much further than financial measures, which required an element of guesswork, and ensured that the value of the system was considered from a relevant set of organisational perspectives.

Summary

- To overcome the limitations of formal-rational evaluation, several alternative methodologies for measuring the value of information systems have been developed.

- The Balanced Scorecard in particular relates IS to strategy, by considering the effects on customers, internal processes and learning, as well as on financial performance.

Organising for IS evaluation

Having reviewed some of the methods for evaluating information systems proposals this final section considers the place of evaluation within the organisational structure.

Evaluating IS at a utilities company: continued

The earlier part of the case described how the company had introduced non-traditional evaluation methods. Success was mixed, and analysis identified these reactions.

The accountants and senior managers viewed the inherent subjectivity of intangible benefits with suspicion and so rejected many outputs from the new methods that incorporated more intangible factors. Stakeholder groups tended to have subjective, informal views and hidden political agendas that influenced their judgement on certain topics. Many methodological changes lacked a champion at a sufficiently senior level to counter objections and to maintain support. Typically, a new method achieved patchy recognition at best and application became a mixture of old and new across different stakeholder areas.

The most successful new method focused on traditional financial elements, and owed its success less to its superiority than to the political influence of its owners – the finance department. It was apparent that proposed new methods did more than challenge the validity of the existing one. They also challenged the traditional roles of the stakeholder groups. So, accountants may have perceived their influence as being usurped, while business managers may have been uncomfortable with new unfamiliar types of accountability.

Due to the large size of the organisation, and the complex nature of its decision-making processes, it was often unclear who should make a particular decision and where accountability lay. During the period of analysis, the company was performing successfully in the market. This may have led staff to be unenthusiastic about the new appraisal methods that were designed to improve performance.

Nevertheless, it was clear that the company had benefited from recognising the importance of IS as a strategic element. The experiment had helped to move it away from exclusive reliance on the formal-rational approach to IS evaluation, and towards a more entrepreneurial style.

Source: Based on Serafeimidis and Smithson (2000)

Central project evaluation teams – a structural solution?

Project sponsors and owners are poor judges of the value of their project. They naturally have a biased preference and are often familiar with only a single area of the business. These factors can lead to sub-optimal investment decisions if the individual project teams are left to fight it out for board funding.

One way of addressing these problems is to establish a central project evaluation team (CPET). Ideally, such a team will be made up of a selection of experienced project managers from different areas of the organisation, with a variety of skills, including marketing, economics, finance and IT. Their role would be to take an objective view of projects and assess their value using a standard approach based on the Balanced Scorecard or something similar. By putting every proposal requiring significant funding through the same assessment, but one more broadly based than the formal-rational approach, boards can be presented with a better set of options.

Another role for the CPET would be to carry out post-implementation reviews of the projects which have been previously approved. This is done very rarely, yet the omission prevents valuable learning. By measuring the actual costs and benefits (broadly defined) of a new system the team can learn useful lessons for future assessments.

However, the CPET approach will have disadvantages for the analysis of IS projects:

- the lack of local awareness and knowledge will detract from the team's ability to understand the less tangible aspects of a project's value

- the systemic approach to evaluation could be viewed as 'bureaucratic' – slow and inflexible

- a central team is less likely to react quickly to changes in the marketplace.

MIS in practice Budget ownership – a plea for business control

IT purchasing policy at Northern Rock Building Society incorporates an unusual stratagem – business units that have proposed an installation are made financially responsible for the projects. 'The onus is on the business side to justify expenditure,' says Neil Wilkinson, strategic development manager. 'This has produced greater cohesion between IT and business managers. We work closely together and it is in the business managers' interests to justify the process.'

Source: *Financial Times IT*, July/August 1999

In many organisations the IS department owns the budget for system developments. Business divisions lobby IS to win part of the budget for their project. The weakness of this approach is that IS departments are not responsible for the revenues of the organisation. This responsibility lies with the business divisions who own the value chains from which revenues flow. For IT budgets to be applied effectively, business areas need to be able to purchase requirements from whichever source, and at whatever price, supports their business.

The CPET may work best where:

- projects are related to a well-established system

- organisations are more formal and risk-averse

- environments are stable.

Localised business budget control may work best where:

- projects are related to new types of opportunity
- organisations are flatter with more decentralised autonomy
- environments are dynamic and uncertain.

Summary

- To manage the costs and benefits of IS effectively, the organisation structure must be aligned to support the needs of the business areas in a technically aware manner.
- Central project evaluation teams have some advantages, but many disadvantages, for the evaluation of IS initiatives.
- Business areas will always claim budget ownership and view the technology departments as suppliers, potentially competing with outside suppliers.

Conclusions

This chapter has discussed the problems of using the traditional formal-rational techniques (rate of return on investment, payback period and so on) for evaluating information systems. The extent to which such systems integrate themselves in organisations, and the complex human interactions involved, require a more holistic approach to be taken that goes beyond simple financial measures.

The costs and benefits of information systems are in themselves complex in nature and require skilled judgement of many indirect and intangible factors. The common approach of ignoring factors that do not easily translate into definite quantities has led to the rejection of many valuable projects, and the acceptance of many poor ones.

In many cases, the costs and benefits of IS projects cannot be viewed in isolation and an organisation-wide view of short- and long-term benefits accruing from all IS investments is needed.

Ideally, a company will evaluate its information systems taking account of organisational factors impacted by each system. Some methods of doing this have been presented, such as the Balanced Scorecard, which is a way of encouraging consideration of the broader range of organisational, human and strategic factors that information systems will inevitably influence. Finally, the importance of ensuring that the organisation structure is aligned to support quality IS decision-making has been discussed.

References

Baker, B. (1995) The role of feedback in assessing information systems planning effectiveness. *Journal of Strategic Information Systems*, 4, 1, 61–80.

Bannister, F. and Remenyi, D. (2000) Acts of faith: instinct, value and IT investment decisions. *Journal of Information Technology*, 15, 231–241.

Bensaou, M. and Earl, M. (1998) The right mind set for managing information technology. *Harvard Business Review*, 78, 5, 119–128.

Brynjolfsson, E. and Hitt, L.M. (2000) Beyond computation: information technology, organizational transformation and business performance. *Journal of Economic Perspectives*, 19, 4, 23–48.

Clemons, E.K. (1991) Evaluation of strategic investments in information technology. *Communications of the ACM*, 34, 1, 23–26.

Computer Weekly (2003) MPs slam Libra as one of UK's worst PFI deals ever [online], http://www.computerweekly.com/Articles/2003/11/11/198520/mps-slam-libra-as-one-of-uks-worst-pfi-deals-ever.htm (accessed 9 February 2009).

Currie, W. (1989) The art of justifying new technology to top management. *Omega*, 17, 5, 409–418.

Currie, W. (1995) *Management Strategy for IT: an international perspective*, Pitman, London.

Doherty, N.F., King, M. and Al-Mushayt, O. (2003) The impact of inadequacies in the treatment of organisational issues on information systems development projects. *Information and Management*, 41, 49–62.

Farbey, B., Land, F. and Targett, D. (1993) *How to Assess your IT Investment: a study of methods and practice*, Butterworth-Heinemann, Oxford.

Farbey B., Land, F. and Targett, D. (eds) (1995) *Hard Money – Soft Outcomes: evaluating and managing the IT investment*, Alfred Waller, Henley-on-Thames.

Financial Times IT, July/August 1999, p. 10.

Cregory, A. J. and Jackson, M.C. (1992) Evaluation methodologies: a system for use. *Journal of Operational Research*, 43, 1, 19–28.

Hawgood, J. and Land, F. (1988) A multivalent approach to information systems assessment. In *Information Systems Assessment: issues and challenges*, Bjorn-Anderson, N. and Davis, G.B., eds, pp. 103–124, North-Holland, Amsterdam.

Hirschheim, R. and Smithson, S. (1987) Information systems evaluation: myth and reality. In *Information Analysis: selected readings*, Galliers, R., ed., pp. 367–380, Addison-Wesley, Sydney.

Johnson, J. (1995) Chaos: the dollar drain of IT project failures. *Application Development Trends*, 2, 1, 41–47.

Kaplan, R.S. (1986) Must CIM be justified by faith alone? *Harvard Business Review*, 64, 2, 87–95.

Kaplan, R.S. and Norton, D.P. (1992) The Balanced Scorecard: measures that drive performance. *Harvard Business Review*, 70, 1, 71–79.

Laudon, K.C. and Laudon, J.P. (2004) *Management Information Systems: organization and technology in the networked enterprise*, Prentice Hall, Englewood Cliffs, NJ.

Peters, G. (1994) Evaluating your computer investment strategy. In *Information Management: the evaluation of information systems investment*, Willcocks, L., ed., pp. 99–112, Chapman & Hall, London.

Powell, P. (1992) Information technology evaluation: is it different? *Journal of Operational Research*, 43, 1, 29–42.

Ross, J.W. and Beath, C.M. (2002) New Approaches to IT Investment. *MIT Sloan Management Review*, 43, 2, 51–59.

Saarinen, T. (1996) An expanded instrument for evaluating information system success. *Information and Management*, 31, 103–118.

Serafeimidis, V. and Smithson, S. (2000) Information systems evaluation in practice: a case study of organizational change. *Journal of Information Technology*, 15, 93–105.

Strassman, P.A. (1999) *Information Productivity*, The Information Economics Press, New Canaan, Conn.

Willcocks, L. (1994) Introduction: of capital importance. In *Information Management: the evaluation of information systems investment*, Willcocks, L., ed., pp. 1–27, Chapman & Hall, London.

Source: Adapted from Boddy, D., Boonstra, D. and Kennedy, G. (2008) *Managing Information Systems: strategy and organisation*, Financial Times/Prentice Hall.

Acknowledgements

Grateful acknowledgement is made to the following sources:

Text

Page 11: Chaffrey, D. and Wood, S. (2005) 'Introduction to information management', Business Information Management, Pearson Education Limited;

Page 49 and 171: Applegate, L. M., McFarlan, F. W. and McKenney, J. L. (1999) Corporate Information Systems Management, McGraw-Hill;

Page 65 and 79: Checkland, P. and Holwell, S. (1998) 'Data, capta, information and knowledge' and 'The processes which information systems support', Information, Systems and Information Systems: Making Sense of the Field. Copyright © 1998 John Wiley & Sons Ltd. Reproduced with permission of John Wiley & Sons Ltd;

Page 89: Orna, E. (2006) 'Organizations and information', Hinton, M. Introducing Management Information, 2006, pp. 75–85. © Copyright Elsevier 2006;

Page 109: O'Brien, J. (2000) Introduction to Information Systems: Essentials for the Internetworked Enterprise. Irwin/McGraw-Hill Education;

Page 133 and 149: Curtis, G. (1998) 'Distributed systems, EDI and the organisation' and 'Strategy and information systems'. In: Business Information Systems Analysis, Design and Practice. 3rd Edition, © 1998. Reprinted by permission of Pearson Education, Inc., Upper Saddle River, NJ.;

Page 181 and 223: Boddy, D., Boonstra, A. and Kennedy, G. (2005) 'Using information systems to rethink business processes' and 'Assessing the costs and benefits of information systems', Managing Information Systems: An Organisational Perspective, 2nd edition 2005, Pearson Education Limited;

Page 205: Rowley, J. (2002) 'Frameworks for e-business', E-business Principles and Practice, published 2001, © Palgrave Macmillan Ltd, reproduced with permission of Palgrave Macmillan.

Tables

Page 193: Davenport, T. H. (1993) Process Innovation: Reengineering Work through Information Technology, Harvard Business School Press, Boston, Mass;

Page 201: Markus, M. L. (1994) 'Preconditions for BPR success', Information Systems Management, 11(2), 7–14;

Page 238: Doherty, N. F., King, M. and Al-Mushayt, O. (2003) 'The impact of inadequacies in the treatment of organisational issues on information systems development projects', Information and Management, 41, 49–62.

Figures

Page 234: Laudon, K. C. and Laudon, J. P. (2004) Management Information Systems: Organization and Technology in the Networked Enterprise, Prentice Hall, Englewood Cliffs, NJ;

Page 238: Saarinen, T. (1996) 'An expanded instrument for evaluating information system success', Information and Management, 31, 103–18;

Page 240: Kaplan, R. S. and Norton, D. P. (1992) 'The Balanced Scorecard: measures that drive performance', Harvard Business Review, 70(1), 71–9.

Index

accountability 74

accounting information systems 33, 125–8, 131

accounts payable systems 126, 128

accounts receivable systems 126, 127–8

active human agent in the world 79–80, 82

adding value 22, 23

advertising and promotion 116, 117

affiliation of information 14

after-sales service 178

agricultural age 14

Amazon.com analysis 109–11

American Airlines 19, 172, 177

applications portfolio 33, 43–4, 167–8
  Nolan stage model 159, 160, 161

appreciative settings 83, 85

automated billing systems 167

B2B e-commerce 215, 217

Balanced Scorecard measure of IS success 239–41, 242–3, 245

band-width 13

bar-coding 74

benefits of information policy 95–6

'bricks-and-mortar' stores 219

brochureware 206

business drivers of process change 195–6

business function-based business models 219–20

business information management
  definition 25–6, 29
  fundamentals of 24–5

business information systems 109–32
  accounting information systems 125–8, 131
  Amazon.com analysis 109–11

cross-functional information systems 111–13

financial management systems 128–30, 131

human resource information systems 122–5, 130–1

manufacturing information systems 118–22, 130

marketing information systems 113–18, 130

strategy 152–68, 169

business information technology strategy 153

business intelligence 19

business models
  choosing 210
  definition 217
  e-business models 217–20

business performance management 19

business plan alignment 41

business process re-engineering/redesign 182, 184, 224

business processes, information systems and 181–204
  approaches to innovating processes 185–90
  definition 183
  examples of IS-enabled process change 195–200
  managing process innovation 200–2
  Redon city council 181, 194, 200, 201–2
  rethinking and innovating processes 183–5
  role of IS in process change 190–4

business relationships, redefining 211

business strategy 149–70
  information systems 152–68
  need for 149–50
  strategic planning 150–2

capital budgeting systems 129

Capital One 20–1

capta 68–71

and information systems processes 79, 80, 84, 85

Carson, Rachel 81, 83

cash management systems 129

central project evaluation teams 242–4

centrally planned strategy 44

channel 215–16

COBIT (Control Objectives for Information and Related Technology) 16

cognitive filters 77, 85

cognitive style, information and 78

collaborative manufacturing networks 120

communication of information 75–6, 82

communities of interest 116

compensation analysis 124

competition, basis of 172–3

competitive forces within an industry 154–6

competitive growth, IT market 54

competitor rivalry 156

computer-aided design 119, 121, 156, 179

computer-aided engineering 121–2

computer-aided manufacturing 119, 156, 179

computer-integrated manufacturing 118–19

computing technology 34–5

consumer e-commerce 213–14, 216–17

contact stage of e-commerce 206, 207

corporate culture 139–40

corporate databases 57

corporate infrastructure 178

cost analysis 57–8

cost benefit analysis 37, 243

cost reduction

in distributed systems 137

in e-business 211

from ICT use 173

from information 22, 23

from information systems 230, 231

costs and benefits of information systems

assessing 223–45

balanced portfolio of project types 233–5

benefits of information systems 229–33, 236–7

costs of information systems 226–9, 235

failing projects, reasons for 235–6

formal-rational methods for evaluating IS proposals 225–6, 235–7, 241, 244

framework for IT investment 234

main dimensions of success 237–9

organising for IS evaluation 242–4

wider criteria for evaluating IS 237–41

creating new reality 22, 23

critical success factors 43, 153

cross-functional information systems 111–13

customer relationship management systems 182, 224

customers 155

and e-commerce 211, 213–14, 216–17

see also user

cybermarketing 205

data 65–72

capta and 68–9, 70, 80, 84

definitions 27, 65, 66, 74

information and 27, 28, 70

see also electronic data interchange

data analysis 74–5

data communications costs 137

data dependency 39

data processing

Nolan stage model and 159

systems 34, 71

data warehouse 103

database management systems 102, 103

databases 36, 101–3

  corporate 57

decision making, location of 140

decision support systems 105, 106

demographics 117

differentiation, information systems and 233

disaster recovery costs, information system 228

discounted cash flow 226, 235

disintermediation 210

disruptive technology 191

distributed computing 134

distributed systems 133–40

  drawbacks of 137–8

  extent of distribution 139–40

  organizational benefits of 136–7

  organizational levels and 138–9

dynamic interaction of internal forces 163–4

Earl model 162–3, 169

e-business 205–21

  consumer and organizational e-marketplaces 213–15

  definition 206

  drivers for 209–11

  models 217–20

  new channel 215–16

  opportunities 210–11

  threats to 210

e-commerce 131

  Amazon.com analysis 109–11

  business models 210

  definition 205–6

  developing 206–9

  features of 212

  most visited sites 213–14

  using the Internet for 109–11, 131, 197–9, 200

ECONOMIST EDI system 144

EDI *see* electronic data interchange

effectiveness 37

efficiency 37

electronic data interchange (EDI) 140–4, 145, 154–5, 167

  benefits of 143

  e-business 213

  examples 141–2, 144

  method 142

electronic data processing system 71

electronic payment systems 131

Elf Atochem 196

email overload 17

e-marketplaces

  B2B e-marketplaces and portals 215

  consumer and organizational 213–15

employees

  behaviour 139–40

  employee self-service applications 123

  see also human resource management; staff

enabler information projects 234

enterprise collaboration systems 105

enterprise resource planning systems 113, 182, 185, 195–7, 224

entry barriers 171, 210

e-procurement 198–9, 200

European Community Information Society 12

Executive Information Systems 94, 105

expert systems 106–7

factory systems 168

failsoft 137

feasibility concerns 56

finance and accounting 33

financial forecasting and planning systems 129–30

financial management systems 128–30, 131

five forces model 154–6, 170
  competitor rivalry 156
  customers 155
  new entrants 156
  substitute products 155–6
  suppliers 154–5

flexibility of systems development 136–7, 233

formal-rational methods for evaluating IS proposals 225–6, 235–7, 241, 244

formulation of information 75

free market strategy 45

general ledger systems 126, 128

generic information systems 101–7
  databases 36, 57, 101–3
  types of 103–7

goal seeking 106

governance 40

governmental reporting 124–5, 179

Grosch's law 133

group decision support systems 106

groupthink 76

groupware 87, 130

hardware
  costs 227
  interoperability of 229

high potential applications 43, 44

homogeneous activities 140

hospital information systems 188–90

human resource information systems 122–5, 130–1
  compensation analysis 124
  and the corporate intranet 123
  governmental reporting 124–5, 179
  and the Internet 123
  staffing 124
  training and development 124

human resource management 179
  ICT and 11, 33
  information systems 122–5, 130–1
  see also employees; staff

IBM 199

ICT
  and barriers to entry 171
  and basis of competition 172–3
  benefits of 36–7
  definition 27
  exploiting through the value chain 164–7, 175–80
  history of 34–7
  human resources and 11, 33
  investment in 94
  management of 31
  new product generation 175
  stages of adoption 41–2
  and supplier relationships 174–5
  and switching costs 172

ICT control, pressures towards 55–8
  corporate databases 57
  cost analysis 57–8
  feasibility concerns 56
  fit with corporate structure and strategy 57
  staff professionalism 55–6

ICT department 32–4

ICT development 49–62
  coordination and location of IT policy 58–61
  examples 51–2
  IT *versus* user dominance 50–1
  organizing issues in 49–52
  pressures toward user dominance 53–5
  pressures towards IT control 55–8
ICT policy, coordination and location of 58–61
  general management support and policy review 60–1
  IT responsibilities 58–9
  user responsibilities 59–60
implementation and ownership change costs 228–9
improvement-based business models 218
inbound logistics 176
industrial age 14
information 65–72
  analysing 74–5
  capta and 69–71, 80, 84
  characteristics of 13–14
  communicating 75–6, 82
  cost of finding 17
  creating value through 20–4
  data and 27, 28, 70
  definitions 27, 65, 67
  gathering 73–4
  organizational definition of 90–2
  processing 77–8
  sale of 13, 14
  storing 76–7
  supporting business processes with 17–26
  technology *versus* 11, 16
  in today's organization 15–17
  in today's world 12–15
information age 14–15

information and communications technology *see* ICT
information economy 13–14
information management 33
  definition 25–6
  expenditure on 13
  future developments 45–6
  introduction to 11–30
  key concepts 40–5
  process of 73–8
information management function
  development of 36–7
  key challenges 37–40
  need for 32–4
information management superiority 40–1
information overload 16–17, 29
information policy 92–7
  benefits of 95–6
  responsibility for 97
  risk avoidance 92–4
information quality 17
information resources 26–9
information society 12–13, 16
information systems
  business processes, rethinking using 181–204
  classification of 105
  definition 27
  evolution in organizations 183
  interorganizational 112, 174, 195
  processes supported by 79–89
  roles of 104
  strategies 44–5
  utility company example 223
  see also business information systems; costs and benefits of information systems; generic information systems
information technology *see* ICT

INFOSCAN 116

innovation, failure of 93–4

intangible benefits of information systems 232–3, 237

interact stage of e-commerce 206, 207

interaction between processes, information systems and people 190–1, 203

interactive marketing 113, 114–15

interactive support 106

interdependent activities 140

internal stages of growth 157–63, 169

   Earl model 162–3

   Nolan stage model 158–61

Internet

   channel 215–16

   growth of 12, 14, 192

   human resource management and 123

   in organizations 38

   start-ups 209

   using for e-commerce 109–11, 131, 197–9, 200

   see also e-business; e-commerce

interorganizational information systems 112, 174, 195

interpretation of information 76

intranet 123, 131

inventory control systems 126, 127

ITEC 184

just-in-time manufacturing 167, 174

key operational applications 43, 44

knowledge

   capta, information and 69–71, 80, 84

   definition 29

   organizational definition of 90–2

knowledge barrier 171

knowledge discovery and analysis 46

knowledge distribution and use 46

knowledge identification 46

knowledge management systems 46, 106–7

knowledge-based work 32

leading edge strategy 44

legacy systems 39, 113

Lo-cost Airline Company 19, 22, 27, 29

long-term information architecture building 58

machine control 120–1

McKesson Pharmaceutical 144

mainframe systems 34–5, 113, 134–5

maintenance, systems

   costs 228–9, 231

   user dominance in 54

management information systems 71, 101–2, 105, 178–9

management support systems 105–7

manufacturing execution systems 119

manufacturing information systems 118–22, 130

   collaborative manufacturing networks 120

   computer-aided engineering 121–2

   computer-integrated manufacturing 118–19

   machine control 120–1

   process control systems 105, 119, 120

   robotics 121

manufacturing resource planning 119

market channel 216

market intelligence 19

market research and forecasting 117–18

marketing and sales 33, 177–8

marketing information systems 113–18, 130

   advertising and promotion 116, 117

   interactive marketing 113, 114–15

   market research and forecasting 117–18

   sales and product management 116

sales force automation 113, 115

targeted marketing 116–17

materials requirement planning 119

m-commerce 197

media channel 216

mini computers 35

mission statement 151

monopoly strategy 45

necessary evil strategy 45

networks 133–6

new entrants 156

new product generation 175

Nolan stage model 41–2, 158–61, 169

critique 161

implications for strategic planning 160–1

Northern Rock Building Society 243

numerical control 120–1

objectives, of organizations 151–2

obsolescence costs, information system 229

online accounting systems 127

online behaviour 117

online transaction processing 131

operating excellence 41

operational support information systems 103, 105

operations, ICT and 33, 176–7

optimization 106

order processing systems 126, 127

organising process innovation 186

organizational e-commerce 213

organizational process in information systems 83–8

organizational setting of information 78

organizations 89–98

activities of 165–6

defining knowledge and information in 90–2

definitions 89–90

environmental influences on 156–7

essential knowledge in 90

information in 15–17

information policy and strategy in 92–7

mission statement 151

objectives 151–2

structure of 138–9

outbound logistics 177

paper-based systems 27

payback period 226

payroll systems 126, 128

personal computers, introduction 36

personal process in information systems 79–81

personnel dependency 39

personnel management 122

PEST (political, economic, sociocultural, technological) analysis 156–7, 169

point-of-purchase (POP) promotions 116

POM (processes for organization meanings) model 85–8

Port of Rotterdam 185

primary activities of organizations 165, 166

process control systems 105, 119, 120

process improvement 41

see also business processes, information systems and

process mapping and modelling 187–90

process support 17–26

procurement 180

e-procurement 198–9, 200

products

new product generation 175

product definitions 176–7

substitute products 155–6

programmable logic controllers 121

'pure play Internet business' 219

quality improvements from information systems 230
quality monitoring 74

reach of information 13, 14
reception of information 76
Redon city council 181, 194, 200, 201–2
relate stage of e-commerce 207, 209
resource optimization 41
response times 137
return on investment 37, 226, 235
revenue increases from information systems 231
revenue-based business models 218, 219
richness of information 13–14
risk avoidance 92–4
risk management 22, 23
robotics 121
Royal Bank of Scotland Group Manufacturing Division 231
rules affected by information systems 191

sales and product management 116
sales force automation 113, 115
scarce resource strategy 45
sensitivity analysis 106
service growth, IT market 54
Silent Spring 81, 83
social process in information systems 81–3
software
  costs 228
  openness of 229
software engineering 35
staff 124
  costs 228
  flexibility and growth 53
  and information systems 199, 228, 230, 231, 235

professional growth 53
professionalism 55–6
  see also human resource management
standardization, information gathering 74
storage of information 76–7
strategic advantage 37
strategic applications 43, 44
strategic grid 167–8, 170
strategic planning 150–2, 169
  see also business strategy
strategic systems 104–7
substitute products 155–6
suppliers 154–5
  relationships with 174–5
supply chain management software 113
support activities of organizations 165–6
support applications 43, 44
support costs, information system 228
support systems 167
switching costs, customer 155, 172
system roles 105
systematic approach to process innovation 187, 190

tactical information systems 103
tangible benefits of information systems 230–2
targeted marketing 116–17
technology
  development 179–80
  driving process change 195, 196
  increased availability of 31
  information *versus* 11, 16
  technology dependency 38–9
telecommunications costs 137
total cost of ownership 227
training and development 124
transact stage of e-commerce 206–7

transaction processing systems 105, 125, 126

transactions 101–2

transborder dataflows 137

transmission of information 75–6

turnaround 168

two-way customer relationships in e-commerce 207

universal product code 116

upgrade costs, information system 229

user awareness 159

user control, IT systems 54

user dominance, IT systems 50–1
  pressure toward 53–5

user responsibilities, IT services 59–60

user satisfaction 136

value activities 165

value-added network 142

value, adding 22, 23

value chain 164–7, 175–80

value creation 20–4

virtual communities 116

virtual organizations 46

Wal-Mart 19, 232

Wayton Haulage Contractors Ltd 241

website functionality in e-commerce 207, 208–9